Wordsworth Education

AS level
English

Wordsworth Education Limited
Cumberland House,
Omega Court,
Crib Street
Ware,
Hertfordshire
SG12 9ET

ISBN: 1-903342-201

Printed by MacKay's of Chatham, Kent

The Publisher's policy is to use paper manufactured from sustainable forests

Wordsworth
Education

AS level
English

a coursebook
for the new specifications

by Adrian Beard and Jean Evans

Contents

Contents

English literature by Jean Evans

contents

An introduction to AS level and this book

About this book

This book is presented in three sections, Language, Language and Literature, and Literature. A glossary of relevant technical terms appears at the end of each chapter, and a comprehensive glossary is included at the end of the book.

Continuity and change

Most of you reading this book for the first time will recently have completed GCSE in either English, or English and English Literature. One of the most pressing things you will want to know is whether the work you are about to do in English at AS Level has any connections with what you have done before.

There are in fact three AS Level English subjects: English Language, English Language and Literature and English Literature.

If you look back to your GCSE English course, you will remember that it consisted of three broad categories:

◆ reading
◆ writing
◆ speaking and listening.

If you also studied English Literature, this involved more reading. Taking these three categories, and then seeing how they are reflected in the various AS subjects, will allow you to get a flavour of how your English will progress from GCSE to AS. It is also worth stressing at this point that although some of the content may be reassuringly similar to what you are used to, the level of difficulty will be raised, first at AS Level, then again at A2 Level if you decide to take all six modules.

Reading

At GCSE you had to study, analyse and respond to different types of text. These can be broadly divided into two categories: literature texts, and non-literature texts such as journalism and advertisements.

Literature texts

From your work at GCSE you will be familiar with reading the following:

◆ a Shakespeare play or plays
◆ a novel or novels
◆ poetry from different authors and periods
◆ other plays, probably written in the 20th century.

It is worth noting here that drama, poetry and prose (usually a novel) are called literary genres.

AS English Language

There will be no compulsory reading of literary texts – no set texts that you must read. Nonetheless the language of literature is an important part of language in general, so you will refer to literary texts from time to time.

AS English Language and Literature

You will have to study at least two literary texts from two different genres, and one of the texts must have been published before 1900.

AS English Literature

You will study further examples in all of the above categories – at least four texts in total. In addition to a Shakespeare play, at least one of the other texts must have been published before 1900. Depending on the course and options you are following, some of this reading may be covered in coursework. You may be allowed to take the set books into one of the exams.

Non-literature texts

From your work at GCSE you will be familiar with studying a range of non-literature texts. Most of you will be familiar with answering questions on 'unseen' texts in exams.

AS English Language

You will be required to read a wide range of non-literature texts and to have a framework, or consistent method, of analysing them.

AS English Language and Literature

You will be required to read a wide range of literary and non-literary texts, and to have a framework, or consistent method, of analysing them.

AS English Literature

You will not be required to study non-literary texts, although they may well be used to teach you good methods of reading literary texts.

Writing

At GCSE you had to write for various purposes and audiences. It is likely that you will have produced:
◆ creative writing, such as a short story, poem, play script etc.
◆ writing for a specific audience and purpose, such as an informational text
◆ argumentative writing where you put forward arguments and ideas
◆ analytical writing, where you analysed media texts, information texts etc.
◆ formal essays, usually on literature texts.

In all three of the English subjects at AS Level you will be expected to communicate accurately and clearly when writing.

AS English Language

You will be required to produce: analytical writing on non-literature texts; formal essays on language topics; and your own writing for a specific audience and purpose (which could include some creative writing) – you will also have to produce an analytical commentary on what you have written here.

AS English Language and Literature

You will be required to produce: analytical writing on literature and non-literature texts; formal essays on language and literature topics; and your own writing for a specific audience and purpose (which could include some creative writing) – you will also have to produce an analytical commentary on what you have written here.

AS English Literature

Most of your writing will be formal essays on literary texts you have studied. Some questions may be broken down into parts, but here too you will be using a formal essay style.

Speaking and Listening

At GCSE, part of your coursework involved you being assessed at various times for the quality of your oral work. In other words you were assessed as a producer of speech. It is highly unlikely, though, that you analysed actual spoken texts. You will have studied many examples of dramatic representation of speech, and you may even have come across transcripts of famous public speeches, such as Martin Luther King's 'I have a dream', but there will not be many readers of this book who are familiar with analysing 'real' conversation.

For most AS English students, regardless of the subject you are taking, there is no oral component – all your assessed work is written. Nonetheless, exploring texts and ideas through discussing them with others is a very valuable way of studying advanced English, and will certainly contribute to your Key Skills profile, if you are submitting one. The more you can contribute to class talk, or, if working on your own, the more you can find someone to discuss ideas with, the better you are likely to do.

AS English Language

The study of spoken texts is as important as the study of written texts. Indeed one of the first things you will need to do on this course is have a clear understanding of some of the essential differences between speaking and writing.

AS English Language and Literature

The study of spoken texts is also important, and again you will need to have a clear understanding of some of the essential differences between speaking and writing. The spoken texts that you study, though, will often be linked by subject matter with written texts, especially literary ones.

AS English Literature

You will continue to study the literary representation of speech, especially in drama and novels.

Overview

you will see that there are considerable inter-connections across the three English subjects. Inevitably you will turn first to those sections that apply most directly to the subject or subjects that you are taking. However, because there is often considerable overlap of content it is well

Introduction

worth reading the other sections too.

There is another reason to recommend that you spend at least some time reading about all three subjects. English is not a totally knowledge-based subject in the way that other subjects you are studying may be. To do well in English there are things you need to know, but more importantly there are skills you need to acquire. These skills always involve your writing, and your ability to think and analyse can be sharpened by all sorts of activities, not just the ones that seem most closely to match your chosen subject(s).

Tasks and Activities

There are a number of tasks and activities in each chapter of this book. As a general guideline, a task should be written work that you do alone, an activity can be pair or group work and can be a discussion or written work.

English language

1 | Introduction

In turning to this section of the book, it is likely that you have chosen to study English Language as one of your AS subjects. We hope that by the time you have worked your way through the following chapters, you will feel fully confident about meeting the demands of the course.

The big picture

Sometimes when you study a subject you get so bogged down in all its details you forget the big picture. Studying English Language at AS Level involves looking at two basic things:

◆ some of the ways English speakers/writers communicate with each other
◆ some of the ways in which that system of communication is organised.

Assessment Objectives for AS English Language

Before looking at some subject matter, it is important that you have a broad sense of how the course and its assessment works. One very important point to make is that different skills – or Assessment Objectives – are assessed in different parts of the course.

This means that you need to know which of the Assessment Objectives are being assessed in each module that you take.

For each AS subject in English there are five Assessment Objectives (or AOs). The English Language AOs are listed below:

AO1

You must be able to communicate clearly your knowledge about language, using correct terms and writing with accuracy and fluency.

This refers to your ability to express clearly and accurately what you know about language. It is a general requirement that when writing about language, especially in exams, you need to be easily understood by an external marker.

AO2

You must show skill and accuracy in writing for a variety of audiences and purposes. You must also be able to comment on your own writing, explaining the various choices you have made.

English language

This refers more specifically to the fact that as part of your AS course you must not only create texts with specific audiences and purposes in mind, but you must also be able to write about some of the methods you used in creating that text.

AO3

You must analyse spoken and written texts in a systematic way, using the structured frameworks that apply to different types of text.

This idea of systematic frameworks is explored later in this chapter, and in the next one too. You must be able to apply these frameworks to texts that you are given in exams.

AO4

You must show that you can understand, discuss and explore the way language is used in everyday contexts.

This refers to looking at the way language works in a social context, and understanding that language does not exist somehow independently of the social situations that surround its use.

AO5

You must show that you can distinguish, describe and interpret different types of text, both spoken and written, and the meanings that these texts contain.

The key thing to notice here is that the words 'types' and 'meanings' are in the plural. Texts mean different things to different people, and there are reasons for this. As you work through this book you will find this idea explored further.

This analysis can now be put to use by taking its essential parts and beginning to build the systematic frameworks that are mentioned in AO3.

TASK

To make some initial moves into the two connected areas mentioned in the section above the big picture, look at the reproductions of two posters that appeared as part of the government's anti drink-drive campaign in December 1999. Write down on a piece of paper anything at all that you notice about them, and then see if you can make a point about language in general, based on your analysis of these posters. Here's an example to start you off:

The posters are made up almost entirely of words, yet they are very striking in appearance;

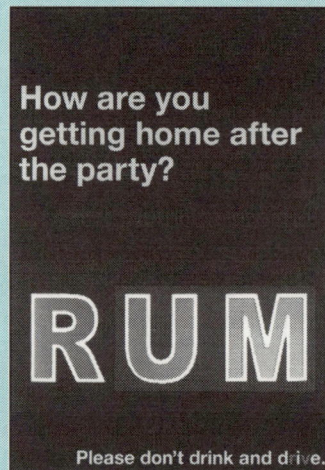

Did you know
you can lose your
licence the
following day?

Beer

Please don't drink and drive.

How are you
getting home after
the party?

RUM

Please don't drink and drive.

texts can involve visual features as well as linguistic ones.

Different readers will have seen different things – and that's part of the way language works. It is good news for you as a student because it means that when studying language texts you are not looking for someone else's right answer. What you are looking for is an understanding of why you have read them in a certain way, and other possible ways in which they might be read.

This book will show you a range of texts and guide you through ways of looking at them. These guides are not, however, the 'right' answers. They are possible answers that you might present if you have a good knowledge of how language works.

CONSIDER

Here are some possible responses to these posters. At this stage you may have noticed the point without necessarily being able to say much else. Don't worry – learning about the bigger issues is what this book is all about.

YOUR POSSIBLE RESPONSE	ANALYSIS
1 The posters are made up almost entirely of words, yet are very striking in appearance.	Texts can involve visual features as well as linguistic ones.
2 Two posters start with questions, one with a statement.	Phrases and sentences do various jobs in a text. Looking at these jobs involves some knowledge of grammar.
3 For a full impact all three posters need to be read, even though each one can also stand alone.	Texts are often arranged so that connections have to be made across more than one text.
4 All three texts are designed to stop people drinking and driving.	Texts are written for a purpose.
5 The texts talk to 'you' as an individual but also as a member of a group – in this case people who drink.	The creators of texts have certain audiences in mind.
6 The texts make certain assumptions about the readers. They go to parties, they drink, they might be tempted to drink and drive.	Texts work within various social contexts.
7 Each of the texts involves aspects of language 'play'. To fully understand the adverts, readers have to work certain things out. Here the most important thing is that certain words are highlighted: UM, ER and POLICE. Also, by shading the letters 'r' and 'v' in the word drive, a further message is created – 'don't drink and die'.	Writers know that readers are active thinkers, keen to understand the message.

English language

Some readers however did not understand the posters and phoned the distributors to ask what they were about. They knew the posters were about drink-driving, but they did not understand the middle bits. This was especially the case if they saw only one of the posters.

Of course not understanding a poster is sometimes as effective as understanding it – it means you think even harder about the message!

What you should have noticed from the seven points above is that some focus on looking at the way the texts communicate with their audience, and others focus on the way the texts are organised. All these factors are working together to produce an effect on the reader.

ACTIVITY

1   In February 2000, the Scottish football team, Inverness Caledonian, caused a major upset by beating Celtic 3-1 in the Scottish Cup. Inverness Caledonian is nicknamed 'Caley'. The *Sun* used the following headline with its report of the game:

Super Caley go ballistic, Celtic are atrocious

Write notes on this piece of text, looking at the different ways in which it 'works'.

2   Now look at the following advertisement that appeared in a Newcastle free paper as part of an anti-smoking campaign.

Make some notes on the way language is used in this advertisement. Keep these handy, and then return to them when you have worked through the next chapter, which begins to look at language in more detail.

2 | Some language frameworks

This chapter offers a more detailed analysis of the assessment objectives through the study of various texts. A framework is provided for you to apply to various texts, with examples and tasks.

Introduction to analysing texts

The opening activity in Chapter 1, page 12 on the drink – driving texts introduced you to the idea that how a text is produced and read depends upon the following factors.

LANGUAGE USE

- Who is writing the text?
- What are they writing the text about?
- For what purpose are they writing the text?
- For what audience are they writing the text?
- What kind of text are they producing?

All of the above form part of the **context** of the text.

LANGUAGE SYSTEM

When talking about language systems these are the words that you will need to be aware of and handle with accuracy in accordance with assessment objective AO3.

- What vocabulary is used in the text? (**Lexis**)
- What does the text look like and how is it structured? (**Graphology/Discourse**)
- What is the text's level of formality? (**Pragmatics**)
- How are the sentences constructed? (**Syntax and Grammar**)
- What does the text mean to you and to other possible readers? (**Semantics**)

The terms in brackets are explained later in this chapter.

Analysing parts of text

The following terms previously mentioned identify some of the main areas worth looking at when you are exploring texts. Taken in isolation, they are not necessarily important. You need to look at their contribution to the whole text to make the analysis worthwhile.

English language

English language

Graphology

The word graphology refers to the visual elements that help to make a written text work. These can be actual illustrations, or the way language is set out on the page. A simple illustration would be **to highlight something in bold type**, to make sure it was noticed. Electronic texts on the Internet also make great use of graphological features.

Graphological elements of written texts are usually quite easy to identify and comment on. Do not spend ages talking about graphology because there are more complex language issues to explore.

Phonology

The word phonology refers to the way sound can contribute to the overall effect of a piece of written or spoken text. In spoken texts heard on television and radio, advertisements may deliberately use speakers with a local accent to convey a certain impression of the product. In written texts, patterns of sound are often worth noting. Blake's poem 'The Tyger' begins with the following lines:

> *Tyger, tyger, burning bright*
> *In the forests of the night*

These two lines contain a number of phonological effects: repetition of words and sounds: a clear, strong rhythm and rhyme.

Vocabulary or lexis

This is to do with words and patterns of words, and so can involve you in looking at texts in a fairly fragmented way. Nonetheless it is often worth commenting on unusual words, technical words, new words, words that belong to a specialist occupation etc.

For example, the following piece of advice appeared in the business pages of a national newspaper:

SPDR are tradable shares in a fund that tracks the S&P 500. Unlike normal index trackers, Spiders are listed on the US market and can be bought and sold like any other shares. They are equivalent to an Index Tracking investment trust. Check with the major investment trust suppliers and compare their products.

Only regular readers of such pages would have any idea what this is about. The difficulty for us is not in the grammar, which is easy to follow, but in the words themselves. Our problem is added to by the use of **initialisms** ('SPDR' 'S&P') which are a common feature of specialist texts, but if not explained are impossible to understand.

Semantics

Semantics involves looking at meanings that can be found in texts. Note the plural use of the word 'meanings' here – recent academic work on reading texts has led to an understanding that texts and parts of texts have more than one possible meaning. A particularly useful way of looking at meanings is to see if you can identify **semantic fields** in texts; these are groups of words or phrases that cluster around the same area of meaning. Other things you might find in a text are: words which have changed in meaning since the text was published; new words whose meaning is known only by certain groups; regional variations in meanings etc.

Grammar

Written texts can be viewed in a developmental way, i.e. from word to phrase to sentence to paragraph to whole text. We have already identified words under the heading of vocabulary/lexis, so grammar is the term we need to use when looking at larger units of text, especially phrases, sentences and paragraphs. The analysis of sentence structure is called **syntax**.

The word 'grammar' has several definitions, but essentially it is about structures, about the way sentences and parts of sentences are built up and cemented together. The metaphor of a building has been deliberately used here; grammar involves the building blocks of language.

Spoken texts also have grammatical structures, although they are often different from written ones. Fluency in speech is maintained by many features of communication, the actual structures of the language being just one of them.

The word 'grammar' puts off some language students. This is partly because of the cultural associations of the word: grammar schools are perceived as 'academic', politicians and others often identify features of language development and change as a product of bad grammar. In fact you do know a huge amount about grammar, and although you may sometimes vary from the standard grammar when writing, you should make good sense. However, what you may not know much about is how to analyse grammar using the correct terminology. This is not something that you can learn overnight, and it is only worth using the terms if you are confident that you are using them correctly.

Analysing a whole text

The parts of the framework mentioned above can all be used to show parts of the structure that is the text. But if you only ever look at the parts and never look at the whole, you are only doing a partial analysis. Two further terms are now needed when you look at how the whole text works.

Pragmatics

Pragmatics is a term used by linguists to describe the way meanings can work beyond the apparent surface meaning. So, for example, if a teacher walks into a room and says 'It's hot in here' and a student sitting by the window then opens it, there has been a pragmatic understanding between teacher and student. What the teacher said carried a meaning beyond what it appeared to carry at face value.

Pragmatics, therefore, involves both the producer of the text, in this case the teacher, and the receiver of the text, in this case the student, in shared knowledge. This shared knowledge often comes from awareness of living in the same culture and so having the same way of understanding things. Another example would be when two strangers acknowledge each other's presence or greet each other by saying 'Are you all right?' or a regional variation of this. It would break the accepted pragmatic courtesy ritual if one of the strangers proceeded to give a detailed account of their recent medical history.

The examples given above are from spoken texts, but pragmatics also operate in writing. A simple example would be the way we begin formal letters, even letters of complaint, with an address to 'Dear …'. Clearly both writer and receiver know that the word is not used in the way lovers would use it.

Another way pragmatics can be seen to operate involves the use of comparison, especially metaphor. Much of our everyday language involves describing something in terms of its being something else; meaning is only communicated effectively if both language user and language receiver understand what is meant. So, when the teacher says to a class 'OK, that's enough' she means that the class should stop talking and start working – and they know and understand this.

English language

One further example is that of a metro train driver announcing to a group of children over the speaker system: 'Have you finished playing with those doors?'

What this really means is: I can see you playing with the doors; stop playing with those doors; we will not start until the doors can be closed. The children of course know this, and do as they have been told, even if they are not actually given a direct order to do so.

Discourse

Discourse can be a difficult term for language students for two reasons: it refers to quite complex ideas; linguists use it in different ways. Essentially it is to do with the way texts hold together, about the way **cohesion** in a text is achieved. So, for example, if a text contains a metaphor which is repeated a number of times, then this metaphorical use will provide a cohesive thread of meaning which runs through the text.

Now look at the previous sentence above. It begins with the words 'so, for example.' This is another way cohesion is achieved, this time by making it quite clear that an example is now going to be given to help make a point. Here the cohesion is achieved by pointing in the text to what has gone before.

It is also possible however for cohesion to be sustained in a text by the ideas it contains. The text suggests that such ideas are assumed to be shared by producer and reader. So, for example, if a car advertisement compares the body of a car with the body of a woman, this is not just an example of a metaphor. It is also an example of the way women are perceived to be objects of desire in our culture.

Or take the following example. An airline wishing to advertisementise a new service between Newcastle and Hamburg placed the following slogan on a poster:

Hamburg
With
Regular
Flies

For this advertisement to work, readers had to understand a number of shared ideas. They had to see the link between Hamburg the place, and the food item, a hamburger. They also had to be aware of the food chain that serves hamburgers with regular fries, and see the phonological joke of flies/fries. The word 'regular' has two meanings here, depending on whether it applies to frequent flights or a medium sized portion of chips. The ultimate message – we fly frequently to Hamburg – works better by involving the readers in some work before they get the point.

A final more specialist use of the word discourse is as an alternative word for conversation. Used in this way, discourse analysis looks at the way conversation works, so in this sense too it is looking at a form of cohesion.

TASK

The following advertisement for the charity Christian Aid was printed in a number of broadsheet newspapers around the time of the millennium in late December 1999/early January 2000. The British Government had just announced that it was going to reduce Third World debts as a gesture of goodwill for the new millennium. Read the advertisement carefully and then write answers to the following questions:

1   How does the design of the advertisement suggest that it is copying other sorts of advertisements?

2   Which words in the various headlines carry more than one possible meaning?

3   What words in the advertisement are to do with time, and how/why are they used here?

4   A pronoun is a word which replaces a noun i.e, 'I', 'you', 'she' etc. Which pronouns are used most frequently in the second column in the smaller print? To whom do they refer?

5   In what ways does this advertisement expect its readers to have some specialist knowledge?

Millennium Madness
1/3 OFF DEBT

STILL *Thousands of child deaths* **DAILY**

DON'T SETTLE FOR CHEAP DISCOUNTS **END THIRD WORLD DEBT NOW**

Wiping one third off the unpayable debt of the Third World means that thousands of children still die needlessly each day. This is not good enough. Third World governments are paying off debts, instead of investing in healthcare. Worse still they have to charge for medicines and treatment, which poor people simply can't afford. And the situation is getting worse, not better. Christian Aid wants the G8, the world's richest countries, to work with the World Bank and the IMF to put an end to all unpayable Third World debt. We need to persuade the G8 countries to get rid of this unacceptable debt burden. The UK Government has taken bold steps. But much more needs to be done. We need to take action now to ensure the G8 makes the right decision when they meet in Japan next July. Contact us by phone or at www.christian-aid.org.uk for your free action guide.

call **0345 000 300** now

Christian ii Aid
We believe in life before death

CONSIDER

(a)   This advertisement appears at first sight to be similar to advertisements for sales that appear in certain tabloid newspapers, but not the broadsheets – so it catches the eye by being out of place. The slogans surrounded by jagged edges are in sharp contrast to the picture, which is of a father burying a child. Here again the reader is surprised by an unexpected set of images put together. The main headline, with its words of command, and its order to act now are also similar to those found in advertisements for shop sales.

(b)   A number of words and phrases are deliberately ambiguous in meaning. 'Millennium madness' in a store advertisement would refer to the offer of ridiculously low prices, but

English language

here it refers to the deaths of children. 'Cheap discounts' also could refer to money-off offers, but here it means the British Government has not given enough to the poorer countries – theirs is a cheap gesture, easily given but carrying little effect. The reference to 'thousands of child deaths daily' is very close to the way a chain store would advertisementise thousands of bargains.

(c)   What we are seeing here is that a particular use of language creates a particular meaning or meanings. A technical term for looking at meaning is **semantics**. Here, semantic double reference has been used to attract the readers' attention, to make them think.

(d)   There are many words here to do with time. Probably the most important is 'still'. 'Still lots of bargains' would mean that the sale goes on. Here though it is the dying that goes on, despite the action by the British Government. Things are 'getting worse'. Action is needed 'now' if the 'daily' deaths are to be halted.

(e)   As is often the case with advertisements, **pronouns** and what they refer to, are an important aspect of this text. A pronoun usually replaces a noun – it refers back to it. In the example, 'The striker saw his chance and he scored', the noun 'striker' is replaced by 'he' the second time. Advertisements, however, often use pronouns that are without any backwards reference. Here the pronouns 'we' and 'us' are left deliberately vague – 'we' could refer not only to Christian Aid, but also the readers, and indeed everybody. This, then, is using the **grammar** of the text to make a point.

(f)   Surprisingly this advertisement is not directly asking for money from its readers, although that may be one result. Its main purpose is to raise awareness of a political point, and in doing so it assumes a fair amount of sophistication from its readers. It assumes that we will know about the IMF (International Monetary Fund) and the G8 (the eight most advanced industrial countries whose financiers meet every so often). This degree of knowledge assumed to exist between text producer and text reader may be a fair assumption, because of where the advertisement is printed, but it also is a good example of the way **discourse** works in a text.

Following this analysis, we are now ready to add to the framework for analysis that has been given so far.

Further examples and activities will consolidate your understanding of the framework.

ACTIVITY

Ten short texts of very different types and on very different topics are reproduced below.

1   For each text note the main linguistic features at work, which give the text its distinctive qualities. Then label each feature by using the terms used in the frameworks given above. Text 1 is done for you as an example.

2   Now see if you can put texts into various groups, using the framework labels as a way of seeing that the texts can be seen to have certain similarities. Each group must have at least two texts in it. Some suggestions follow after the exercise.

Text 1 – Advertisement from newspaper

A pain in the neck for planespotters.

The shuttle. 106 flights daily. That's worth looking up. **BRITISH AIRWAYS**
The world's favourite airline

Example:

◆ Some of the features you may have noticed here are as follows:
◆ informal words ,e.g. 'pain in the neck' (lexis)
◆ double meanings ,e.g. 'pain in the neck', 'worth looking up' (semantics)
◆ implied meaning for reader to work out (pragmatics)
◆ a 'sentence' without a verb and the use of noun phrases, e.g. 'The world's favourite airline' (grammar)
◆ strip advertisement (graphology)

Text 2 – Poem by 10-year old in local newspaper

I think that planes will fall from the sky
I think there will be a cure for those who die
I think all computers will close down
The shops will be busy in town
There'll be a big party
I'll bake a cake which looks arty
Everyone will celebrate the millennium in a special way
Because it is Christ's 2000 birthday

English language

English language

Text 3 – A recipe

Moroccan Preserved Lemons

10 large fat lemons
500g/1lb 2oz sea salt
a good handful of thyme
a good pinch of fennel seeds
½ stick cinnamon
a pinch of cumin
1 bay leaf

Get your ten lemons and make deep, star-shaped cuts (about three-quarters of the way into the lemon). Mix your herbs and spices with the salt, then stuff some of this mixture into the lemons. Sprinkle some salt into the bottom of an airtight jar – the bigger the better – then add your lemons to the jar.

Pack them in as tightly as possible with the salt-and-herb mixture between them, then seal the jar and leave in the cupboard for at least a month (warn the recipient not to open it straight away!) The salt will draw the water out of the lemons, leaving you with a briny liquid. The lemons will be salty, but you will have preserved their zesty fragrance. Use them chopped up in salads, rice and couscous.

Jamie Oliver – Radio Times, December 1999

Text 4 – A music review

Oasis: Rich retro rock

Repeating the same monkey business practiced on its first two releases, Oasis continues to ape the Beatles on glorious third album *Be Here Now* (★★★½ out of four).

Out today, *Be Here Now* goes Way Back Then to rummage the Fab Four's attic. What better place to find inspiration? As copycats go, brothers Liam and Noel Gallagher can't be lumped with cloned Elvis and neo-hippie Grateful Dead impersonators. Oasis honors the Beatles in soaring rock anthems and swelling ballads that are as engaging and confidently executed as the vintage blueprints.

What the Beatles have over Oasis, of course, is originality. But in today's world of retro ripoffs, the young Brit band brings far more commitment, personality and musicianship to its borrowed sound than

Music Review
By Edna Gundersen

the parade of Nirvana-be bands.

The hair apparent to the Mop Tops doesn't limit itself to surface imitations. Rich arrangements, gentle melodies and rosy lyrics characterize Noel's exquisite songcraft, bolstered by a brawny rhythm section, shimmering guitars and the charismatic, combative voice of Liam.

Be Here Now's uplifting tone is set by eight-minute opener *D'You Know What I Mean?*, a supple midtempo rocker drenched in feedback. In tracks like *It's Gettin' Better (Man!!)* and *Stand by Me*, Oasis displays boyish energy, grand hooks and a fearless drive to create bullying, arena-friendly rockers that goad listeners to sing along.

Be Here Now may be a shameless amalgamation of the Beatles, the Rolling Stones and deja Who, but it's also a joyous noise of brilliant simplicity that places Oasis among a tiny coterie of bands sure to remain relevant into the next millennium.

Washington Post 1999

Text 5 – A letter from Northumbrian Water

NORTHUMBRIAN WATER

NORTHERN CUSTOMER CONTACT CENTRE
NORTHUMBERLAND DOCK ROAD,
WALLSEND, TYNE AND WEAR,
NE28 0QD.
TELEPHONE 0345 171100.
FAX + 44 (0)191 234 2098.
MINICOM TEXT + 44 (0)191 295 1530.

Our Ref. : Leakage control work
28 October 1997

Dear Customer

Church Road area - Gosforth

In line with our current leakage reduction initiative, valving work will be carried out in the above area.

This work will be carried out on **Saturday 8 November 1997** and will last for one day only, starting at 12.00 noon and finishing at 20.00 hrs.

There is a slight possibility of supplies being discoloured and therefore we would ask that all customers check their supply before using it.

The supply can be checked by running a tap for a few minutes and washing machines and dishwashers should only be used if the supply is running clear.

If your supply is discoloured and you require water for a special reason e.g. preparation of babies bottles, taking medication etc. or if you have any queries about the above works, please contact our Customer Services Department on **0345 171100** where our staff will be pleased to help.

Please accept our apologies for any inconvenience this work may cause and be assured that every effort will be made to minimise disruption.

Yours sincerely

Joe Jones

Joe Jones
Community Manager North Tyne

NORTHUMBRIAN WATER LIMITED.
REGISTERED IN ENGLAND & WALES No.2366705.
REGISTERED OFFICE: NORTHUMBRIA HOUSE, REGENT CENTRE,
GOSFORTH, NEWCASTLE UPON TYNE NE3 3PX.

Text 6 – A speech by Tony Blair on election night May 1997

The following is a brief extract from a speech by Tony Blair to party workers:

'This vote tonight has been a vote for the future, for a new era of politics in Britain, so that we can put behind us the battles of this past century and address the battles of the new century. It will be a Britain renewed, where through education, technology and enterprise we equip our country for the future in a different new economic world.'

Text 7 – Two 'Personal' ads

Lady of Shalott
Attractive, tactile, loving lady, 50, 5'6", slim with GSOH, loves fun, the arts, silence, the outdoors and travel, seeks 'Lancelot', to restore passion to her life.

Perfect Winter Soup
Simmer impish male, 29, 177cm, season with arts, theatre, hectic professional life, mix with lively female, for perfect result.

English language

Text 8 – A male hairdresser speaking to a male customer

H   **Hairdresser (male)**
C   **Client (male)**

H: how would you like it doing
C: right (.) erm (3) short round the sides (2) just a good trim all over really
H: do you want it shaved at all
C: (.) erm aye (.) aye that would be nice (2) not lots [off
H: [not sort of er (2) very short anyway (.) number [three
C: [yeah (.) number three
H: would that be all right
C: aye (.) that's fine
H: we'll bring it forward aye
C: aye
H: allright
C: aye (.) aye

(Text from Nayeema Chowdhury)

Text 9 – A post-it note advertisement stuck inside *Radio Times*, Christmas 1999

New Year's Resolution

Must make better use of my local pharmacist:

1. No appointments necessary.

2. In the High Street and open during shopping hours.

3. Free expert advice about everyday health problems:- like colds & flu.

NHS
CHOOSE THE RIGHT REMEDY THIS WINTER.

Text 10 – Horoscopes

TAURUS *(April 20-May 20)* The kinds of questions you're privately asking yourself now have other-worldly, spiritually enriching answers, no matter how startling or annoying that may sound. Sorry to say it, but the solutions you're looking for simply cannot be found in this material world of refined sugar, gas-chugging cars, cheesy pizza, or fame. You have to turn to new sources for solace.

GEMINI *(May 21-June 21)* Well, of course you don't have the vaguest idea where you're going now. You're not supposed to. Your course is being drastically altered, guided, determined, and set by a force much greater than yourself — your need for a relationship with someone who knows you inside and out, has seen all your tricks, and is still talking to you. Love hurts.

CANCER *(June 22-July 22)* Careerwise, for the moment at least, everything has seemed to stop cold. Your work and mission may be shifting more toward physical and mental health services and education. And as if that weren't enough to deal with, there are big changes going on at home that are reaching right down into your core and stretching and twisting you like saltwater taffy. All in all, a fun time.

BY MICHAEL LUTIN

You should be aware of some of the main features of each text.

Text 2 – Poem
◆ rhythm and rhyme (phonology)
◆ verse format (discourse)

Text 3 – A recipe
◆ recipe format (discourse)
◆ verbs of instruction (grammar)
◆ verb tenses present/future (grammar)
◆ specialist food terms (lexis)

Text 4 – A music review
◆ use of metaphor e.g. 'monkey business'/'ape' (discourse and pragmatics)
◆ noun phrases e.g. 'neo-hippie Grateful Dead impersonators' (grammar)
◆ specialist music terms (lexis)
◆ informality (discourse)
◆ double meanings e.g. 'hair apparent' (semantics)
◆ opinion/argument/cohesion (discourse)

Text 5 – A letter from Northumbrian Water
◆ letter format (discourse)
◆ formality (discourse)
◆ pronoun reference (grammar)
◆ paragraphing and cohesion (discourse)
◆ noun phrases e.g. 'current leakage reduction initiative' (grammar)
◆ specialist terms (lexis)

Text 6 – A speech by Tony Blair
◆ use of pronouns 'we/our' (grammar)
◆ metaphor of battles (discourse)
◆ features of argument – three part list (discourse)
◆ repetition of words/phrases (discourse)
◆ speech rhythms (phonology)

Text 7 – Two 'Personal' ads
◆ ellipsis i.e. omission of words (grammar)
◆ metaphor (pragmatics/discourse)
◆ format and details (discourse)

Text 8 – A male hairdresser
◆ implied meaning (pragmatics)
◆ adjacency pairs (discourse)
◆ informal and technical vocabulary (lexis)
◆ presumed intonation (phonology)

English language

Text 9 – A post-it note
◆ format of note (discourse)
◆ ellipsis (grammar)
◆ appearance of being hand-written (graphology)
◆ one text pretending to be another (pragmatics)

Text 10 – Horoscopes
◆ format (discourse/graphology)
◆ use of pronouns (grammar)
◆ modal verbs e.g. 'must' (grammar)
◆ metaphor (discourse)

It will be clear from the analysis above that discourse is a feature of most texts, almost by definition. It is therefore not enough simply to lump together all texts where discourse is a feature. Instead you should look for similar features of discourse. Some possible groupings, based upon similarity rather than difference, are as follows. If writing these up as an answer for exam purposes, you would need to give clear examples and show that you understand the terms you are using.

Texts 2, 3, 7, 10 (discourse)
All have a known format which the reader expects to find in this sort of text.

Texts 3, 10 (grammar)
Both use verb forms which are directing the reader to do something.

Texts 1, 4 (semantics)
Both use double meanings. You could also add **7** here, as both 'Personal' ads have sustained metaphors that clearly mean something else as well.

Texts 1, 8, 9 (pragmatics)
All contain examples of implied meaning which the reader of the text has to work out.

Texts 2, 6 and maybe 8 (phonology)
All depend upon features of sound for their full effect.

Texts 5, 6, 10 (grammar)
These texts all make significant use of pronouns and pronoun reference.

Texts 3, 4, 5 (lexis)
These texts all make use of specialist terms.

Texts 1, 9, 10 (graphology)
These texts all, to some extent, depend upon their layout and appearance for their effect.

Texts 1, 6, 7, 8, 9 (purpose)
All to some extent at least are written in order to persuade.

Texts 5, 6 (formality)
Both texts are formal in their use of language.

Texts 4, 8, 9
These are informal.

TASK

Now that you have explored some key areas of language more closely, return to the notes you made on the anti-smoking advertisement at the end of chapter 1 on page 6.

Describe some of the language features you can find at work in this text. Try to do this without further help, but if you need some hints, they follow below.

Think about :
- Who has produced the text?
- Why it has been produced?
- Who it has been produced for?
- What does the text look like?
- How is its language similar to other texts that look like this – and how is it different?
- What language here is very unlike that found on a gravestone and why is it used?
- Which lexical items are formal and which are informal? Why?
- Which lexical items are dialect words? Which ones are invented words?
- How is the life of a pensioner presented here? What could his 'life' have been?
- What meaning does the text have for you?
- Does the text achieve its purpose?

TECHNICAL TERMS

cohesion   refers to the way texts hold together, the way parts connect. This connection can be through words, grammar and ideas

discourse   used in various ways by linguists. It can refer to a continuous piece of written or spoken text, but as used here it refers to more than this. Here it refers to the way texts cohere (see cohesion above) and the ways in which readers recognise this

formality   involves a scale of social use relating to situations which are 'tight' or 'loose'. Linguists talk of 'levels' of formality

genre   a word for types of texts. It can refer broadly to such things as poetry, prose, drama, but also more specifically to types of text within those broad areas, such as crime fiction, narrative poetry etc.

grammar   the system by which texts and meanings are constructed

graphology   involves looking at the way the appearance of a text influences how it is read and understood

initialisms   a collection of the initials of the name of a group or organisation to form a short title. Unlike an acronym they do not form a word.

lexis   the vocabulary of a language

phonology   the study of the way sound operates in a language

pragmatics   the way meanings in a text, written or spoken, can work beyond the apparent surface meaning

pronouns   words which substitute for nouns and noun pharases, e.g. 'mine'

semantic field   a group of words that are related in meaning through being connected in certain contexts

syntax   the way in which sentences are constructed

English language

3 Speaking and writing

This chapter begins by explaining how analysis of speech has tended to be ignored in favour of analysing writing. It also used to be assumed that speaking and writing were distinct and therefore easily categorised. This chapter provides a model that allows you to apply certain questions to a text, whether it is spoken or written.

Assessment Objectives

The previous chapter began with a look at the Assessment Objectives which apply to your AS course in English Language. Look again at AOs 3–5, as written in their 'simplified versions'.

AO3

You must analyse spoken and written texts in a systematic way, using the structured frameworks that apply to different types of text.

AO4

You must show that you can understand, discuss and explore the way language is used in everyday contexts.

AO5

You must show that you can distinguish, describe and interpret different types of text, both spoken and written, and the meanings that these texts contain.

You will notice that AO3 and AO5 specifically draw attention to the fact that spoken and written texts must be analysed, and AO4 does so by implication. This is a major development from your work at GCSE. Although you were assessed for your ability to speak and listen, it is unlikely that you did any analysis of how spoken texts work. On the other hand you probably did lots of work on written texts.

Since the age of five, your schooling has placed a huge amount of emphasis on reading and writing texts that are produced on paper – and perhaps to a much lesser extent on screen. You will have received many formal lessons on how to read and write, your work will have been checked and corrected.

Speaking, though, will have had much less attention. You will almost certainly have been

English language

able to talk when you started school, but can you remember any lessons on how to talk effectively? There may have been a few on formal bits of speaking like giving a talk, reading/acting a play, but it is unlikely that you have ever looked very closely at conversation. Indeed there will have been many times when conversation was specifically banned. 'Talking in class', 'chatting', 'gossiping', are all likely to have been used as terms of disapproval, of doing something you ought not to.

In one sense this is easy to understand. A room full of children all talking at once is very difficult to manage. But remember that talking comes before reading and writing in your language development, and talking is the most common form of communication. You should not be surprised, therefore, that talking is seen as so important at AS Level English Language. The real surprise should be that it has been overlooked for so long.

One reason has already been given – managing large numbers of children. Another reason for the way talk is undervalued in our system is because it is hard to assess. Writing can be parcelled up and sent away to examiners. Talk, though, cannot be preserved in this way. Tape recorders are no answer, as we do not respond naturally if we know our words are going to be recorded. The way talk disappears so fast is actually one of its pleasures!

So, at AS English Language, talk at last appears on equal terms with writing – at least in what you study it does. However, unfortunately, your ability to analyse (and produce) spoken texts is still going to be assessed by written examination. Speaking may be given equal billing as a topic, but writing is still what matters most when it comes to the exams!

Key points

One of the inevitable by-products of this emphasis on writing is that students who analyse speech for the first time find it very difficult not to look at speech as though it is writing. Making this adjustment will be a major task for you during this course, so it is worth making a few clear statements at this point:

1   Speaking and writing are different forms of communication, although modern technology is often blurring these differences – an Internet chat room is written communication using many forms typical of informal speech.

2   Speaking and writing are not in competition with each other – one is not better than the other in terms of merit. There are, however, occasions when choosing whether to speak or write has clear advantages for you. If you are in a hurry you may choose to phone a friend; or, if they own a mobile phone you may choose to send a text message. On the other hand, if you want to remember something later you may choose to write it down.

3   Texts, whether spoken or written, must be analysed using certain criteria. The most common mistake made is that informal speaking is analysed, and judged, by the standards of formal writing.

ACTIVITY

Before giving a framework of the main differences between speaking and writing, it will help to use an example of each form.

This can be done through using data provided by a role-play. There are obviously some problems with this, in that the data is not strictly authentic – it has not been produced in an actual context. On the other hand, it is relatively easy to collect and record and will at least give some indications for further possible research.

You will have noted above that we are rarely in the position to choose between speaking and writing. Using a role-play allows the research to overcome this problem by directing different students to do different things.

Essentially the role-play was about a pair of trainers that had been bought, but which soon turned out to be defective. The purchaser wanted the money back!

1   In pairs students were asked to compose letters of complaint to an imaginary shoe shop. Some argued that they would be unlikely to write, when they could go into the shop, but such is the power of writing, when told to compose a letter, they got on with it without any problems. Here is one example:

```
                                    15 Mendip Road
                                    Kingston Court
                                    Newcastle Upon Tyne
                                    NE3 8GH
                                    January 4th, 2000

Pearsons Shoes
51, Argyle Street
Newcastle Upon Tyne

Dear Sir/Madam,

After purchasing a fairly expensive pair of Acto trainers from the
above store on December 11, 1999, I wore them for a very short
period before the sole completely detached itself from the left
shoe.
   This goes against the consumer rights act, which states that all
goods sold should be suitable for the expected use. These trainers
were of such a low quality that they did not comply to the required
standards.
   I am aware that I have the right to a full refund, and I assume
this will be paid directly to me on the return of these faulty
goods. Please inform me when it will be convenient to come into your
store and collect my refund. I look forward to hearing from you as
soon as possible.
Yours faithfully,


...................
```

English language

2   Meanwhile a number of individual students were asked to role-play customers going into the shop to complain. The shopkeeper was a male researcher, so his contribution is less spontaneous, perhaps, than the complainer's. Here is an example of how the conversation went.

Some basic conventions of transcription have been used here. These include:

◆   most of the punctuation associated with writing is not used, but apostrophes are used to help when reading
◆   using ( ) to mark pauses. (.) means a small pause (2) means a pause of two seconds etc.
◆   using [to indicate when two people speak at once.

A: is the (male) customer and
B: the (female) shop assistant

A: erm (2) well could I speak to the manager please
B: I'm sorry the manager isn't based in the shop
A: erm (1) I've got a complaint about [a pair of shoes
B: [yes
A: um um that I bought last Saturday (2) they're they're a pair of Aviator shoes um (1) um (1) they cost £70 I've only been wearing them a week one of the soles has fallen off I've still got the receipt I haven't (1) I haven't (.) done anything stupid with them
(3)
B: well (.) well (1) well I (.) I'm not really sure what I can do about that (1) where exactly were you wearing the shoes
A: er (.) er to work (.) I just work in an office nothing that should make the sole fall off they're supposed to be a pair of quality shoes
B: they are they are are one of our best makes we haven't had any other com[plaints
A: [well I'm sorry I'm making a complaint about them

Using the evidence above make a list of as many of the differences between speaking and writing shown here.

CONSIDER

The letter
(a)   The letter contains a number of formal conventions: the addresses and the way they are set out; the opening and closing 'Dear Sir/Madam', 'Yours faithfully'; the date etc. These can be described as **phatic conventions**, the word 'phatic' referring to social connections rather than any meaning as such.
(b)   This high degree of formality is also evident in the lexical choices made, for example: 'purchasing', 'detached'; 'states', 'comply with' would rarely be found in conversational speech.
(c)   Formality is also found in the grammatical structures of the letter, especially in the **syntax**, or sentence structure. For example, the opening clause beginning, 'After purchasing a fairly expensive pair of …' delays for some time reference to the subject of the sentence, 'I'. In speech it is likely that we would start with 'I'.
(d)   Finally, the structure of the argument is very clear and logical. One thing follows clearly on to the next, helped by the use of paragraphs. With no one to interrupt, and plenty of time to

draft their ideas, this pair of students had little trouble in making their point clear.

The role-play

(e) When writing about spontaneous speech it is important that you do not see speech as an inferior version of writing. Speech and writing work differently, but they do both work. You cannot, therefore, just describe speech in terms of what it does not do.

(f) One obvious feature to notice here is that speech comes in bursts, punctuated either by pauses or by **fillers**, 'words' like 'erm' and' um'. There are also a number of false starts. Another feature is that the syntax, or sentence structure of speech is different from that of writing. If you look at the third utterance by character A you will see that various chunks of meaning all run into each other, without the formal organisation found in writing. However this does not mean that the utterance has no organisation, because it would not make sense – it is just different. Some linguists are unhappy that the idea of a sentence should be used at all when discussing speech; others refer to speech syntax, recognising the difference between this and written syntax.

(g) An implied meaning, rather than a stated one, can be seen when A mentions the cost of the shoes. Although he mentions a price, the full implication is not stated, i.e. that this is a lot of money to pay for shoes that fall apart.

(h) Notice also the ways in which the speakers sometimes overlap. Two people cannot speak simultaneously for long – one has to back down and let the other speak. This happens twice here, both times when the word complaint is being used. The second time they speak together, A anticipates the full word after hearing only one part of it; he is determined to assert his rights.

(i) It is worth repeating at this stage that this conversation is taken from a role-play; it is not a fully authentic situation. Nevertheless it is different from a drama script, in which an author would produce a very different simulation of talk.

Categorising the differences

Earlier textbooks on English Language have tended to suggest that the different qualities of speaking and writing can be easily categorised and even learned. However this approach can be misleading. Take for example levels of formality. It used to be assumed that speech was less formal than writing, and indeed it often is; nobody would argue that casual classroom chat is less formal than a written essay. However what about the difference between a formal speech in a debate, and a scribbled note to a friend? In this case, the writing would be informal.

Look at the idea of permanence. It used to be suggested that writing tends to be permanent and speaking more impermanent, and this is indeed often the case. On the other hand a note to the milkman will be destroyed as soon as it has been read, whereas a recording of the police interviewing a suspect will need to be kept for a long time.

Just to make the situation even more complex, there are some texts which can be seen as both written and spoken: when newsreaders speak the news, for example, they are usually reading from a written version. Or when contributors meet in an Internet chat room, they are writing down their 'spoken' contributions.

English language

So, much as it would be convenient to make lists of labels that can be attached to speaking and writing, we have to employ more subtlety. What we can do is list some descriptors that can be used when describing various spoken and written texts.

Where on a line between the following opposites does a text come?

formal --- informal?	
permanent -- temporary?	
planned -- spontaneous?	
grammatically standard ---------------------------------- showing non-standard features?	
delayed in its communication with others --------------- immediately shared with others?	

Let's take as a possible example a teacher addressing a Year 10 class. (See chapter 4, page 35 for a transcript of this.) Now let's look at the categories of descriptions above to assess the chosen text. The level of formality would have to be quite high, but not too much so. The speech would be temporary, unless recorded for research purposes. Grammatically it would be largely standard – maybe with some regional variation. The communication would have to be immediate rather than delayed. In conclusion this sort of utterance has some features at the end of some lines, and others are somewhere near the middle.

ACTIVITY

Printed below are the top and bottom parts of a continuous list. The top, number one is an informal kind of speech, the bottom, number 12 a formal type of writing. Where would you place the others listed below, according to their levels of formality? There are no right answers to this exercise, and hence no commentary, but discussing your answers with others will be useful.

1 Typical speech: conversation with mates

12 Typical writing: this text book

- a political speech
- a TV quiz show
- Internet chat
- a talk by the head in school assembly
- a discussion, with an appointment, with your personal tutor
- a discussion with your tutor met by chance in a corridor
- a message on an answer phone
- an e-mail to a friend
- a fax to a business address
- a personal statement on a UCAS form.

The effect of new technology

Recent technological advances, in particular, have begun to blur some of the over-simple distinctions between speaking and writing that were once made. The answerphone makes speakers talk to somebody who is not there (unless of course they are sneakily listening without picking up the phone). The fax machine allows writing to be delivered instantly, without the previous time delay of delivery. These factors are bound to change the nature of the language used.

Consider also the role of the Internet. Emails are written and delivered quickly across the whole world; a reply can be sent just as quickly. Emails are more informal than traditional paper letters, and some people are less preoccupied with being fully correct in matters such as spelling. Meanwhile chat rooms and other means of simultaneous communication allow friends and/or strangers to chat to each other in electronic written form. The old distinctions between speaking and writing, no longer apply here. They are no longer perceived as distinct and separate – writing and talking are happening at the same time. Although this is unlikely, at least yet, to appear as part of your work in AS exams, there is plenty of opportunity for you to write texts using 'electronic language' in your Original Writing, or to research its use in coursework research projects at A2.

An example of an answerphone message comes from the role-play about shoes, described earlier. A third group of individuals were asked to telephone the shop and complain over the phone. Unknown to them in advance, when connected they were faced with an answerphone message. The following Task gives an example of a response.

TASK

How does the language used here differ from the complainant's language in the face-to-face extract above?

yeah (2) I bought a pair of trainers a few days ago and (.) er (.) and the stitching's coming away on the sole (.) I was wanting a refund so I don't want (.) my shoes replaced (.) because (.) because of what's happened (.) so I want my money back which is quite a lot compared to the trainers I got (.) so if I leave my phone number I'll be hoping you get back to me....

CONSIDER

Answering machines put a lot of pressure on the caller, who is usually expecting a conversation. With little time to prepare, the caller must attempt to be clear and coherent. One strategy the caller uses here is to use a lot of **connectives**, especially the word 'so' which allows him to string his ideas together. You will also notice that there are more pauses than in the conversation transcript, but that they tend to be briefer. **Verb tenses** also become a problem for the caller, who has to try to work out if and when their message will be heard. Hence 'I was wanting a refund' instead of 'I want a refund' and 'I'll be hoping you get back to me.'

Planned/unplanned speech: public/private speech

So far in this chapter, you have looked at speech that is unplanned and private, in the sense that it was intended for the ears of only one person. However speech can be either planned or unplanned, and it can be either private or public. It is possible to come up with potential examples using all the permutations available. So:

- unplanned and private: a conversation
- unplanned and public: a teacher giving a general lesson
- planned and private: a formal warning as to future conduct by an employer, teacher etc.
- planned and public: a political speech or a formal lecture.

Some examples of speech in the other categories can be found in the next chapter.

TASK

This chapter ends with a transcript of part of a 'real' conversation, recorded and transcribed by a student as part of her A2 coursework project. Lauren (L) and Nicola (N) are also discussing trainers.

Here you are faced with the nearest a written exam system can give you to real speech – a transcript, which gives you the words spoken, and some indication of pauses. What you cannot get any sense of are those features of the conversation that cannot be written down in this form. These include features of local accent, body language, facial gesture, and what are called prosodic features such as pace and emphasis.

Read the transcript through carefully and respond to the following points.

1   List the features of the planned/unplanned and public/private list (see above) that can be seen here, and give examples of where they are seen.

2   Which utterances might mean different things depending on the way they are stressed?

3   Look at how the two women take turns in contributing to the conversation. Make a list of what each of the two participants contributes to the overall conversation.

L: I bought some new trainers today
N: oh I thought they were new
L: yeah
(1)
N: you bought Fila
L: pardon
N: you bought Fila trainers
L: well they were cheap so (.) I got them for twenty one seventy eight altogether with my discount [so
N: [yeah
L: I can't afford I mean I like the ones I like sort of [I think
N: [yeah
 (1)
L: I think it's the ones Sarah's got are quite nice (1) but I wouldn't fancy (.) I can't afford to pay eighty pounds for a pair of trainers so (1)
N: do you get a discount on everything you buy
L: apart from sales stuff (.) but sometimes its selected sales sales stuff that you don't know
N: do friends get it
L: well if you pay for it
(1)
N: oh

TECHNICAL TERMS

connectives   words which connect different parts of sentences or utterances. They are also known as conjunctions.

fillers   short 'words' or sounds which are used by speakers during an utterance. They provide thinking time, while letting you keep your turn.

phatic conventions   utterances such as 'how are you?' which establish and maintain social contact

prosody   prosodic features refer to aspects of sound such as rhythm, speed, pitch

verb tenses   these indicate the time in which something happens / happened / will happen

4 | Some social aspects of language

Key areas of study in AS English Language involve looking at **sociolinguistics** — the way language works in a social context. In this chapter you will sample some aspects of sociolinguistics, in particular those of language and occupation, and language and gender. Issues surrounding authority and power significantly influence both of these topics.

The term sociolinguistics can be simply defined as the relationship that inevitably exists between language and society. All the language that we use, whether spoken or written, whether public or private, is governed by our social identity and the social situations that we find ourselves in.

It is sometimes thought that language is neutral, that it can describe the world 'as it really is'. There is, however, no such thing as neutral language, and no such thing as a form of reality existing outside the world of language. Different languages encode objects and ideas differently. This difference in the way language represents objects and ideas is part of the difference that we find in various cultures. This means, for example, that there is no such thing as 'real' masculinity and femininity; they are terms used to describe social constructions. These constructions can differ across cultures. If you compare, for example, the way in which Japanese women are traditionally represented with the way warrior tribeswomen are shown, you will see that there is no single understanding of the term 'femininity'.

Language users

In the previous chapter you learned about language systems. This chapter identifies some issues concerning language users. Consider for example the different ways that you talk to and about your teachers in the following contexts:

◆ to their face in a formal lesson
◆ to their face in a private conversation

- to teachers who are the same sex as you
- to teachers who are the opposite sex to you
- about them to other teachers you know well
- about them to other teachers you do not know well
- about them to your friends of the same sex
- about them to friends of the opposite sex.

It is likely that you will use subtly different language in each of the above situations. But what are some of the factors that determine this difference? A very obvious one is that teachers are in an institutionalised position of authority. From the time you first went to school, it was made clear that the teacher is in charge, they are allowed to tell you what to do. This power comes as a result of their occupation. Whether or not they gain respect, will in part depend upon the way they project their personality. The first reason for their authority is that it comes with the territory of being a teacher. Both teachers and students are acting out social roles in their language interactions.

This authority is most obvious when teachers are in front of whole classes. It is also present in some written situations such as the school or college report home to parents. It can be less obviously powerful in one-to-one conversations, although again this depends on the context – whether, for example, the student is being praised or told off.

Teachers, as a rule, are older than students, and as our culture suggests that age should be respected, this is another factor that will affect the language used. Teachers have been educated to a certain level and in some cases, they may be seen to belong to a different social class from their students. Of similar importance is the gender of those involved in the various permutations listed above. When speaking to a friend of the same sex, your language use is likely to be different from that if you are speaking to a friend of the opposite sex. You could research this with your own friends. We live in a multi-racial society and ethnicity may also be an influence on the language used. Two Afro-Caribbean students may use different language with each other than when talking to English students, for example.

Finally, it is likely that regional variations in language will be evident. These are in part to do with factors such as dialect and accent, but they are also influenced by issues of power. When students are speaking respectfully to their teachers, they are more likely to use standard forms than when they are talking to their friends. If Geordie pupils were to reply to a question with 'I divvent na', they themselves would be throwing out a challenge to the teacher; not only might they not know the answer to the question, but they are possibly not particulary interested anyway. This situation could well lead to conflict – the teachers seeing themselves challenged by language that may be seen as off-hand or even offensive.

To summarise, when we are exploring language within a social context, the following factors can be applied. It must be stressed, though, that they do not usually operate independently of each other.

SOCIOLINGUISTIC FACTORS TO LOOK OUT FOR:

- authority/power
- occupation
- gender
- social class
- age
- ethnicity
- regional variation.

Occupational language

The following extract comes from a speech made by Tony Blair on the night his party won the General Election in May 1997. Having won his own constituency in Sedgefield, he travelled down to London and spoke to party supporters at the Royal Albert Hall in London. The speech was made by a professional politician, and hence is an example of occupational language. However politics is about power, so in one sense of the word at least, it also shows language reflecting a certain sort of power.

TASK

Answer the following questions based on the extract below. Set out your answers in whatever form is most suitable; for instance you could use tables to present the features you have found. Each question gives you features in brackets from the framework described in previous chapters.

1   What features of vocabulary are most noticeable here? Why do you think they are used? (lexis/semantics/pragmatics)

2   What do you notice about the pronouns in this speech? Why do you think they are used? (grammar)

3   What features suggest that this speech was planned in advance? (discourse)

> 'Today, on the eve of this new millennium, the British people have ushered in this new era of politics, and the great thing about it is that we have won support in this election from all walks of life, from all classes of people, from every single corner of our country. We are now today the People's Party. The party of all the people, the many not the few, the party that belongs to every part of Britain, no matter what people's background, or their creed, or their colour. The party that can work for what is a great country. We want everyone to feel pride in their country tonight because all have a stake in its success. I believe in Britain and tonight the people of Britain are uniting behind New Labour. They are uniting around basic British values, uniting to put the divisions behind us, uniting to face the challenges of the future, uniting at long last as one nation.'

CONSIDER

(a)   So many words and ideas are repeated here, it should not be difficult to find areas of common meaning, or **semantic fields** as they are sometimes called. These include:
   - new
   - all/every/everyone
   - party/People's Party/New Labour
   - country
   - uniting/one nation
   - Britain/British

(b)   Spotting the semantic fields is one thing, but to gain full marks you need to comment on what they contribute to the overall effect of the text. Tony Blair is celebrating success and looking towards the future. The future is new, it includes us all, it is good news not just for his party but also for the whole country. Whereas previously we had been divided, we will now be united. This is a triumph for Britain – one nation happy together with this election result.
   Of course this is not necessarily the case, but it is the way politicians talk, especially when

English language

they have just been elected. You may have noticed how cleverly he links the success of his party to the whole country. His party, once the 'Party of the People' (i.e. socialist) has now become the 'People's Party', no longer belonging to one social class, but to all social classes.

(c) The pronouns that are used in political speeches are always important. The two most frequent pronoun sets that are used are those which are called 'first person pronouns': 'I/me/myself/my/mine' and 'we/us/ourselves/our/ours'. How and where they are used, can reveal a great deal about the politician's intentions. So, when he or she refers to himself or herself alone, using the 'I' form, he or she is willing to show a clear sense of personal involvement and is usually delivering good news.

Using the 'we' form, on the other hand, can achieve a number of things:

◆ it can share the responsibility if it refers to the speaker and other senior colleagues
◆ it can go broader than this and refer to the speaker and his whole party
◆ it can go still broader and refer to the speaker and the whole country
◆ it can go yet broader still and refer to the speaker and all humanity.

In the extract above Blair is speaking to his own party which has just won the election, so to begin with he uses 'we' to refer to his audience of party workers and all other party members. He moves on from the party workers to talk of 'everyone', and by the end of his speech he is using 'us' to refer to all the British people. He also at one point uses 'I', making his own belief in Britain central to his message.

(d) Although this speech appears to have been made in the moment of victory, it has features that suggest it has been written and planned in advance – as most speeches these days are. Blair knows that the real audience is the country at large, watching on television, or seeing edited highlights later. The repetition of words, already commented on above, is one obvious feature of the speech's discourse. So too are the patterns of grammar that he uses. A very common feature of speeches is the use of three part lists, and here we have:

from all walks of life
from all classes of people
from every single corner of our country.

and:

the party of all the people
the party that belongs to every part of Britain
the party that can work for what is a great country.

(e) Another point of clear emphasis is the repeated use of the 'ing' form in the word 'uniting'; it is used five times. Twice he uses short sentences for effect, following much longer ones that have gone before. The cohesion of his speech, the way it all holds together without any major pauses or re-starts, suggests that he is reading words that have been previously written.

Dialects

The term **dialect** refers to a regional variety of speech, and occasionally to writing. A Geordie dialect word for cigarette is tab. When a news report stated that the Canadian government were going to place health advice on a tab inside a cigarette packet, not unnaturally some Geordie listeners at first thought the cigarettes themselves were somehow going to contain warnings. In fact a standard Canadian meaning of the word was being used, referring to a piece of paper.

A simple definition of the term dialect is as follows:

> **dialect** – a language variety in which vocabulary and/or grammar identifies the user as belonging to a certain historical, regional or social group.

Roughly speaking, dialect can be divided into four different parts.

idiolect	the individual features that we all have, especially in our speech; a sort of linguistic fingerprint, which can place our age, gender, regional and social background etc.
regional dialect	regional variations in speech patterns in different groups of people
historical dialect	the way different language patterns have been used in different times
social dialect	the way certain groups of language users collectively reflect their gender, social class, age, ethnicity, occupation through their language patterns.

As you would expect, these do not operate independently of each other. People of a certain age and occupation may well also show regional features of dialect, for example.

Occupational dialect

This term is used to describe distinctive language features associated with the way people earn a living or spend organised leisure. This means that they are temporary in their use, in a way that a regional accent, for example, is not. Lawyers throughout Britain will communicate with each other when working using certain occupational language, but if they meet socially they are unlikely to do so – unless of course, they are so hooked on work that they 'bring it home with them' or 'cannot stop talking shop'.

Most occupations have their own dialect features, not just the high prestige ones such as the legal profession or the language of religion. As a general rule, though, the more specialised the occupation, and the more senior the post, the more technical the language is likely to be. It is also often the case that a long-established occupation will have various accepted language rituals. How well the workers can deliver these rituals will probably be a factor in how well they are seen to be doing their jobs. Vicars, for example, are working within a long tradition of ceremony and ritual. An example of religious language is shown on pages 36,37.

Reaction against what some see as the extremes of occupational English – sometimes called **gobbledygook** – has led to such groups as the Plain English Campaign which identifies what it sees as both good and bad practice within organisations.

English language

English language

The following features are often found in examples of occupational language:

SOME SUGGESTIONS FOR LOOKING AT OCCUPATIONAL LANGUAGE

When looking at examples of occupational language you could consider:
- vocabulary, especially technical language
- grammar
- discourse/pragmatics
- ritual

When looking at the vocabulary of occupational language you are likely to find technical language understood only by those using it. For example, the following appeared as part of an advert for a lecture at Newcastle University on computing:

The ESPRIT-funded High Performance Banking (HYPERBANK) project brought together the technologies of business modelling, data warehousing, data mining (in a parallel environment) to improve customer profiling. This talk will briefly overview the project, with the main emphasis being on the data mining activity undertaken.

Some features of the technical language that are worth noting here include:
- use of capital letters
- use of **acronyms**, or words which are made up of initial letters e.g. ESPRIT
- invention of single words formed from other words i.e. Hyperbank (HIGH PERformance BANKing)
- use of metaphors which are unfamiliar, e.g. 'data warehousing' and 'data mining'
- changing the usual grammatical function of a word, e.g. 'overview' as a verb not a noun.

While such technical language can often exclude outsiders who will not understand it, it can serve positive functions. Fellow experts can communicate quickly, briefly, and precisely, without needing long explanations, and in a social sense it can lead to a form of bonding between those who are in the know. It also gives people who know and use such language power over those who do not. The power, though, lies in the social situation, not the people themselves. So if a client goes to a lawyer, the situation will give the lawyer power. If they then meet and speak to each other in the pub later that day, there will be much more equality between them.

The **grammar** of occupational language often involves subtle differences from grammar used in a standard way, and frequently reflects issues of language change. So, for example, employee references often begin with the rather old-fashioned words:

To whom it may concern …

Whereas in the text quoted above, what was originally a noun, 'overview', itself a compound of the two words 'over' and 'view', is here being used as a verb – the lecture will 'overview the project'.

Discourse features in occupational language involve the way the language is constructed and bound together. For example, in everyday use most question and answer exchanges are two-part:

- Is there any marmalade left?
- It's in the fridge.

However in the world of teaching three-part exchanges are common:

- What's the capital of France?
- Paris?
- Yes, well done!

ACTIVITY

For a longer example of how discourse works within an occupational context, look at the following extract which shows a teacher beginning a lesson with a class of mixed sex Year 10 pupils. Any suggestion of pitch and tempo in the teacher's voice, or the body language which would inevitably accompany the utterances are missing from the transcript.

Make some notes on how the teacher establishes authority at the beginning of the lesson, and features of discourse and pragmatics that you notice here.

> come on then lads let's have you sitting down (.)
> coats off(.)
> bags off the table (1)
> morning Richard (2)
> looking slightly casual today (2)
> no it's all right (.)
> it's cold in here (2)
> Tom missing yesterday but saw you around (4)
> morning all (2)
> morning ()
> come on Daniel sit down please (1)
> I'm gonna bring you round some paper because you're going to need one sheet each later (.)
> er names on the top quickly Jack come on (.)
> let's get cracking Jenny please (8)
> OK are we ready (2)
> OK let's get started

(Source: Graham Roberts, Gosforth High School)

CONSIDER

(a) In terms of **discourse**, the teacher uses a mixture of greetings, encouragement (usually signalled by saying 'let's'), pauses and commands, often directed at specifically named students.

The greeting of 'good morning' is also a first attempt at a call to order. Saying 'let's', short for 'let us', is a way of saying that teacher and students are in this process together. Long pauses are used to establish that the teacher will only talk when the pupils are quiet; they are almost certainly accompanied by stern looks. Identifying individuals is a way of adjusting their behaviour, and of warning other students that they may be named too, if they catch the teacher's eye. The final two parts of the extract show a rhetorical question ('OK' are we ready) and then again the use of 'OK' to signal a beginning.

(b) There are also some examples of **pragmatics** at work here. We can work out that when the teacher tells Richard that he is looking casual, what he really means is that Richard is not wearing what he should be – his uniform presumably. Then when he says 'it's all right it's cold in here' the implied meaning is that Richard can continue to wear the offending item.

English language

(c) Although there is an appeal to shared interest here, and the pupils do in fact co-operate quite quickly, the fact that they say nothing to the teacher, and he/she does all the talking and directing, shows that he/she is in a position of authority. There is also a sense of ritual behaviour and language here too. A ritual is a repeated pattern of behaviour, sometimes formally ceremonial as in the church or the law, sometimes more informal, as in the example above. The references to such things as bags off the table suggest that this is an expected and regular command/request that the pupils will obey.

Occupation and ritual

There are obvious areas where you can find examples of ceremonial ritual – attend any ceremony such as a wedding, funeral, or any traditional event such as a court trial or a debate in Parliament and you will find plenty of evidence of ritual language.

The term ritual is used here in two ways:

◆ to describe the use of ceremonial language which is special to a certain occupational area
◆ to describe a certain frequently used method of using language which is common in a certain occupational area.

The traditional Christian marriage service contains the following exchange of vows between the bridegroom and the bride.

Bridegroom
I (name) take you (name)
to be my wife
to have and to hold
from this day forward;
for better, for worse,
for richer, for poorer,
in sickness and in health,
to love, cherish and worship,
till death us do part,
according to God's holy law;
and this is my solemn vow

Bride
I (name) take you (name)
to be my husband,
to have and to hold
from this day forward;
for better, for worse,
for richer, for poorer,
in sickness and in health,
to love, cherish and obey,
till death us do part,
according to God's holy law;
and this is my solemn vow

The language here is ritualised in a number of ways. It seems to belong to an earlier time (from this day forward instead of onward) and in this version has survived, immune from language change. It has many patterns and repetitions, especially in its balancing of good and bad things. It has religious vocabulary, not just the reference to God, but also words like 'holy', 'solemn' and 'vow'. It also requires ritual behaviour – in the order of service the groom always gives his vows first.

This version also contains a social requirement about male and female behaviour. Indeed the vows are identical, except for the groom promising to 'worship' his wife and the bride promising to 'obey' her husband. Here the ritual language is part of the social behaviour of an earlier age. Not surprisingly, these vows are frequently omitted nowadays.

Other examples of ritual language are the terms of address that are used in courts and Parliament. There are precise ways in which a judge must be treated and addressed, and barristers will refer to each other as 'my learned friend'. Failure to do so can lead to trouble – and it will usually be people who are ignorant of the conventions who will get them wrong. Here again we have not only an example of ritual, but also of the way in which issues of power underpin so much occupational language.

Debates in Parliament involve language rituals. Members of Parliament are only allowed to address each other using certain terms, and some terms are banned. You are not, for instance allowed to call someone a liar, even though that is what you are implying. Even school or college debates are likely to follow certain language rituals, such as having a 'motion' which will usually begin with the words 'this house believes' and which will involve formal speeches and contributions from 'the floor'.

As an example of occupational language, the following extract looks at the way a football manager responds in a post-match interview.

TASK

Read the following extract from an interview with Manchester United manager Sir Alex Ferguson.

1   Describe any features of occupational language that you can find.
2   Explore the way Ferguson replies to the interviewer's 'question'.

> **Interviewer**: In the end it was quite a nervous finish.
> **AF** : I think so. I think that you've got to give credit to Villa (.) they have a lot of pace up front and introduced the young boy Vassel I think his name was (.) and they kept us they started stretching us a bit and er they have returned to form Villa (.) so I mean it's not I don't think we've seen anything unexpected (1) I said that to the players they came here in a confident mood because you know they're not fearing about languishing in the middle of the table (.) they've still got a chance to go for that UEFA place …

(Source: Graham Wright, Gosforth High School)

CONSIDER

(a)   There is plenty of evidence of the specialist language of football, sometimes called **jargon**. 'Pace up front' 'stretching us a bit' 'languishing in the middle of the table' etc. This last phrase is also an example of **collocation**, a term used to describe words that often go together: a team can languish in mid-table but never near the top of it.

(b)   Another feature you may have noticed in Ferguson's reply is the relatively small and infrequent pauses that are used.

(c)   The most notable feature of discourse, though, is the way that Ferguson does much more than respond to the prompt he is given. The fact that he is not technically asked a question – although the interviewer's rising inflection could have suggested one – shows that the

English language

interviewer expects far more than a simple response. And that is what he gets.

(d)   What Ferguson does is give a short speech, uninterrupted by the interviewer in the way a politician would have been. In effect he is asked to comment on whether his team were struggling to win. He replies by saying the following:

Yes, they did struggle to win

Villa are a good team

When Villa used a sub he turned out to be dangerous

Villa have returned to form

he told his players that Villa could be dangerous

Villa had an incentive to win.

What this means is that if other football managers do the same – and there is evidence to suggest they do – that one of the language rituals of the post-match interview is to make a short speech in reply to a general prompt. If you watch football on television you can check to see if this is true.

Language and gender

So far in this chapter, we have seen examples of occupational language, and how power can often be seen to operate through the language that is used. This language of power tends to arise as a result of the authority that the person has in the job that they do. As women often do jobs of lower status than men, and men in authority treat women in institutions differently from the way they treat men, it is frequent to find that work-place language provides evidence simultaneously for all three of the sociolinguistic areas covered in this chapter – occupation, power and gender.

It needs to be said at the outset that the topic of language and gender is not an easy one. A brief section like this cannot do anything more than introduce one or two ideas for you to consider. Although many of you will have strong views on issues surrounding gender, and gender and language, sorting your ideas into a coherent form can be difficult. In their excellent book *Language and Gender*, Goddard and Patterson (Routledge), from which many of the ideas in this section come, argue that with research in this area going back over thirty years, it is possible to have old ideas on this topic which are now out-of-date. Ideas about gender, like all issues in language, are subject to development and change.

It is also important to stress that investigating language's contribution to the way society constructs gender must involve looking at representations of men as well as women.

The difference between sex, sexuality and gender

An important point to grasp at the outset of this section is that each of the three terms 'sex', 'sexuality' and 'gender' has different meanings.

Your 'sex' is something that is biological; you have certain biological features that lead you to being male or female.

Your 'sexuality' describes your projection of sexual feelings and your sexual orientation or preference(s).

The word 'gender' is used to refer to the socially expected characteristics that belong to your sex, rather than the biological ones. So when we talk of language and gender, we are looking at the way language supports and reflects social attitudes. Although the words 'man' and 'woman' define your sex, the words 'masculine' and 'feminine' suggest certain characteristics that are seen as typical. For example, 'masculine' is often associated with strength and power, 'feminine' with smallness and delicacy.

Connotation and collocation

Connotation refers to the level of meaning based on association we attach to words. A building might be described as large, or imposing, or towering, or monumental, or an eminence, or an eyesore, or a carbuncle, or a blot on the landscape. The word 'large' denotes size and little else, but all the other terms, which are in a sense metaphorical, connote approval or disapproval.

The word 'collocation' has already been used in this chapter, with reference to the Sir Alex Ferguson text. Collocation refers to frequently occurring words that appear in the vicinity of each other. Sometimes this refers to word order, so 'fish and chips' is the accepted order, never 'chips and fish'. 'Men and women' are always put with 'men' first, but 'ladies and gentlemen' reverses this order.

As a further example of collocation, read again part of the following sentence from the second paragraph of this chapter:

'This means that there is no such thing as 'real' masculinity and femininity; they are terms used to describe social constructions.'

You will notice that masculinity is mentioned before femininity. It is not impossible to put them the other way round, but it would seem strange to most readers. This is because we always put masculinity first, reflecting a mind-set that sees one word order as being more natural than the other. In putting the words in one order, we are putting what they represent in one order too – with maleness coming first.

Language use is in a constant state of change. Thirty years or more of attention to the way language reflects gender, and the difference in the way men and women are treated and perceived, is bound to have an effect. Legislation has helped, but this does not mean that men and women are no longer gendered in language; it just means that the process is less obvious.

In a UCAS reference which a school or college provides for university applicants, there is usually a comment about the personality of the student. Comments on female students used to say things like:

Neat and attractive in appearance, she …
She is a very presentable young lady who …

Reference was not however made to the way male students looked. Looks were deemed as significant when describing a woman's suitability for university, but not for a man's. Men's personalities were commented on by referring to qualities such as their 'strength' of character and their willingness to challenge accepted views.

Such obvious references to female appearance would be unlikely in a reference now, at least from an institution with some awareness of gender issues. This does not mean, though, that connotations of gender no longer exist when men and women are described – they are just a little less obvious.

English language

English language

ACTIVITY

1   The following descriptions of students' personalities and attitudes were used by male and female teachers from a mixed comprehensive school in recent UCAS references. Can the sex of the student be identified from the connotations associated with these words and phrases? There is no right answer here, but analysing these terms in mixed groups may lead to some interesting discussion.

a refreshing personality   a determined character   a bubbly personality
a solid character

very industrious   very conscientious

embraces life wholeheartedly   is a lovely student   is a charming student

is very serious with little time for small talk people   is good with people

has a zany personality   is very sincere   is very much their own person

2   Now consider the following:
   ◆   What connotations arise from 'a solid character' being written about a woman?
   ◆   What connotations arise from 'is a charming student' being written about a man?
   ◆   Does the sex of the writer and/or reader of the comment affect the way it is understood?

3   The process of change can also be seen in the way young men and women refer to each other as objects of sexual interest and attraction. Language textbooks, when exploring language and gender, in the past would highlight the way men would refer to women using words such as 'crumpet' 'dish' and 'tart' – words which all carry the suggestion that women are items of food, suitable for consumption.

   There was rarely any reference, however, to the way women referred to men, thus endorsing the view that while men were the active pursuers of partners, women were the passive receivers of attention. Whether or not this was the case then, it is certainly not so now.

   A straw poll conducted among a group of 17-year-olds in a Newcastle school, showed the following terms being used to describe a member of the opposite sex:

dishy, slapper, tart, totty, top totty, bit of all right, fit, tasty, talent.

   All of the words were used interchangeably, by men about women and by women about men. The following questions can be the basis of some research/discussion.
   ◆   Are any of these words used in your school/college/region?
   ◆   Can you work out what the derivation of the words may be, and say what connotations go with the words?
   ◆   What are the current words used by you and your friends?

4   The sports pages of newspapers are a useful resource for descriptions of men and women. Writing in the *Independent on Sunday*, Alan Hubbard had the following to say about the gymnast Lisa Mason:

   ❝ She has a sparkle in her eyes, a stud in her nose and silver-ringed hoops dangling from her ears. Then there's her looks and personality … a bubbly, chatty youngster … she's usually mistaken for a model with her sculptured shape and curves …❞

   (Independent on Sunday 13.2.00)

Look at a variety of newspapers over the space of a week and compile a list of quotations and pictures that use language and images to suggest gendered characteristics. This can then be used as data to explore the issues raised here.

5   Men now spend ever-increasing amounts of money on cosmetic products such as face creams – but advertisers do not regard men and women as an identical market. This reflects in part the way men and women are gendered, and it contributes in part to that process. Advertisers sell what is essentially the same product in very different ways.

The following words and phrases were used in advertisements specifically for face creams: what connotations can you find for each one, and what do they show about the way men and women are gendered in our culture?

For women	For men
fragrance	stops shine
freshness	grease
smooth skin	clogged up pores
gentle cream	re programme your skin
pure moisturising	leaves no stickiness
soothing	helps heal cuts
softer skin	firmer skin
	it doesn't mean you're soft

Representing masculinity

Whereas most work on language and gender used to look at how society and language constructed views of women, more recent work has looked at representations of masculinity too. The following two advertisements raise some issues about the ways in which men are represented. Both advertisements appeared in magazines aimed directly at men.

TASK
What ideas about masculinity can be found in these two advertisements?

English language

YES, THEY LOOK DAFT.
BUT THEY GET THE JOB DONE.

NEW: THE CLEAR
PORE STRIP

NIVEA FOR MEN WHO DARE TO CARE.

CONSIDER

(a) The Nivea advertisement is trying to get men to buy a face-care product. Although it is a known fact that men do buy such products, the advertisement nonetheless constructs a view that men will only buy a face cleaner if there is a vaguely medical condition which needs treating. Men are not in the business of looking good just for the sheer hell of it. In paying attention to their skin they know they are going to look foolish in front of their mates, but at least they will be buying something that gets the 'job done' without too much fuss. The idea of getting a job done, of being active is an important part of the advertisement's message.

In the cartoon instructions of how to use the strips again suggest that men are not used to doing this sort of cosmetic thing – they need help if they are going to end up smiling. But nonetheless, if they are brave enough, the treatment will work – they will take up the 'dare'. For after all, 'who dares wins'.

(b) This means that although the two adverts apparently present different aspects of constructed masculinity, they are actually much closer than may at first appear. In the Suzuki advert the first word of the text, 'action', placed on its own, without qualification, takes the reader into a world where he is in control, at speed. He acts, and his ride reacts; 'the throttle opens and the grin broadens.' Here we are at the 'cutting edge', with man and machine blending into perfect harmony. The technical specification details suggest that a man needs some facts if he is to cause a 'reaction'.

(c) The exact nature of this reaction is left at the level of implication only, but there is a strong sense that this man is not only riding a bike, but riding a woman too. The most obvious reason for thinking this is the fact that the biker is seen with the Cerne Abbas giant chalked on the hillside behind him. This lone ancient figure, part hunter, part sexual symbol of male power, is linked with the lone biker – they are both primed for action.

It may well be that you have read these advertisements rather differently to the views expressed here. And how you have read them will depend upon your own sex and cultural background. Nonetheless, with a boom in published material aimed directly at men, and with men now being targeted by the lucrative cosmetic markets, there is lots of material around which is now placing masculinity at the centre of its attention.

Markedness

If a word is said by linguists to be **marked**, it means that it signals to the language users that there is something not normal or standard in its meaning. An obvious group of words that show this are words which end in 'ess' to show they refer to a female:

waiter	waitress
actor	actress
manager	manageress
singer	songstress
host	hostess

In this case the words in the second column are all marked, because they specifically refer to women. The words in the first column are unmarked because they refer to the norm, by implication a man.

The words 'seamstress', 'seductress' and 'temptress' could also be put in the list above, except they do not seem to have an unmarked word to go alongside them. A 'seamstress' is a woman sewer, and there was once a word 'seamster' which is no longer used, presumably because such work is not seen as something men do. The word 'seductress' used to be matched by the word 'seductor', but that too is no longer used while the word 'temptress' does not have an unmarked parallel. This suggests that our language accepts that only women sew, seduce or tempt.

Another suffix, or word ending which can suggest a female is 'ette'. The New Oxford Dictionary gives three possible meanings for the suffix 'ette':

something small e.g. kitchenette, laundrette

something that is an imitation or substitute e.g. flannelette, winceyette

denoting female gender e.g. usherette.

ACTIVITY

There are other ways of showing markedness than the use of suffixes. One way is to place a marked term in front of an occupation, i.e. male nurse.

Listed below are some occupations. Discuss, in a group if possible, how many of these would be prefaced by a marking term – such as woman, female, lady – if the job referred to is done by a woman. There is no right answer here, but it should encourage you to think of why some occupations, but not others, are more likely to show women marked in this way.

1	Doctor	6	Judge
2	Dentist	7	Football referee
3	Consultant	8	Managing Director
4	Psychiatrist	9	Police officer
5	Vicar	10	Teacher

Not all markedness shows the male as the norm. Markedness in language reflects conventional ways of seeing things, the 'normal' state of affairs. Consider the word 'nurse'. A

English language

man who is a nurse is known as a 'male nurse', but once you go higher up the ranks that way of marking is not available. It would sound strange to talk of a 'male sister' or a 'male matron'. It would seem that within the language system at least, you have to be a woman to be a senior nurse. This means that we take a stereotypical view of nursing, largely seeing it as a role fulfilled by women.

Meanwhile one group of Newcastle women that took part in the survey on terms for sexual attraction referred to earlier in this section, were asked by their teacher to define the meaning of the word 'slapper' as applied to a man. Their definition was 'a male slag'.

The English language, therefore, has a way of normalising men in some roles, and women in others. In an attempt to counteract this inequality, deliberate attempts have been made in some areas to find words that can be unmarked. Many schools and colleges now have a 'Head' or a 'Headteacher', rather than a 'Headmaster' or 'Headmistress'. The word 'chair' is now often used in place of the generic chairman (which can be both male or female) or the obviously marked 'chairwoman'. Deliberately avoiding marked terms is not universal, though: some schools and colleges retain the marked terms headmaster or headmistress.

ACTIVITY
Research the way names and titles are used in the institution you attend. To what extent do they show the use of marked forms?

The pronoun problem

We can examine how issues of language and gender change over time by looking at the grammatical problem raised by the fact that traditional English grammar has no gender- neutral third person singular pronoun. Although 'he/him/his' and 'she/her/hers' are usable when the sex of the person referred to is known, it becomes problematic when either the sex of the person is not known or it can refer to a member of either sex.

The third person plural pronoun 'they/their/theirs' does not indicate gender – it is gender neutral. So, for example, if a teacher says: 'I'd like four students to volunteer to give up their free period to help me ...', there is no indication of the sex of those students. Assuming it is a mixed class they could be boys and girls, or just boys, or just girls.

The same does not apply, though, when one unspecified student is required. Traditionally, the teacher would have to say: 'I'd like one student to volunteer to give up **his** free period, and if **he** would like to give me **his** name I'd be grateful ...'.

Another example of using the male form in the singular is still seen on many buses:

> Do not stand forward of this notice or speak to the driver as **he** will be distracted.

When writing, the problem can sometimes be avoided by using alternative forms such as 'he/she' or 'she/he' or '(s)he'. However this option is not available when speaking. This has led to the practice, in the interests of equality, of certain rules of grammar being relaxed. Increasingly, therefore, people are using 'they/them/theirs' for singular and plural reference. This would give: 'I'd like one student to volunteer to give up **their** free period, and if **they** would like to give me **their** name I'd be grateful ...'.

This use is not universal. Sticking absolutely by the grammatical rules, even though it is possible that some of the audience could be offended, is still practised.

Political correctness

This chapter closes then, in a sense, where it began; looking at issues of language and power. The notion of political correctness is a complex one. Perhaps the closest definition is that found in the New Oxford English Dictionary, reproduced below.

ACTIVITY

The New Oxford English Dictionary, published in 1998, defines political correctness as follows:

The avoidance of forms of expression or action that are perceived to exclude, marginalise or insult groups of people who are socially disadvantaged or discriminated against.

The words 'that are perceived to' carry a lot of weight here – one person's perception is not the same as another's. This means that while some people might applaud political correctness as a sensitive use of language, others might ridicule it for its over-attention to fashionable causes. To what extent are the following usages politically correct in your view, and are you using the expression with approval or disapproval?

1 She is a mistress of her craft (instead of the male marked 'master')
2 She is a master of her craft (refusing to use the female marked 'mistress' which has another meaning anyway)
3 One person's perception is not the same as another's (instead of one man's)
4 Visually impaired (to describe people with sight problems)
5 Ethnic diversity (to describe people of different races/cultures/religions)
6 Students with special needs
7 Students with learning difficulties
8 Patwa (a form of Black English, deliberately spelt this way rather than 'patois')
9 Poems from other cultures (i.e. not white English mainstream)

Recommended Reading: *Language and Gender* by Angela Goddard and Lindsey Mean Patterson. Published by Routledge, ISBN 04151772

TECHNICAL TERMS

acronyms a word composed of the initials of other words, and pronounced as a whole word e.g. ASH, Action on Smoking and Health

collocation the way certain words frequently appear together, often in a certain order

connotation the connotations of a word are the associations it creates

dialect a language variety in which features of vocabulary and grammar show the user belonging to a particular social or regional group

gobbledygook a word used to describe occupational language that is impossible for outsiders to understand

jargon the technical language of a certain occupation. The word is often used critically, as with gobbledygook above.

markedness this is when a word indicates that it is not the norm, e.g. 'waitress' is marked by the 'ess' denoting a female waiter

sociolinguistics the study of the ways in which language is used in social contexts reflecting its influence on, and by, different social groups

English language

5 | Original writing

In this chapter you will be introduced to some ideas surrounding texts that you produce. Your work on reading and analysing texts by others should help here, but particular focus is placed on creating a voice, using data, planning, and writing a commentary.

Producing texts

By now you have probably read most of the material in this section of the book dealing with AS English Language. Much of the work so far has been based upon the analysis of texts written by other people. Now, however, the situation is reversed: this time it is you who will be producing the texts.

This certainly does not mean, that you forget all that has gone before. The very same frameworks that you applied to the analysis of texts can now be applied to your own writing. Sometimes these frameworks will be applied very consciously, as you make key decisions about how your writing will be shaped. At other times the process will be on a less conscious level, with the flow of your writing leading you to make certain choices as you go.

Making choices is a key phrase as we move on to looking at the third component of AS courses. When faced with the blank page that has to be filled with your own ideas, you will start to fill that page by seeing a set of choices before you, and then making your decisions.

A WRITING FRAMEWORK

A range of technical terms can be used to describe the writing process, but in this book we will use the following writing framework. For each piece of writing that you produce you will have to make choices within the following areas:

Field	What topic are you covering in your text? What is your subject matter? Does it involve the collection and presentation of data? Is data already provided?
Function	What is the main purpose of your text? Is it to entertain, persuade, inform, or instruct/advise? Or, more probably, does it combine more than one element of these?
Mode	What sort of text are you producing? What genre will be you be using? How will it reflect other similar texts? How will it be different from other similar texts?
Tenor	What voice or voices will you create in your text? What will be its overall tone? What relationship will you create between the text and the reader? How formal will the writing be?

English language

Depending on the specification you are following, your Original Writing component will either be assessed as an examination, or as coursework. Clearly there are some differences between the two approaches, and it will help if they are made clear at the start. As far as you are concerned, find the column which applies to you, and make sure that you understand its implications.

Coursework	Examination
You choose topic	Topic chosen for you
You choose the genre	Genre probably chosen for you
You choose the target audience	Audience chosen for you
You research relevant data	Data is provided or not needed
You have time for a number of drafts	Only time for one draft
You can use ICT	Must be handwritten
You produce a finished product	You produce a working draft

Writing to inform

To see how this works, consider the following sample question:

Your school/college provides an induction programme for students joining the post-16 courses. You have been asked to present a lively, informative talk about the extra-curricular and other services provided by the institution. Suggested topics include leisure facilities, societies and clubs, work experience, careers advice, counselling services, events and trips. The text should be sufficiently clear and detailed to be given by someone else, if need be. Do not write it as a transcript of a live talk.

In terms of doing this question in an exam, the following apply:

Field

Extra-curricular activities in your school/college. Data can be 'true' or a version of the truth.

Function

To inform, in a lively way, possible recruits, so elements of persuasion and entertainment too.

Mode

Lively, informative talk for 16-year-olds. The final product will be a handwritten draft.

Tenor

Aiming to establish a warm, relaxed, quite informal voice, but with clear elements of persuasion and rhetoric.

If, however, you decide to do a piece of informative writing for coursework, based upon the same field or topic, you will have choices on how you deliver this.

So, for example, you might decide to do:

Anytown High School: An unofficial guide to life in our sixth form.

The way this would work within our framework is as follows:

Field

Extra-curricular activities in your school/college. Data can be 'true' or a version of the truth.

Function

To inform, but with entertainment almost as important. Could be some persuasion too.

Mode

An 'unofficial' guide, but still requiring certain values if it is to be published, especially if the school is to allow it to be distributed. It may be based upon the reading of unofficial guides to universities.

Tenor

Very informal, speaking directly to 16-year-olds. Deliberate use of teenage slang, but not rude – too offensive and authorities will ban it.

Here then, we have two different models for producing a piece of writing, one for examination, the other for coursework. It is worth stressing, though, that in both of the above cases there is an element of role-play. In terms of examinations, all tasks set will be simulations – the examiners cannot assume that you have much specific knowledge in advance. This, incidentally, is why so many exam questions take your own educational experience as a starting point. The fact that you are being educated is one thing they can guarantee!

However, despite the fact that you will go to a lot of effort in terms of production quality in your coursework, it is still likely that all, or most of, your writing will be a simulation rather than a real text for publication. The closer you can get to areas of your own research and interest the better, but in the end the mode you choose with which to present your text - radio script, play for performance, pamphlet for doctors' surgery etc. – is likely to mean that your text is produced for your AS module rather than for 'real' production.

Finding a voice

Introduction

Once you have established the field and function for your piece of writing, you then face further key choices. The first of these is to establish the mode of your piece of writing; just what precise form is it going to take? What genre of writing, or speaking as writing, are you going to produce?

Although within coursework finding the field/function/mode cannot be dismissed as a simple task, the most challenging part of the process is still to come (in an exam situation, it is possible that all three will be specified in the question itself). This challenge involves creating the right tenor – of finding a voice.

A number of different terms are used to describe this process of creating the right tenor. Register, tone, and style are all words that are used to describe the way a written text is constructed to communicate with its readers. In reality it does not really matter which of these terms you use to describe the process as a whole; far more important is to know about and be able to manipulate the different elements that make up the process.

Look at these brief quotations.

Road safety is important. If you know your stuff, you'll be safe wherever you go. Traffic lights help you when you are out walking or biking. Why not try to remember this riddle. R 3D Remember to stop O = Only have a look; G = Go on over

Don't talk to me about traffic calming. The real people in danger are the car drivers. Let's have some thought for the motorist for once.

> I am writing to express my concern about road safety in our area. I have three children, all under the age of 13, and I get very worried when they are near roads, even quiet roads.

It is immediately obvious that they are about the same topic, road safety, yet they 'sound' very different.

The first one is addressing children. How do we know? Partly, of course, because of the content; it is hardly likely that adults would require something to help them remember the sequence of traffic lights. But also because of the way language is used. The frequent address to 'you', the uncomplicated lexis or vocabulary, the straightforward syntax or sentence structure all contribute to the created voice.

The second is part of a script for a radio broadcast. How do we know? It has examples of the **rhetoric** of persuasive speech: 'Don't talk to me'; 'the real people'; 'let's have some thought for'. It argues a case through a series of short sentences. The speaker refers to self, and to 'us' (in 'let's').

The third is part of a letter to a local councillor. How do we know? It has the pragmatic convention of much letter writing which begins by saying 'I am writing to express my concern.' This in one sense states the obvious – 'I am writing' – but also states the main function of the text. Here there is a sense of calm, measured argument which can be seen in the more complex syntax.

TO SUCCEED WITH ORIGINAL WRITING YOU NEED:

- good content and ideas
- suitable vocabulary
- suitable sentence structures, paragraphs and cohesion
- effective use of genre conventions
- a clear sense of who is talking the text – the narrator
- a clear sense of who is reading or 'hearing' the text – the narratee.

In order to explore these ideas in more detail, some data is required. The following was used by the students from whose work the above extracts are quoted. It involves road accident figures for Newcastle Upon Tyne from 1990-98.

Using data

Selecting what you need

Data 1

The following data applies to road accident statistics for Newcastle Upon Tyne from 1990-1998.

Year	Slight Accident	Serious Accident	Killed	Total Accidents
1990	924	221	29	1175
1991	838	189	20	1047
1992	821	184	11	1016
1993	724	147	16	887
1994	784	156	13	953
1995	783	152	16	951
1996	829	122	10	961
1997	925	120	10	1055
1998	914	103	3	1020

(Source : *Road Safety 2000* - Newcastle City Council)

However good the technical aspects of your writing, you can only do well if you have good material to work with. If you are using factual material, such as the road accident figures in the above data, you need to have an angle on them, an interpretation that you can work with. You need to have a good 'spin' to use a word currently associated with politics. All the various features referred to in the box above will deliver this spin.

TASK

Using the information in Data 1, find the statistics that you would use to support the following original writing exercises:

1   A press release from the city council, saying Newcastle roads are getting safer and safer.
2   A press release from RoSPA (Royal Society for Prevention of Accidents) saying road accident figures are getting worse.
3   A local news story hailing Newcastle as a safety success story.
4   A local news story accusing Newcastle of being a safety disaster.
5   A pamphlet for local school children urging greater attention to safety.

Now plan and/or write a version of at least one of these tasks.

CONSIDER

(a)   Although you should have few problems selecting figures to suit your case, how you use them is vital. Take question 3 above. Here are figures you could use:
   –   Only 3 killed compared to 29 in 1990
       Many fewer serious accidents: 103 compared to 221 in 1990

   However what is now needed is a 'spin' on these figures if we are to produce a text for a local newspaper. This could begin as follows:

Safety Cracked

Official figures released by Newcastle Council show that the streets are safer than they have ever been. A staggering reduction of nearly 1000% in fatalities over the last nine years indicates that safety policies are working.

Add to this the fact that serious accidents have more than halved in the same period, and it is no wonder that local councillors are celebrating making Newcastle the Safety Capital of the North.

(b)   Even from this short extract, we can see how the text is taking shape. With its punning headline, and its short paragraphs it reads like a piece of journalism (suitable vocabulary suitable sentence structures and paragraphs/effective use of genre conventions). It takes the reduction from 29 deaths to 3, but makes it more sensational by using a very high percentage figure and talking of a 'staggering' reduction. Likewise 'more than halved' gives an arguably greater impact than using the actual figures (good content and ideas).

   The 'speaker' of the text (or narrator) is also leading the 'reader' of the text (or narratee) to certain points of view. Opinions are presented as facts – policies are working, Newcastle is the Safety Capital of the North – and we are told it is 'no wonder' that councillors are pleased. The narrator of the text is clearly establishing a point of view, and the 'reader' is expected to follow it (a clear sense of who is talking and hearing the text).

English language

Narrator and narratee

You will have noticed in the paragraph above that the words 'narrator' and 'narratee' are used to describe who is speaking the text and who is reading it. These are important terms to describe what is going on in the texts that you, and others produce. Just as a text is a constructed thing, then so are the narrator and narratee. It should be pretty obvious that when an author invents a first-person narrator to tell a story, then the author and narrator are not the same person. Chaucer wrote *The Merchant's Tale*, but the invented character, the Merchant, tells the tale. This is equally the case if the story is told in the third person. The voice behind the text is not the author's voice, but a voice the author has invented.

Just as there is a difference between the author of a text and a narrator, so there is between the real reader of a text, and the invented reader, or narratee. The narratee can be invented to have a certain background, set of values, etc. in just the same way that a narrator can. When producing a commentary on your original writing it is always worth talking about how you have created narrators and narratees.

Sequencing

The first set of data was used to show how selective choice from a mass of statistics could lead to the spin most suited to purpose, task and audience. The second set of data will also show how a point of view can be put across, but this time the focus will be on the cohesion of the text that is to be produced – how it all holds together. This will involve looking at:

◆ sequencing of material
◆ how sentences work
◆ the need for paragraphs which link together.

To help to illustrate these points, historical data will be used. This will be based around the story of Henry VIII and his six wives.

In broad outline, the following list gives details of Henry VIII's six wives, in chronological order.

Name	How marriage ends	Religion	Children
Catherine of Aragon	marriage annulled	Catholic	Mary
Anne Boleyn	executed	Protestant	Elizabeth
Jane Seymour	died after childbirth	Protestant	Edward
Anne of Cleves	divorced	Protestant	
Catherine Howard	executed	Catholic	
Catherine Parr	outlived Henry	Protestant	

This is how a school reference history book writes about Henry's wives.

The king and his wives

The story of Henry VIII's six wives is closely linked to the story of the changes in the English Church. By the time Catherine of Aragon died in 1536, Henry's feelings towards Anne had cooled, especially as she had recently given birth to a dead son. She was accused of being unfaithful, probably falsely, and executed with a sword, as a sign of 'mercy'. The king then sent her two-year-old daughter Elizabeth away from court.

Jane Seymour was quiet and modest, quite the opposite of Anne. The Seymours were an ambitious Protestant family already in favour at court, and when the king married Jane immediately after Anne's execution, their influence grew. Jane gave Henry his longed-for son, Edward, in 1537 but she died twelve days later.

In 1540 Cromwell organized Henry's fourth marriage, to Anne of Cleves, a German princess, as part of an alliance with some German Protestant princes. Henry soon tired of the German alliance, and divorced Anne, saying she looked like a 'Flanders mare', a thickset farm horse. Then Cromwell's enemies at court brought about his fall. Henry's hard-headed, efficient minister was executed a month later.

On the day that Cromwell was beheaded, Henry married Catherine Howard. She was the young niece of the powerful Duke of Norfolk, a Catholic who, although he had accepted Henry as Supreme Head of the Church, had worked against Cromwell, and opposed Protestant changes in the Church. Henry soon regretted the loss of Cromwell, who had served him faithfully for eight years, and he regretted this marriage too. Catherine was foolish enough to be unfaithful to the unhealthy, irritable old king, and she was executed in 1543.

The king's last choice was Catherine Parr, a sensible widow and probably a Protestant. She looked after the elderly king and his three children, who by this time were all back at court, and she outlived Henry.

ACTIVITY

Make notes on the following:

1   How does this account sequence events in terms of time? Why do you think this is the case?
2   Using the reading skills you worked on in earlier chapters, what do you notice about the way the wives are described to school children?

CONSIDER

(a)   The wives are presented chronologically – in other words in the strict time sequence in which they occur. The precise dates reinforce this point that is only to be expected in a basic history reference book, where facts are important.

(b)   However this is not just a factual account. It contains a lot of attitudes and values held towards the king and his wives. The very fact that they are called wives – not queens – is a good example of collocation (see the previous chapter). 'The six wives of Henry VIII' as a phrase suggests that they have status only in being married to him. The women are not really seen as individuals, more part of a process of kingship. The king requires certain things: sexual interest; sexual faithfulness; male heirs; political allies. If any of the wives fail in these departments, they are disposed of in various ways.

English language

English language

(c)   The text's attitudes to the wives can be seen at various points. Anne Boleyn is not 'quiet and modest', so, by implication deserves to have her head cut off. Jane 'gives' Henry a son, losing her own life in the process – but the history text does not comment on this. Anne of Cleves is dismissed by Henry as a 'Flanders Mare' and our history book kindly tells us that this is a 'thickset farm horse'. Henry himself, of course, was by this time massive in size and petulant and unpredictable in behaviour. Meanwhile Catherine is 'foolish enough' to be unfaithful, thus meaning, presumably, that she is therefore responsible for her death. Catherine Parr is 'sensible' enough to survive.

Note too how the connectives 'but' at the end of paragraph 2, and 'and' at the end of paragraph 4 imply that nothing special has happened, just a normal sequence of events.

Planning your own text

The history book account is one version of the story, but there are others that could be written. Most of them would require some further research, but here are some possibilities for original writing; all of them involving an element of role-play and an element of historical research.

◆   The secret diaries of Catherine Howard
◆   Letters home from Anne of Cleves
◆   Newspaper accounts of the execution of Anne Boleyn
◆   Catherine Parr writing on the last days of a tyrant
◆   Extracts from a magazine series called 'From Catherine of Aragon to Diana – Royal Wives through the Ages'

As an example of how to plan a piece of writing we will work on the last task quoted above: an extract from a magazine series called 'From Catherine of Aragon to Diana - Royal Wives through the Ages'.

The planning needs to be in several stages. The first is an outline plan which identifies some key features. It can be used as a framework for all your planning of original writing.

Example of outline plan	
Audience:	mainly women readers of a newspaper supplement
Purpose:	to inform, entertain and persuade
Genre:	journalistic feature
Narrator:	journalist with own ideas and opinions
Narratee:	readers who are willing to accept an alternative view of history

Now we require a more detailed plan, which again involves making choices. There are usually lots of ways to write a text but what we need is a method which best serves our purpose.

Example of detailed plan
(1) Establishment of main point/ attitude right at start – Henry as object of scorn
(2) Overview of Henry's reasons for marriage
(3) Anne of Cleves as first example
(4) Anne Boleyn/Catherine Howard – the executed wives, linked by supposed adultery
(5) The quiet sufferers – Catherine of Aragon and Catherine Parr

What this plan does is give us a working outline. It begins to give a sense of the shape of our writing. Now it is time for a first draft. This will be all you have time for in an examination, whereas with coursework you will be able to do at least one more. The following is the opening section only.

The London Boor

In our series on royal wives, we now turn to a serial marrier, Henry VIII, and take a fresh look at the treatment given to royal wives in the sixteenth century.

No king is more famous for his wives than Henry VIII. And no king deserves more scorn for the way he treated his wives than Henry VIII.

He married them for a variety of reasons. He wanted healthy male heirs to succeed him; he wanted political allies and the wealth they would bring; he wanted sexually attractive women to sleep with.

Of all the wives, the one who most highlights the sickening abuse of women in those times is his fourth wife, Anne of Cleves. A German princess, she was spotted by Henry's then chief minister Thomas Cromwell as a potential bride. Legend has it that Henry was persuaded into the marriage by seeing a flattering oil-painting of her. What she certainly brought with her, though, was much needed wealth and political influence in Europe.

But Henry soon tired of the political alliance, and so of Anne – or was it the other way round? This king, grotesquely overweight himself, and certainly no oil-painting, had the power to dismiss her from his presence with the dismissive description that she was 'A Flanders Mare'. Such hypocrisy!

At least Anne of Cleves survived. Not so lucky were second wife Anne Boleyn and fifth wife Catherine Howard. Both were accused of adultery and beheaded. Henry, of course, could do what he wanted sexually. Only wives were expected to be faithful …

Writing a commentary

The Assessment Objectives for AS English Language make it clear that you must do more than write your own text. You must also:

◆ draw on knowledge of linguistic features to explain and comment on choices made
◆ discuss and explore concepts and issues relating to language use.

Some students produce excellent texts, but then write poor commentaries, which seems surprising given that they should have a pretty good idea of what they have done.

The first point to make about writing a commentary, especially if time and/or space is limited, is that you should look at the major issues involved, rather than making highly specific comments on individual words. And the more important issues will involve looking at the choices you have made. These choices will be linked back to your original planning. You will need not only to identify what choices you made, but also you will need to say why.

English language

Here is our original broad plan for the article on Henry's wives. As usual, circumstances will be slightly different from examination to coursework.

Outline plan	
Audience:	mainly women readers of a newspaper supplement
Purpose:	to inform, entertain and persuade
Genre:	journalistic feature
Narrator:	journalist with own ideas and opinions
Narratee:	readers who are willing to accept an alternative view of history

The first three of these categories may have been given to you in a task, but the last two, involving narrator and narratee are well worth commenting on, because they are at the heart of all texts. You might say:

> Here the narrator is sharp, has opinions, takes sides. The narrator expects the narratee to want to be challenged, to be reasonably well-informed already and to have sympathies with a different view of history than is found in school text books.

Now we need to look at our detailed plan to comment on further choices.

Detailed plan
(1) Establishment of main point/ attitude right at start – Henry as object of scorn
(2) Overview of Henry's reasons for marriage
(3) Anne of Cleves as first example
(4) Anne Boleyn/Catherine Howard – the executed wives, linked by supposed adultery
(5) The quiet sufferers – Catherine of Aragon and Catherine Parr

This plan, when it was made, focused essentially on the sequence of ideas, and these are worth commenting on:

> The attitude of the narrator is established at once, and this is followed by an outline of Henry's reasons for marrying. It implies that these reasons all centre on his desires, with little thought for the women involved.
>
> Rather than take the wives chronologically, more emphasis is given to the main point about male royal behaviour by looking first at Anne of Cleves. She shows clearly the way women were traded for power and influence, and the very sexist way in which she was simply discarded can be seen to be as cruel as the executions of two wives for supposed adultery. Putting these two first would lead to sensationalism; starting with a less obviously violent story makes the main point better.

You will notice so far that the commentary has focused on choices that have affected the main point of writing the text. Without such comments, any details about language used become pointless.

So far then the commentary has looked at:

◆ main purposes

◆ narrator and narratee

- openings (and closures for a completed text)
- sequences
- choice of content.

Now it is time to turn to some linguistic features used. These are best addressed by looking at:
- use of genre conventions
- sentence structures, paragraphs, and cohesion
- significant vocabulary.

Commenting on sentences, which are key building blocks of text, is vital. It will help you at this point if you can identify four types of sentence structure that occur frequently in writing. These are:

Simple sentences
These contain one verb. An example from above is 'No king is more famous than Henry VIII'.

Compound sentences
These use connecting words like 'and', 'but 'etc. An example from above is 'Both were accused of adultery and beheaded'.

Complex sentences
These have subordinate clauses as well as a main clause. An example from above is 'This king, grotesquely overweight himself, and certainly no oil-painting, had the power to dismiss her from his presence and did so with the unkind comment that she was 'A Flanders Mare'. Here, 'grotesquely overweight himself' and 'and certainly no oil painting' are subordinate to the main clause 'This king had the power to dismiss her ...'

Minor sentences
These are not fully sentences at all, but nonetheless stand alone. An example from above is 'Such hypocrisy!'

Now we are ready to pick up the commentary on our article again.

In terms of genre conventions, there is a punning headline. The word 'boor' means someone who behaves uncouthly, but it also sounds like 'boar' which is an animal and so links to Anne being called a 'mare' and also 'bore', someone who is not as interesting as they think.

After a trailer into the article, the first paragraph contains two simple sentences with lots of repetition of words and phrases. Although this could be one compound sentence, by using 'and' to start the second sentence there is more emphasis on the key word 'scorn'.

Each paragraph is designed to have a close link with the one that has gone before - a strong feature of most journalism. So from reference to Henry at the end of paragraph 1, the second paragraph opens with 'he'. Paragraph 3 moves the story on, and 'but' at the beginning of paragraph 4 shows a change of events. Paragraph 5 begins with mentioning Anne of Cleves but then connects her, through difference, to Anne Boleyn and Catherine Howard.

To support the anti-Henry approach, certain rhetorical devices have been used. Repetition in the first paragraph has already been mentioned. Repeating 'he wanted' in the second paragraph

English language

highlights his selfishness. The idea of an oil-painting has been played with – again to make Henry seem unpleasant. The rhetorical question in paragraph 4 deliberately casts doubt on Henry's real motives, whereas using 'of course' in the final paragraph is an address to the narratee saying you agree, don't you?

This commentary is on part of a text only. To finish a commentary for AS, you would comment honestly on how well you feel you have achieved your task. You can also use the 'I' form when writing, which can make the effect more personal and convincing. Here, is the full commentary on the Original Writing extract used above:

Here the narrator I have used is sharp, has opinions, takes sides. The narrator expects the narratee to want to be challenged, to be reasonably well-informed already and to have sympathies with a different view of history than is found in school textbooks.

The attitude of the narrator is established at once, and this is followed by an outline of Henry's reasons for marrying. It implies that these reasons all centre on his desires, with little thought for the women involved.

Rather than take the wives chronologically, I have given more emphasis to the main point about male royal behaviour by looking first at Anne of Cleves. She shows clearly the way women were traded for power and influence, and I wanted the very sexist way in which she was simply discarded to be seen to be as cruel as the executions of two wives for supposed adultery. Putting these two first would lead to sensationalism; starting with a less obviously violent story makes the main point better.

In terms of genre conventions, I have used a punning headline. The word 'boor' means someone who behaves uncouthly, but it also sounds like 'boar' which is an animal and so links to Anne being called a 'mare' and also 'bore', someone who is not as important as they think.

After a trailer into the article, my first paragraph contains two simple sentences with lots of repetition of words and phrases. Although this could be one compound sentence, by using 'and' to start the second sentence there is more emphasis on the key word 'scorn'.

I have designed each paragraph to have a close link with the one that has gone before – a strong feature of most journalism. So from reference to Henry at the end of paragraph 1, the second paragraph opens with 'he'. Paragraph 3 moves the story on, and 'but' at the beginning of paragraph 4 shows a change of events. Paragraph 5 begins with mentioning Anne of Cleves but then connects her, through difference, to Anne Boleyn and Catherine Howard.

To support the anti-Henry approach, I have used certain rhetorical devices. Repetition in the first paragraph has already been mentioned. Repeating 'he wanted' in the second paragraph highlights his selfishness. The idea of an oil-painting has been played with – again to make Henry seem unpleasant. The rhetorical question in paragraph 4 deliberately casts doubt on Henry's real motives, whereas using 'of course' in the final paragraph is an address to the narratee saying you agree, don't you?

This chapter has looked at some approaches to Original Writing. If you wish to read about creating your own literary texts, now turn to the section on Original Writing in Chapter 2 AS Language and Literature, on page 75.

TECHNICAL TERMS

field   the topic of a text, its subject matter

function   the purpose of a text, why it has been produced

mode   the sort of text being produced, and its possible genre

narrator   the constructed voice that 'speaks' a text

narratee   the 'ideal' constructed reader who reads the text

rhetoric   methods used to persuade in speaking and/or writing

tenor   the tone used in a text

English language and literature

1 Making connections

This chapter outlines the assessment objectives for AS Level Language and Literature, introduces you to the idea of studying language and literature as a combined course, and argues that the distinction between so-called literary texts and non-literary texts is an artificial one. Using examples from various diaries, it shows how the same frameworks for analysis can be applied to fictional texts and non-fictional texts.

Assessment Objectives for English language and literature

One very important point to make is that different skills – or Assessment Objectives – are assessed in different parts of the course. What this means is that you need to know which of the Assessment Objectives are being assessed in each module that you take. English Language and Literature will not be studied as different subjects, but in an integrated way. Whatever exam board you are taking, the course will be designed so that language and literature are seen as part of the same process.

The Assessment Objectives condensed here make reference to the work on diaries in this chapter, where they help to show more clearly what is required of you.

AO1

This states that you must communicate what you know about the combination of language and literature, using appropriate technical vocabulary and writing accurately yourself.

Here you would show, for instance, how personal diaries use a certain type of language, and how fictional diaries echo this language but also do other things too.

AO2

This states that you must respond to literary and non-literary texts, describing and interpreting how they vary in meaning and form. The word 'form' relates to the shape and structure of a text. Work in the previous chapter on diaries refers in part to form – the way a diary is structured.

Note that this Assessment Objective looks at the term 'non-literary', shown to be problematic in this chapter.

AO3

This states that you must analyse texts, using literary and linguistic concepts and frameworks. Whereas AO2 looks specifically at meaning and structure, this AO involves looking at other features such as the way a text is narrated, how the reader is constructed, how metaphorical language is used and so forth.

An example from this chapter would be analysing the way Adrian Mole's diary uses language that we would expect from a teenager in the 1980s.

AO4

This states that you must show understanding of the way meaning is affected by context. Context is an important term, which ideally requires more than a brief definition. Essentially, though, context refers to all the possible factors that can affect a way a text is read and understood. These will involve issues surrounding the writer or speaker of a text, the reader or hearer of the text, and the text itself.

An obvious example involves the Donald Crowhurst diary earlier in this chapter. You could read the diary without any knowledge whatsoever about the circumstances in which it was written. Once you are aware that he was under huge psychological strain, that he had been alone for months, and that he died soon after he wrote it, however, you are likely to see the text in a very different light. This means that texts are not fixed in single meanings, but that meanings shift and alter according to various contexts.

AO5

This states that you must identify and consider attitudes and values which are shown in speech and writing. Attitudes in speech and writing should not be too difficult to identify, but 'values' is a more difficult term until you are familiar with it. It relates to the beliefs and principles held by the producer of a text, often assuming that the text receiver holds them too. A useful term to describe a person's, or indeed a culture's, beliefs and principles is **ideology**.

An example of this can be seen in the Captain Scott diary. Through what he says we can see that he believes in certain notions of being English, which include the idea of being a gentleman, of being brave, of sacrificing yourself for others.

AO6

This states that you must show that you can write for specific audiences and purposes, drawing on your knowledge of literature and language, and commenting on the choices you have made in your writing.

Creating a fictional diary of your own, and then writing a commentary on how you have used the diary form, and created a character and events within it, could be one example.

As the title of this AS Level subject suggests, it involves elements of both language and literature study. This is a logical combination of elements because, in the real world distinctions between the two areas of study are much less obvious than is sometimes suggested.

Consider the following statements.
- Some of the most creative use of language play is found in advertisements as well as poems.
- Advertisements, as well as poems, often contain cleverly constructed metaphors.
- Fictional diaries (e.g. Adrian Mole and Bridget Jones) sell as many copies as real diaries (e.g. Alan Clark, various sports players).

◆ In telling a friend about a recent night out, you use many of the strategies used by a fictional story-teller.

In each of the above examples, the so-called distinctions between language and literature become blurred. Traditionally literature has been seen as a 'higher' form of expression, but more recent research has shown just how much everyday writing and speaking have in common with literature – or how much literature has in common with everyday writing and speaking.

Many elements of your AS course also appear in the separate Literature course and Language course. You are not therefore allowed to study either or both of the two separate subjects in addition to the combined course. Nonetheless, it is strongly recommended that you read the other two sections in this book, which will give you plenty of ideas on how to study the combined course.

Course Content

Reading

You will be expected to have read a variety of texts, at least some of which must have been written before 1900. Some texts will be literary; usually these will be poems, plays and prose texts. Other texts will include such things as journalism, letters, transcribed spoken texts and so on. These are sometimes called non-literary texts, but this is a tricky term because:

◆ not all texts can be neatly categorised as being literature or not literature
◆ calling something 'non-literary' suggests it is not as good as literature, that something is lacking. One of the things you need to bear in mind in this combined course is that all texts should be judged on how effectively they fulfil their purpose.

Writing

You will be expected to produce a piece, or pieces, of original writing for a specific audience and purpose. You will also be expected to produce a commentary on what you have written. Depending on the specification you are following, you will either be writing for a coursework folder or in an examination.

Getting started

The following tasks are designed to:

◆ get you thinking about how a specific **genre** of writing works
◆ show you that investigating texts, regardless of whether they are called literary or non-literary, involves using a similar framework
◆ show you how to comment on changes in language use over time.

It will use various diaries as its data. Some have been written by real people and some have been written by authors inventing fictional characters.

TASK

Most people at some stage in their lives have tried keeping a diary, even if they do not persist for very long. Make a list of what you consider to be some of the main features of a personal diary.

English language and literature

CONSIDER

What follows is a framework, which is applied to three different types of diary. Check your ideas against it.

(a) A personal diary for personal consumption

1. Time

You will try to write every day. If you use a pre-packaged diary the dates will be done for you and there will be a space to write in.

2. Style

You will tend to use an **elliptical** form of writing. In other words you use various short forms, both in words used (e.g. 'vg' instead of very good) and grammar (e.g. 'went to cinema' rather than 'I went to the cinema today.'). There may be secret codes in the diary to make sure someone else does not read it.

3. Events and places

You will include a mixture of events and personal feelings and reactions to these events. You work on the assumption that they are of interest to you now, and in the future, but to nobody else. You will also assume that most places are known, unless you go somewhere unusual.

4. Characters

You will generally refer to people you know, so you will not establish their appearance, age, character etc. in the way a novel would.

5. Readers

It is likely that the reader of the diary will be you in the future.

Listed above are features of a personal diary. It is only intended to be read by you. Many famous people such as politicians write diaries that they intend to be publish. Look at how the above categories apply in this case.

(b) A personal diary for public consumption

1. Time

Not every day will necessarily be recorded or published and different amounts will be written depending on the topic.

2. Style

You are likely to use a full style of writing, rather than an elliptical one. It will probably be quite conversational, though, and there will be no secret codes and references, because your readers will not understand them.

3. Events and places

You will record events that your readers are likely to have heard about, but want to know more about from an insider, from someone who was there. You may well describe places, because your reader will not be familiar with them.

4. Characters

You will refer to people much more in the way novelists do. You are likely to say much more about yourself as a person, and you will sketch the appearance, character and habits of others you meet, especially if they are already famous.

5. Readers

You know, even as you write, that you are writing not for yourself but for a much wider set of readers. This sense of wide readership may also lead you to highlight some moral or religious points, some lessons to be learned, in much the same way that certain types of novels do.

What we have here, is a sort of text that is rooted in a real set of events, but which at the same time is using many of the techniques of literature, in particular story-telling.

Now consider the possibility that you are going to write a fictional diary, based upon an entirely imaginary character. Your purpose is to entertain and amuse, creating a character who is somehow 'typical' of, for example, an age, an occupation, or a social class. How do the original categories apply in this case?

(c) A fictional diary pretending to be a personal diary

1. Time

You do not need to make an entry every day because you are writing fiction, and you can vary the amount written.

2. Style

To sound authentic you will use some elliptical devices, but to make sure that the reader understands them, and to help establish your invented character, you will tend to repeat them frequently. You may have some codes and 'secret' references, but actually the readers will understand these – or they would be pointless.

3,4. Events, places and characters

You will be inventing in much the same way a novelist does. Some of these characters will appear frequently and will have a profound affect on your diarist's life. At least some of the events are likely to become exaggerated, even farcical.

5. Readers

How your diarist responds to the events and characters will be part of the entertainment for your readers.

What we have done so far is to establish a few features of works that fall within the broad umbrella of the diary genre, works that have some common features but in other ways are very different. We have established a framework for looking at different diaries, some of which have authors writing about their own experiences, and others that are written by authors who create invented diarists and experiences. We are now ready to look at some examples.

Diaries

If you have a personal diary, you can at this point see to what extent your diary corresponds to the framework in **(a)** above. For obvious reasons this book cannot print an example of a personal diary, intended for personal consumption only; if it did so, it would cease to be personal. Instead we will look at examples from categories **(b)** and **(c)**, beginning with extracts from two diaries written in similar circumstances.

English language and literature

Personal diaries for public consumption

Captain Scott and Donald Crowhurst

Captain Scott led an expedition to the South Pole, hoping to be the first to get there. Although they arrived there on 18 January 1912, they discovered that a Norwegian team had reached it before them. Scott and his team set off to return, but did not make it back. Searchers found a tent with frozen bodies, and Scott's last diary. Partly because of the diary, Scott's expedition became famous, in Britain at least, for its sense of heroic failure.

Donald Crowhurst entered a race in 1968 to be the first man to sail round the world non-stop. His journey was dogged by misfortune, so he hit upon the idea of falsifying his ship's log and pretending to have sailed round the world without actually doing so. He, like Scott, did not make it back. Quite why is not clear, but it seems that the enormity of what he was doing overwhelmed him. His boat was found drifting and empty. As his story was being faked, some of his earlier diary entries could have been made up too. These extracts come from his last entries.

ACTIVITY

For each of the two extracts below, consider the following questions.

1   To what extent do the diaries seem to be written with a wide audience in mind?
2   How do the diaries present a sense of time and place?
3   What do the diaries tell us about the people who wrote them?
4   Both diaries were written at a time of crisis. How do they differ in their presentation of this crisis?

Captain Scott's diary

Friday, 16 March or Saturday, 17. Lost track of dates, but think the last date correct. Tragedy all along the line. At lunch, the day before yesterday, poor Titus Oates said he couldn't go on; he proposed we should leave him in his sleeping-bag. That we could not do, and induced him to come on, on the afternoon march. In spite of its awful nature for him he struggled on and we made a few miles. At night he was worse and we knew the end had come.

Should this be found I want these facts recorded. Oates's last thoughts were of his Mother, but immediately before he took pride in thinking that his regiment would be pleased with the bold way in which he met his death. We can testify to his bravery. He has borne intense suffering for weeks without complaint, and to the very last was able and willing to discuss outside subjects. He did not – would not – give up hope to the very end. He was a brave soul. This was the end. He slept through the night before last, hoping not to wake; but he woke in the morning – yesterday. It was blowing a blizzard. He said, 'I am just going outside and may be some time.' He went out into the blizzard and we have not seen him since.

I take this opportunity of saying that we have stuck to our sick companions to the last. In case of Edgar Evans, when absolutely out of food and he lay insensible, the safety of the remainder seemed to demand his abandonment, but Providence mercifully removed him at this critical moment. He died a natural death, and we did not leave him till two hours after his death. We knew that poor Oates was walking to his death, but though we tried to dissuade him, we knew it was the act of a brave man and an English gentleman. We all hope to meet the end with a similar spirit, and assuredly the end is not far.

I can only write at lunch and then only occasionally. The cold is intense, - 40° at midday. My companions are unendingly cheerful, but we are all on the verge of serious frostbites, and though we constantly talk of fetching through I don't think any one of us believes it in his heart.

English language and literature

Donald Crowhurst's diary

As his crisis mounted, Crowhurst's mind, increasingly confused, expressed itself in disjointed philosophies, and once again in writing:

The shameful secret of God. The trick he used because the truth would hurt too much. If it had been known before, the necessary perfect shining instrument would not be what it is today.

The quick are quick, and the dead are dead. That is the judgment of God. I could not have endured the terrible anguish and meaningless waiting, in fact.

There must be much we can learn from each other. Now at last man has everything he needs to think like a cosmic being.

At the moment it must be true that I am the only man on earth who realises what this means. It means I can make myself a cosmic being, by my own efforts, but I have to hurry up and get on with it before I die!

Man is forced to certain conclusions by virtue of his mistakes. No machine can work without error!

The only trouble with man is that he takes life too seriously.

Eventually Donald Crowhurst wrote these lines:

11 15 00   It is the end of my
                 my game the truth
                 has been revealed and it will
                 be done as my family require me
                 to do it

11 17 00   It is the time for your
                 move to begin

                 I have no need to prolong
                 the game

CONSIDER
Captain Scott's diary

(a) Scott's diary contains very obvious clues that he is writing for a wider audience than himself. 'Should this be found', 'I take this opportunity of saying' address future readers, and there is a strong sense that Scott is shaping the way his expedition will be viewed, even as it is reaching its close. The first paragraph contains enough ellipses to make it sound like a diary, but for most of the time Scott writes very formal English, in carefully constructed paragraphs and sentences.

(b) In terms of time, he gives alternative dates, but still, even at this stage wants to be 'correct'. Place is evoked by occasional references to weather and cold.

(c) Scott therefore seems to be a very ordered person. He knew that the end was near, and made sure that he tied up the loose ends, and set the story straight. This is especially the case when he talked about Titus Oates – this account has become famous and many people who have never read the diaries have heard of him. Scott helped to create the legend, even as it was

English language and literature

happening. Oates' last thoughts were of his mother and his regiment – but how would Scott know this? Oates is constructed by Scott in exactly the way a novelist constructs a character. Scott tells us that he died as 'a brave man and an English gentleman'. Oates is represented as portraying ideals of English nationalism, just two years before the outbreak of world war.

(d) The fact that some have died and the rest soon will is told with remarkable calm. The language structures stay intact and there is no admitted sense of despair. Scott is writing his own history, even as he knows it is coming to an end. This is not a personal diary; it is the creation of his own legend.

Donald Crowhurst's diary

(e) The same cannot be said for Crowhurst, who was totally alone on his boat. The two extracts here, although very different in the way they are written both show a man who seems to be cracking up. The first section, giving no idea of time or place, consists of a series of abstract thoughts, which appear to be religious. The problem for the reader, though, is that they lack **cohesion** – in other words they do not seem to connect with each other. It is very hard for us to make sense of them.

(f) The second extract from Crowhurst gives very precise timings, right down to the precise minute, but no actual dates. This defining of time so precisely suggests that Crowhurst is about to do something decisive. What he writes in this second extract makes some sense but is still hard to pin down. Who is referred to when he talks of it being time for 'your move to begin.'? Is he talking to himself, to God? The writing has no conventional structure to it, looking a bit like poetry without quite being so.

(g) The final words are particularly interesting. Whereas Scott ended his diary with a sense of **closure**, Crowhurst both does and does not. These could be his consciously written final words, yet the absence of a full stop makes it seem as though he intended to write more. However we answer the questions raised by this diary, Crowhurst comes across as being much more disturbed than Scott by the situation he finds himself in – and therefore, perhaps, more human too.

Fictional diaries pretending to be personal diaries

Mr Pooter and Adrian Mole

The Diary of a Nobody by George and Weedon Grossmith was first published in book form in 1892, having originally been a feature in *Punch* magazine. *The Secret Diary of Adrian Mole aged 13 ¾*, by Sue Townsend was first published in 1982. Despite being separated by ninety years they have much in common, the most obvious similarity being that they are the fictional writings of unexceptional male 'heroes'. Although Mr Pooter, the 'nobody' of the title, and Adrian Mole both take themselves very seriously, they are very ordinary people, as their names suggest. This allows their authors to create humour at the expense of their creations and at the same time to highlight aspects of the political and social times in which their characters live.

TASK

Two extracts follow, one from each text. Look for similarities and differences in a range of different areas. These are:

1   the **characterisation** of the diarist
2   how the characterisation is shown specifically through language

3   **culture specific references** which place the text in terms of time.

Before reading the extracts, some of the above terms need to be explained. Although you may be aware of how to comment on characters in literature, a more advanced way of looking at fictional people is to see how the author has created the character. This means that you are looking at how a character has been created rather than what a character is like. How a character is established and developed is known as the process of characterisation. Clearly in a book of fictional diary entries, the character emerges slowly, but nonetheless these extracts show enough of the process at work.

It is in some ways artificial to separate the process of characterisation from the use of language – how else can an author invent a character? But for the purposes of this task there is a separate section on language on p 00 to make sure that you talk about the way the characters are explored through their fictional language, rather than just commenting on what they do and how they interact with others.

'Culture specific references' are references in a text which mean more to those who are in a particular culture at that particular time, than to others who read the text from a different stand-point. In fictional diaries in particular, where the main purpose is usually to be comic, these are likely to be references to popular culture at the time the book is written.

The Diary of a Nobody

APRIL 27. Painted the bath red, and was delighted with the result. Sorry to say Carrie was not, in fact we had a few words about it. She said I ought to have consulted her, and she had never heard of such a thing as a bath being painted red. I replied: 'It's merely a matter of taste.'

Fortunately, further argument on the subject was stopped by a voice saying, 'May I come in?' It was only Cummings, who said, 'Your maid opened the door, and asked me to excuse her showing me in, as she was wringing out some socks.' I was delighted to see him, and suggested we should have a game of whist with a dummy, and by way of merriment said: '*You* can be the dummy.' Cummings (I thought rather ill-naturedly) replied: 'Funny as usual.' He said he couldn't stop, he only called to leave me the *Bicycle News,* as he had done with it.

Another ring at the bell; it was Gowing, who said he 'must apologize for coming so often, and that one of these days *we* must come round to *him*'. I said: 'A very extraordinary thing has struck me.' 'Something funny, as usual,' said Cummings. 'Yes,' I replied; 'I think even *you* will say so this time. It's concerning you both; for doesn't it seem odd that Gowing's always *coming* and Cummings always *going*?' Carrie, who had evidently quite forgotten about the bath, went into fits of laughter, and as for myself, I fairly doubled up in my chair, till it cracked beneath me. I think this was one of the best jokes I have ever made.

Then imagine my astonishment on perceiving both Cummings and Gowing perfectly silent, and without a smile on their faces. After rather an unpleasant pause, Cummings, who had opened a cigar-case, closed it up again and said: 'Yes – I think, after that, I *shall* be going, and I am sorry I fail to see the fun of your jokes.' Gowing said he didn't mind a joke when it wasn't rude, but a pun on a name, to his thinking, was certainly a little wanting in good taste. Cummings followed it up by saying, if it had been said by anyone else but myself, he shouldn't have entered the house again. This rather unpleasantly terminated what might have been a cheerful evening. However, it was as well they went, for the charwoman had finished up the remains of the cold pork.

Wednesday   April 15th

Went to youth club with Nigel. It was dead good. We played ping-pong till the balls cracked. Then we had a go on the football table. I beat Nigel fifty goals to thirteen. Nigel went into sulk and said he only lost because his goal-keeper's legs were stuck on with Sellotape but he was wrong. It was my superior skill that did it.

A gang of punks passed unkind comments about my flared trousers but Rick Lemon, the youth leader, stepped in and led a discussion on personal taste. We all agreed it should be up to the individual to dress how he or she likes. All the same I think I will ask my father if I can have a new pair of trousers. Not many fourteen-year-olds wear flared trousers today, and I don't wish to be conspicuous.

Barry Kent tried to get in the fire-doors to avoid paying his five-pence subs. But Rick Lemon pushed him back outside into the rain. I was very pleased. I owe Barry Kent two pounds' menaces money.

Thursday   April 16th

Got a birthday card from my Auntie Susan, two weeks late! She always forgets the right day. My father said she's under a lot of pressure because of her job, but I can't see it myself. I'd have thought that being a prison wardress was dead cushy, it is only locking and unlocking doors after all. She has sent a present via the GPO so with luck I should get it by Christmas. Ha! Ha!

The Secret Diary of Adrian Mole aged 13¾

CONSIDER

(a) Both characters, Mr Pooter and Adrian Mole, are seen by the reader to be ineffective when confronted by other people. Pooter is dominated by his wife Carrie, is exploited by his perpetually visiting 'friends' Cummings and Gowing, and served badly by his servants. Mole is bullied and exploited by Barry Kent, forgotten by his Auntie Susan and sulked at buy his 'friend' Nigel. Even his dog is a constant source of embarrassment.

(b) Both are seen to have poor 'taste', a word used in both extracts. Pooter paints the bath red, only to be criticised by his wife, while Mole wears flared trousers, which are mocked by punks. Both are defensive about their taste, which the reader recognises as being unfashionable. This reader response is vital to the way the texts work; the fictional narrators are naive in many ways, never as aware as the reader that they are objects of ridicule. So Pooter cannot see that his friends and servants are spongers. Mole, while being partially aware that Barry Kent is demanding money with menaces, refuses to acknowledge this fully.

(c) This naiveté is especially evident when they try to be funny – both characters are presented as thinking that they have a sense of humour. The joke for the reader comes in the fact that they are distinctly unfunny, but do not see this themselves. The reader is therefore always superior to the narrator. These are innocents in a world that we understand and they do not. The long-term effect of this, if you read the whole books, can be interesting. However, we can only condescend to these characters for so long. Then we become either tired of them, or sorry for them, or a bit of both.

(d) Both characters 'write' their diaries in language that suits their age, gender, and social context. There is some ellipsis at the start of an entry, but otherwise they tend to write in full sentences. This allows the authors more scope for using words and sentences to particular effect. Pooter tends to be very formal, even pompous: the sentence 'This rather unpleasantly terminated what might have been a cheerful evening' is a good example of an office clerk being very precise, even in his personal diary. He also tends to use **euphemisms**, i.e. mild terms, which the reader sees as avoiding the harsh truth. So when he says that he 'had a few words' with Carrie, we assume that she yelled at him.

(e) Mole writes in a less formal way because he is a teenager of the 1980s. His language is also euphemistic and literal though: he talks of being hit in the 'goolies' and says Barry Kent was sent for an early shower, when the usual phrase is early bath. He sometimes uses exclamation marks – Pooter does not – and also uses short sentences, especially when his feelings are involved.

(f) The Adrian Mole extracts are full of culture-specific references, although because the text is still relatively modern, you might not necessarily have noticed them. He uses expressions like 'do me over', 'Mars bars', 'notes for games', 'Woolworth's perfume counter', 'gangs of punks' and 'youth leaders'. Mole's world is full of specific detail, which he takes for granted, and which Sue Townsend assumes we will understand. Inevitably such references are harder for us to spot in the Pooter extract. But did they really paint baths in those days? Was Bicycle News quite a risky magazine? Did relatively humble people have so many servants?

What these cultural references show is that for a fictional diary to work, the created character has to be placed in a recognisable world. The risk here is that these references date, and that new readers fail to pick them up so readily.

'Literary' and 'non-literary' texts

At the start of this chapter we noted that the so-called distinctions between language and literature can easily become blurred. The terms 'literary' and 'non literary' texts to distinguish between different types of writing can be misleading. Traditionally 'literature', when referring to 'literary' texts has been accepted as a 'high' cultural form of expression as distinct from 'other' or 'popular' texts which have been assumed to be 'non-literary' and thereby marked in a negative way. The assumption that one is standard and the other inferior carries over to the implication that writing and written texts are more worthy of consideration than the spoken word and spoken texts.

This notion has also led to the idea that literature uses literary devices that are the province of literature alone. But if we look and listen carefully, poetry uses metaphorical language, and so does everyday speech. Poetry uses sound effects like alliteration and assonance that are as likely to appear in rap lyrics or football chants. Advertisements, too, can be as clever and complicated as many poems, and can be clearly understood.

When studying a course that so clearly labels two strands of study – language and literature – you will be tempted to see texts as belonging in one camp or the other. In one sense, of course, it doesn't really matter, but it would matter if you thought they had to be approached in different ways. As the work on diaries has shown, the same questions can be asked of 'fictional' and 'actual' diaries. The most important thing is to recognise features of genre, authorship and readership, rather than to attach hierarchical labels. Is Scott's diary literature? Is *The Secret Diary of Adrian Mole aged 13 ¾*, literature? It really doesn't matter. What does matter is that as readers we understand how these texts work on us.

English language and literature

English language and literature

TECHNICAL TERMS

characterisation   the way characters are presented by an author

culture specific references   references to objects and ideas which have a certain meaning within a culture or cultural group

closure   the way a text comes to an obvious conclusion

cohesion   the way a text is organised, where parts of the text connect together to make a whole.

ellipsis   the omission of part of a word, or of a word or words from a sentence, while still making sense

euphemism   the use of a mild word or phrase instead of one which carries more force in its meaning

genre   a word for types of texts. It can refer broadly to such things as poetry, prose, drama, but also more specifically to types of text within those broad areas, such as crime fiction, narrative poetry etc.

ideology   a set of ideas and values held by a group or an individual

2 | Producing your own texts

The subjects of AS English Language and AS English Language and Literature, have much in common. They come closest together in the field of text production. In English Language the term 'Original Writing' is favoured, whereas in the combined course it is more often referred to as 'Text Production'. The Assessment Objectives in the two subjects require similar skills.

You are advised to read Chapter 5 on Original Writing in the English Language section of this book on pages 47-58, as well as this section.

The following aspects of writing were covered in Chapter 5 of English Language:
- A writing framework
- Writing to inform
- Finding a voice
- Using data
- Planning your own text
- Writing a commentary

In this chapter, particular emphasis will be on the following:
- The purposes of writing
- Travel writing
- Making choices
- Writing prose fiction
- Writing a commentary

The purposes of writing

Although the terms are not mutually exclusive, the following purposes of text production are usually presented to students as broad areas within which to work. The examples given are by no means a full list, but are included to give you an idea of what each category could contain.

Writing to entertain

◆ a short story
◆ a collection of poems
◆ a radio drama script

Writing to persuade

◆ a piece of journalism
◆ a text for an advertising campaign
◆ a text of a political speech

Writing to inform

◆ an account of a sports event
◆ a piece of travel writing
◆ an article about the cost of living away from home for students

Writing to advise/instruct

◆ an explanation of how you construct a web page
◆ advice on health issues
◆ an article for a college newsletter on how to revise for exams

Travel writing

The four categories above are not mutually exclusive because many forms of writing have more than one purpose. Take for example a piece of travel writing that has been placed in the 'Writing to inform' section. Travel writing comes in many forms. Three of these are listed as follows.

1. When it is written to describe one person's travels, often in exotic places, it is as much about entertaining the reader as informing them. Indeed travel writing appears in English Language and Literature courses among the lists of literary texts. You could try reading the travel writings of Bill Bryson, Colin Thubron, P J. O'Rourke and Bruce Chatwin among others.

2. The text of a travel brochure is a piece of travel writing in which readers of the text are being persuaded, it is hoped, to spend their money on going to a particular location themselves.

3. The writers of a guidebook will be setting out to inform their readers about what to do and see in a certain place. They will also want to give advice about the best places to stay and eat, and what to do if things go wrong. At the same time, though, they will want to entertain their readers, to make their text lively and opinionated. See, for example, *The Rough Guide* and *Lonely Planet* series of books.
    You can sample these on the following web sites:
    ◆ www.roughguides.com
    ◆ www.lonelyplanet.com.

English language and literature

TASK

The three texts below are all taken from what can loosely be called travel writing. Identify what genre of travel writing each text comes from, and say what key language features you have identified which helped you make your choice.

Text 1

… anyone coming in search of the glories of the Bay of Naples is likely to be disappointed. Industry has eaten into the land around the city so as to render it almost unrecognisable, and even in the city the once-grand vistas are often cluttered by cranes and smoke-belching chimneys. Most people take one look and skate right out again, disappointed at such a grimy welcome.

But give the area time. Naples is the obvious focus, an utterly compelling city and one that dominates the region in every way. You need a fair few days to absorb the city properly, before embarking on the remarkable attractions surrounding it … It's the kind of city laden with visitors' preconceptions and it rarely disappoints: it is filthy, it is very large and overbearing, it is crime-infested, and it is most definitely like nowhere else in Italy.

Text 2

Everything in Europe is lukewarm except the radiators. You could use the radiators to make party ice. But nobody does. I'll bet you could walk from the Urals to the beach at Biarritz and not find one rock-hard crystal clear, fist-sized American ice cube … And the phones don't work. They go 'blat-blat' and 'neek-neek' and 'ugu-ugu-ugu. No two dial tones are alike. The busy signal sounds as if the phone is ringing. And when the phone rings you think the dog has farted …

The Europeans can't figure out which side of the road to drive on, and I can't figure out how to flush their toilets. Do I push the knob, or pull it, or twist it, or pump it? And I keep cracking my shins on that stupid bidet thing. (Memo to Europeans: try washing your whole body; believe me you'd smell better) Plus there are ruins everywhere. The Italians have had two thousand years to fix up the Forum, and just look at the place.

I've had it with these dopey little countries and all their pokey borders. You can't swing a cat without sending it through customs. Everything's too small. The cars are too small. The beds are too small. The elevators are the size of broom closets. Even the languages are itty-bitty. Sometimes you need two or three just to get you through till lunch.

Text 3

… the towns and villages of the Neapolitan Riviera are tucked into folds of the cliffs, with fabulous views across the limpid blue Mediterranean to the Isle of Capri and a stunning backdrop of rugged hillsides climbing to the peak of Mount Vesuvius. Enjoy the unique atmosphere of Italy and the Italians, lively and expressive, yet relaxed, warm and welcoming.

From the Bay of Naples, a boat trip to the Isle of Capri or quieter Ischia is a must. A trip to the summit of Vesuvius provides fabulous views, and remember to plan for a visit to incredible Pompeii, lost for two thousand years under the ashes of Vesuvius.

English language and literature

Text 1

The extract comes from the *Rough Guide to Italy*, a guidebook which claims to be 'authoritative and opinionated'. The extract begins by belittling expectations of Naples, saying that 'the glories' do not exist, and that 'most people' take one look at the cranes and the smoke and 'skate right out again'. However the audience is encouraged to be different, to avoid superficial judgements. The **imperative** verb form is used to persuade readers that they should 'give the area time'. From this point onwards the vocabulary changes; connotations of ugliness are replaced by the idea that the city, if 'absorbed properly', is 'utterly compelling'. The use of the **superlative** term 'utterly' strengthens the view that this is indeed a place to visit, provided you are patient and know what to expect.

The final sentence quoted here is a long one, pivoting on the idea that it 'rarely disappoints'. We are given a list of three reasons why the place lives up to our worst expectations, yet the last clause of the sentence, saying it is 'like nowhere else in Italy', makes it clear that the city is well worth visiting.

This guide is indeed opinionated, giving information, yet also adopting a persuasive voice as well. Its audience is constructed as being discerning, thoughtful, more than the average tourist – someone who will take time to get to know a place.

Text 2

This is taken from PJ. O'Rourke's book *Holidays in Hell* (published in 1988). Its blurb says it is 'a package tour of traveller's tales from places as appealing …as the inner circles of Dante's Inferno'. A traveller's tales suggests this is one man's account of his visits abroad – in this case an American in Europe.

There is an immediate sense here that the writer wants to shock, to deliberately offend. He deals in extremes – 'everything is lukewarm', 'the Europeans can't figure out which side of the road to drive on', 'there are ruins everywhere'. He ridicules everyday items such as phones and toilets. He says that Europeans smell. Above all, Europe is depicted as small in area and small in mind.

He refers frequently to himself, rather than other travellers. This time it is the narrator who is most obviously constructed – a man who is American, not fooled by cuteness, he thinks America is bigger and better than anywhere else. He is certainly not telling his readers to go to Europe.

It would be hard, though, to take this seriously. His constructed narrator is not discerning, just full of bias, and the intention here is to mock the Americans as well as the Europeans. A key clue in this is when he talks of fixing up the Forum. We know that he knows that the Forum is a historical site – but he pretends otherwise.

This then is a text whose main purpose is to entertain; there is little if any information, and no attempt to persuade the reader to go to Europe.

Text 3

This comes from the Thomson holiday guide for 2000. Although it is apparently informative, it is really persuading people that this is a good place to visit. Not only are there many adjectives – 'fabulous', 'limpid', 'stunning', 'unique' etc. – they all carry connotations of warmth and excitement. Imperatives are again used, along with saying a boat trip is 'a must'.

Notice in particular how the Italians themselves are depicted. Presumably Italians are like any other people, a mixed bunch, but here they are stereotyped as being all things to all people. If you like your natives to be noisy, then the Italians are; if you like them warm and relaxed, they are that too. Everything is perfect, nothing can be criticised. The audience for this text is also very generalised – everyone who goes there will love the place.

We have three texts which could all loosely be described as travel writing, but which are in fact distinguished by having very different purposes and audiences. Only the travel guide fits in the 'Writing to inform' section, suggesting that topics can be shaped differently depending on their audience and purpose. How you shape your content will involve the use of distinctive language and forms that your readers will recognise.

Making choices

As was noted in Chapter 5 in the English Language section on Original Writing on page 47, 'making choices' is a key phrase to consider. When faced with the blank page that has to be filled with your own ideas, you will start to fill that page by seeing a set of choices before you, and then making your decisions. The following two boxes are repeated from Chapter 5.

A WRITING FRAMEWORK

A range of technical terms can be used to describe the writing process, but in this book we will use the following writing framework. For each piece of writing that you produce you will have to make choices within the following areas:

Field	What topic are you covering in your text? What is your subject matter? Does it involve the collection and presentation of data? Is data already provided?
Function	What is the main purpose of your text? Is it to entertain, persuade, inform, or instruct/advise? Or, more probably, does it combine more than one element of these?
Mode	What sort of text are you producing? What genre will be you be using? How will it reflect other similar texts? How will it be different from other similar texts?
Tenor	What voice or voices will you create in your text? What will be its overall tone? What relationship will you create between the text and the reader? How formal will the writing be?

Depending on the specification you are following, your Text Production component will either be assessed as an examination, or as coursework. Clearly there are some differences between the two approaches, and it will help if they are made clear at the start. Find the column which applies to you, and make sure that you understand its implications.

Coursework	**Examination**
You choose topic	Topic chosen for you
You choose the genre	Genre probably chosen for you
You choose the target audience	Audience chosen for you
You research relevant data	Data is provided or not needed
You have time for a number of drafts	Only time for one draft
You can use ICT	Must be hand-written
You produce a finished product	You produce a working draft

Now look back to the work earlier in this chapter on travel writing. If you decide to do travel writing as a topic for coursework, you will need to be sure of the precise form of travel writing you wish to produce, and what are its purposes and audience. You will then need to be clear about your decisions when you come to write your commentary.

English language and literature

If travel writing is an exam topic, then you need to read the task carefully and ensure that you fulfil the requirements of audience and purpose, while at the same time being aware of how specific these are. If the task is open-ended enough to allow you to be entertaining as well as informative, this will help you to gain higher marks.

Writing prose fiction

The rest of this chapter will focus on writing to entertain; the most obvious links to literature are evident here. Although there are many ways to write entertainingly, this chapter will focus on writing your own stories, giving you insights into how other writers have produced their texts.

For many years in school you probably produced a story at the drop of a hat. The teacher would give you the title, and you would be able to finish your story in half an hour. Teachers, parents and babysitters would have read you lots of stories. Your ability to write, read and understand stories will have been a major factor in your developing literacy.

You will also probably have watched lots of stories on television, especially in soaps and drama series. Yet if your lecturer asked you to write a story about a place and the people who lived in it, you might protest that it was much too difficult. You would want lots of help – despite the fact that most soaps work on exactly that format. Why might you find it hard?

- ◆ Because you're out of practice writing stories?
- ◆ Because you have no ideas?
- ◆ Because you don't know where to start?
- ◆ Because you don't know how to start?

In theory you should be much better at writing stories now than you were when younger, yet somehow it might seem more difficult. This section will attempt to give you some ideas to help you get started.

The word 'story' comes from the Latin 'historia', meaning narrative. We use the word 'story' in at least two distinctive ways. These can seem contradictory: a story can be defined as a description of imaginary events and people, or an account by someone of important events that have happened to them. So a story can be about imaginary events or actual events. The connection between these two apparent opposites, lies in its Latin origin – whether you are telling an imaginary story or a 'real' story, you will give it shape and organisation in an attempt to make it appealing to your listener or reader.

Note the inverted commas around the word 'real' in the paragraph above. Although something may have happened to you, in re-telling the story, you are in a sense creating a new series of events, by giving them a narrative shape that they did not originally have.

Finding a way to give your story shape is crucial to its success. The most amazing events possible will lose their impact if told ineffectively, while the most unexciting of events can have impact if told with skill and flair. Looking at some ways of telling a story forms the next part of this chapter.

The basics of a story

Word limits and time limits mean that for your AS course you are going to have to write a short story if you choose story-writing as your option. A short story has relatively little narrative space, which means that you have to establish certain things quickly. You may leave your reader a considerable amount to work out, and it may be that you do not even begin or end the story in the way a novel might, but there are some basic things that you will have to do.

One problem with discussing stories in the abstract is that you can nearly always find a story that breaks the rules, but as an absolute minimum, you would expect a story to have:

- at least one 'character' – usually but not necessarily a person
- a setting – a place or places inhabited by the character(s)
- a time frame – the character(s) and places(s) must be positioned at a point of time or times.

It is just about conceivable that you could have a story with only these three ingredients, but it is also likely that you will have:

- action
- events
- something happening.

Once you have action, then you probably need to combine the events and the characters. This means that you will have:

- motives for actions, if instigated by your characters
- or responses to events if they come from outside your character.

In addition you will have a certain readership in mind; no story can appeal to everybody, even if some prove incredibly popular. This means that you will:

- consider the needs and interests of your readers in shaping your narrative, presuming that you have some idea what your readers will like.

STORY INGREDIENTS

So far, then, the following have been identified as ingredients that will begin to shape the way you tell your story:

- at least one 'character'
- a setting
- a time frame
- action, events
- motives for actions and/or responses to events
- the needs and interests of your readers.

In addition to these basic requirements, you also need to decide whether you are going to work within a certain **genre**. The sense of genre here relates to a recognised type of story – in other words crime, horror, fantasy, romance etc. If you do decide to write within a specific genre, then you will have choices to make, but these choices will be informed by the genre **conventions** within which you will be working.

So if, for example, you decide to write a crime story then certain things will have to be done:

- at least one of your characters will be a criminal and one will be a detective
- the action will involve a crime being committed and a crime being solved
- setting will be crucial to the action
- motives will be clearly explained.

English language and literature

Within these categories, though, you have lots of choice. Here are a few examples:

- what age/gender/ethnic origin will the detective have?
- what will be the nature of the crime? How will it be solved?
- will the setting be local, grim, exotic?
- will the motives of the criminal be in part justified?

TASK

What follows is the opening of a novel called *Northern Lights* by Philip Pullman. Read it carefully at least twice and then write answers to the following questions, which reflect what has been discussed so far in this section on writing stories.

*L*yra and her dæmon moved through the darkening Hall, taking care to keep to one side, out of sight of the kitchen. The three great tables that ran the length of the Hall were laid already, the silver and the glass catching what little light there was, and the long benches were pulled out ready for the guests. Portraits of former Masters hung high up in the gloom along the walls. Lyra reached the dais and looked back at the open kitchen door and, seeing no one, stepped up beside the high table. The places here were laid with gold, not silver, and the fourteen seats were not oak benches but mahogany chairs with velvet cushions.

Lyra stopped beside the Master's chair and flicked the biggest glass gently with a fingernail. The sound rang clearly through the Hall.

"You're not taking this seriously," whispered her dæmon. "Behave yourself."

Her dæmon's name was Pantalaimon, and he was currently in the form of a moth, a dark brown one so as not to show up in the darkness of the Hall.

"They're making too much noise to hear from the kitchen," Lyra whispered back. "And the Steward doesn't come in till the first bell. Stop fussing."

But she put her palm over the ringing crystal anyway, and Pantalaimon fluttered ahead and through the slightly open door of the Retiring Room at the other end of the dais. After a moment he appeared again.

"There's no one there," he whispered. "But we must be quick."

Crouching behind the high table, Lyra darted along and through the door into the Retiring Room, where she stood up and looked around. The only light in here came from the fireplace, where a bright blaze of logs settled slightly as she looked, sending a fountain of sparks up into the chimney. She had lived most of her life in the College, but had never seen the Retiring Room before: only Scholars and their guests were allowed in here, and never females. Even the maidservants didn't clean in here. That was the Butler's job alone.

1 Looking at the box 'Story Ingredients' above, make a list of references/quotations that show any of these ingredients being introduced to the story.

2 Similarly, make a list of references/quotations that show how the author is establishing the story within a certain genre.

CONSIDER

(a) Two 'characters' are identified at once, a girl Lyra and her 'daemon' who is later identified as Pantalaimon. The names writers give characters are not arrived at by chance, they act as a sort of cultural code. We know only the girl's first name, but it is unusual, suggesting that she too is unusual. 'Lyra and her daemon', the story's first words, immediately suggest some sort of fantasy story. The word 'her' suggests belonging, while the spelling of the word 'daemon' is deliberately archaic, again giving an effect of something unusual. When we are given the daemon's name, it is like no name that we would recognise – 'Pantalaimon' contains the 'mon' ending to match 'daemon', but otherwise we can construct no obvious meaning around it.

(b) At once we begin to think that this is fantasy genre, and because it involves a young girl (suggested by the fact that she 'darted') we may suspect that the apparent audience is children or teenagers. This is enhanced by the jokiness of the dialogue, the reversal of what might be expected. It is Lyra who is brave and carefree, the daemon who is urging care and attention.

(c) The setting has lots of specific references without being fully identified. 'Hall', 'masters' 'dais' 'college' 'scholars' and other references indicate that this is a school or college. The fact that females are not allowed in, and the network of servants imply that we are in a traditional college, probably in Oxford or Cambridge.

(d) The time in which the story is set is not clear yet, but the dialogue sounds modern, despite the references to old furniture and old customs. The action has already started, the girl is where she shouldn't be and people could come in and find her at any moment.

(e) Motives, as you would expect at the very start of a novel, are not clear. Readers are engaged, however by being thrown straight into some intriguing material that raises a series of questions.

Shaping your narrative

So far this chapter has guided you with some ways of answering the question 'who and what am I going to write about?' Now it is time to turn to the vital question 'how am I going to tell the story?'. In other words, you are going to have to decide some issues around narrative. These can best be explored through a series of questions. It is also worth noting that in *writing* fiction you are considering many of the issues that you will already have addressed when *reading* fiction. This means that in addition to thinking about the questions below, look also at those sections of this book which explore ways of reading fiction.

1. What will be the distinctive features of the narrative voice?

The 'narrative voice' refers to the idea that there is a voice speaking the text. This is quite easy to understand if you begin by thinking about what is called **first person narrative**. This term refers to the way a story is told when it is narrated by one of the characters, and is most obviously marked by the fact that the first person pronoun 'I' is used.

There are several variations on the method:

◆ the narrator can be at the centre of the story as it unfolds – hence a number of fictional detectives narrate the stories they appear in, as with Holden Caulfield in *Catcher in the Rye*

◆ the narrator can be involved in the action but not really understand it fully – consider the role of Dr Watson in the Sherlock Holmes stories, or of Huck Finn in *Huckleberry Finn*

◆ the narrator can be perceptive but not fully involved in the action, watching it from a certain distance – as with Nick Carraway in *The Great Gatsby*

◆ there can be more than one narrator, each giving a different perspective on the same events.

There are several advantages to this method of narration:
◆ the narrator can use a voice that is informal, writing as if speaking
◆ the narrator can help guide the narratee (see later) in seeing the point of the story
◆ the narrator can explore their own inner thoughts and motives and speculate on the thoughts of others.

There are also some disadvantages to this method:
◆ the narrator can only write about what they have seen or been told
◆ the perspective cannot alter if one narrator is used.

The second option is to use a **third person narrative**. This is marked by the use of third person pronouns such as 'she/he' etc.

There are many variations on this method. Some are:
◆ the narrative can be very distant from the action, knowing everything and looking into the motives of all the characters
◆ the narrative can have the 'author' commenting on what they are doing in the story
◆ the narrative can be through the perspective of one or more of the characters
◆ the narrative can shift from distant to close and back again as James Joyce does in his stories *Dubliners*.

There are several advantages to this method of narration:
◆ the narrative can move freely around characters and places
◆ the narrative can employ a variety of voices and moods
◆ the narrative can employ shifts of time and place.

There are also some disadvantages to this method:
◆ the narrative voice can be distant and uninvolving
◆ the overall effect can be rather formulaic and moralising.

A third method is to create invented texts such as letters and diaries through which a story can be told. This has been seen at work already in this section with the diaries of Adrian Mole and Mr Pooter for example. Novels consisting entirely of letters – known as epistolary novels – were among the first sort of novels to be written in English.

2. How will time be used in the story?
There is a temptation to begin at the beginning when writing fiction, but this can be too predictable. If you consider the action of a story occupying a line of time going from A to B, it can often be effective to start some way along the time line, and then move back to the beginning later in the story.

Working out an interesting **chronology** for your story will be a vital part of your planning.

3. Who is reading your story?
Parts 1 and 2 above have been concerned with telling the story, but you must also consider who is reading the story. This idea of readership works on two broad levels. If you are writing a story for children, or teenagers, or women, or men, then your content, your narrative method and the language you use will all be influenced by this special audience that you have in mind.

You also need to consider, however, the notion of the narratee. Just as the narrator of a story is constructed by the writer, so is the sense of the reader – or the narratee – constructed too. So, for example, if you are writing a piece of romantic fiction in the style of a Mills and Boon novel, the narratee will be female, interested in heroes and heroines, looking for escapism etc. This does not mean that only such people read the books in reality though. Advertisements for cosmetics construct their readers as beautiful people, whereas the 'real' readers are the masses of ordinary people who are rather less than beautiful. You do not have to believe in romance to enjoy reading about it!

4. Serious or comic writing?

The section above has noted that the narratee is not the same as the 'real' reader. This gap between an idealised reader and a reader who is 'really' reading the text allows authors to play with readers' expectations for comic effect.

As readers we are experienced in how texts work and have certain expectations about them. So, if we are reading romantic fiction, we expect there to be dashing heroes, beautiful women languishing for love etc. Playing with these expectations, by altering the typical representations we expect, can either entertain the reader, or make a point about the original type of story, or both. So if you wish to highlight how far from reality such stories usually are, you might create a wimpish hero being pursued by a voracious female, yet telling the story in the style of the originals.

This idea of using some aspects of a genre convention, but changing others, is known as a **pastiche**. Pastiche can be both fun to write and to read, but it is sometimes more difficult to do than people imagine. Broad pastiche is relatively easy, but the joke can soon run thin. Subtle pastiche, which keeps the reader guessing as to what is really going on is usually more effective.

Writing a commentary

When writing a commentary on a piece of fiction, it is important to remember and consider the choices that you have made. These choices must include the major ones that have been highlighted in this chapter; it is much more effective to talk about the narrative that you have tried to construct, than it is to talk about a word you used in the second paragraph.

As a reminder of what has been discussed in this chapter, and as a checklist for you to consider when writing a commentary, the following areas have been explored.

CHECKLIST FOR WRITING A COMMENTARY

- character
- setting
- a time frame – chronology
- action, events,
- motives for actions and/or responses to events
- genre conventions
- narrative voices
- narratees and real readers

This checklist is not a list of requirements, however. There will always be writers who find an original way of doing things. Indeed finding a way of doing something new, of bending the rules, is the sign of a really creative mind.

English language and literature

English language and literature

I want to tell you a story

David Giles

I want to tell you a story, a true story, which was told to me and which you can pass on to your friends. The moral of the story is to never make presumptions about people by their appearance, everyone has something to offer in different ways. It all took place in my school when I was about your age. It was Tuesday and the lesson was about to begin. The class were humming with whispers of excitement. We had been told of a surprise and I couldn't wait to find out what it was.

As the teacher walked in she was followed by a tall gangly man dressed in a large orange coat. His eyes were dark and he was carrying some sort of package. The teacher introduced him as Mr Ashley Wood, a student from the local high school. She tried to carry on but was interrupted by his booming voice. "Thank you, I'll take it from here". The class lights were turned off giving the room a cold, damp feel.

"I want to tell you a story", he said, "a true story, which was told to me and which you can pass on to your friends. The moral of the story is to never make presumptions about people by their appearance, everyone has something to offer in different ways. It all took place in my school when I was about your age. It was Tuesday and the lesson was about to begin. The class were humming with whispers of excitement. We had been told of a surprise and I couldn't wait to find out what it was.

As the teacher walked in he was followed by a short fat lady dressed in a bright white lab coat. Her eyes were masked by a large pair of spectacles, which she kept pushing up her nose. The teacher introduced her as Mrs Ashley Wood, a student from the local high school. He tried to carry on but was interrupted by her positive voice. 'Thank you, I'll take it from here'. The class lights were turned off giving the room a cold, damp feel."

"I want to tell you a story", she said, "a true story, which was told to me and which you can pass on to your friends. The moral of the story is to never make presumptions about people by their appearance, everyone has something to offer in different ways. It all took place in my school when I was about your age. It was Tuesday and the lesson was about to begin. The class

were humming with whispers of excitement. We had been told of a surprise and I couldn't wait to find out what it was.

As the teacher walked in she was followed by a man dressed in a suit. His eyes were tight and he was carrying a smart black briefcase. The teacher introduced him as Mr Ashley Wood, a student from the local high school. She tried to carry on but was interrupted by his harsh voice. 'Thank you, I'll take it from here'. The class lights were turned off giving the room a cold, damp feel."

"I want to tell you a story", he said, "a true story, which was told to me and which you can pass on to your friends. The moral of the story is to never make presumptions about people by their appearance, everyone has something to offer in different ways. It all took place in my school when I was about your age. It was Tuesday and the lesson was about to begin. The class were humming with whispers of excitement. We had been told of a surprise and I couldn't wait to find out what it was.

As the teacher walked in she was followed by an African lady clothed in her native dress. Her eyes were dark and her hair made her face look very round if not slightly fat. The teacher introduced her as Miss Ashley Wood, a student from the local high school. He tried to carry on but was interrupted by her booming voice. 'Thank you, I'll take it from here'. The class lights were turned off giving the room a cold, damp feel."

"I want to tell you a story", she said, "a true story, which was told to me and which you can pass on to your friends. The moral of the story is to never make presumptions about people by their appearance, everyone has something to offer in different ways. It all took place in my school when I was about your age. It was Tuesday and the lesson was about to begin. The class were humming with whispers of excitement. We had been told of a surprise and I couldn't wait to find out what it was.

As the teacher walked in he was followed by an elderly white male dressed in an old shabby suit. His eyes were glazed and he was carrying a brown paper bag in a distinct bottle shape. The teacher introduced him as Mr Ashley Wood, a homeless person from the shelter in the town centre. She tried to carry on but was interrupted by his slurring voice, 'Thank you, I'll ... take it from here'. The class lights were turned off giving the room a cold, damp feel"

(David Giles – Gosforth High School)

CONSIDER

(a) David Giles establishes at the start that this is a first person narrative – the first word of his title and story both begin with 'I'. Much of the effect of the story, though, comes from the way the narrative is passed on like a relay baton, with repeated structures giving the effect of a hall of mirrors.

(b) The initial audience within the story appears to be a group of young children being told a story in class, but the audience outside the story needs to be more sophisticated.

(c) The moral of the story appears very early, although it could be that the moral of the story is not really about human appearance at all, but is instead about stories themselves. Placing the moral this early, when we would expect it chronologically to come at the end, alerts the reader to the fact that this may not be as conventional a story as it first seems. There are other 'hints' at conventional stories too. The 'cold damp feel' to the room hints at mystery genre for example.

(d) As each variation of Ashley Wood – a name which can be both male and female – comes into the story, they are described physically, but do not sound like students from a high school. However, appearances are deceptive, we are told, which accounts for the puzzle. Note too the way that the gender of the teacher alternates with the gender of Ashley Wood, until the last visitor.

(e) The story has a sort of closure, although it could go on endlessly. It leaves the reader slightly puzzled, and most fellow students, when shown David's story, read it a number of times in an attempt to 'work it out'. In encouraging readers to read again, he had succeeded in capturing his audience.

Other creative forms

The story reproduced above looks like a formal traditional story, but is playing with that idea. If writing to entertain, you too will be faced with the challenge of originality, especially if you are taking a specification which involves coursework. Coursework gives you time to think and plan, and hence the expectation of something a bit different will be higher.

Although most of this chapter has focused on writing stories, there are many other forms of writing to entertain too. Within the sphere of poetry you could write, for example:

◆ a brief collection of shorter poems
◆ a single narrative poem
◆ poems for children.

Within the sphere of drama scripts you could write, for example:

◆ a script for film/tv
◆ a playscript for stage
◆ a radio playscript
◆ a dramatic monologue.

If you choose drama scripts as a general form, there are some issues to consider carefully. These include:

◆ film scripts, and tv scripts to an extent, are hard to write and read on the page, because they are for production in a visual form. You will need considerable skill to manage all the elements of dialogue, vision etc.
◆ stage plays are bound by the limits of what can be shown on stage. This places a much higher premium on speech.
◆ radio plays, although not especially fashionable, can offer some of the best opportunities for writers, because of the nature of radio as a medium. It offers a focus on dialogue, without the constraints of a stage. With a few judicious sound effects, the action can be moved wherever you want.

The examples above are some of the more obvious alternatives for creative writing. If you can find an interesting way to use one of these forms, then that is fine. Sometimes a hybrid piece of writing, something that crosses either genre or purpose, can work especially well. One student who wrote an illustrated recipe book for young children later had it published.

One final tip for producing something original for coursework is that ideas rarely come when you are pushed for time and have urgent deadlines. The blank page is most daunting when it needs to be filled by tomorrow. Instead, give yourself plenty of time to think, plan and write. Even carry a notebook so that if you get an idea, you can make a note of it and return to it later.

English language and literature

However this will not be the case for those of you writing under exam conditions. Your responses have to be much more instant, relying on adrenalin for inspiration. Nonetheless, there must always be time to plan before you write and allow time to re-read your writing afterwards.

TECHNICAL TERMS

chronology   the sequence of time, a traditional chronology arranges events in the sequence in which they occur

genre   a word for types of texts. It can refer broadly to such things as poetry, prose and drama, but also more specifically to types of text within those broad areas, such as crime fiction, narrative, poetry etc.

genre conventions   these are features typically found in a certain type of text, e.g. crime writing

imperative   a form of command

narrative/first person   a story told using the 'I' form

narrative/third person   a story about others using she/he etc.

pastiche   imitating some aspects of a genre convention, but changing others for comic or satirical effect

superlative   the highest degree of comparison

3 | Literary and non-literary texts

In this chapter we shall look at literary and other (non-literary) texts that relate to war. We shall consider such aspects as the differences between spoken and written English, how language is used for different purposes and how it shapes attitudes and values.

Assessment Objectives

We shall be analysing the various texts in relation to AO1, AO2, AO3, AO4 and AO5. First remind yourself of these:

AO1

This states that you must communicate what you know about the combination of language and literature, using appropriate technical vocabulary and writing accurately yourself.

AO2

This states that you must respond to literary and non-literary texts, describing and interpreting how they vary in meaning and form. The word 'form' relates to the shape and structure of a text.

AO3

This states that you must analyse texts, using literary and linguistic concepts and frameworks. Whereas AO2 looks specifically at meaning and structure, this AO involves looking at other features such as the way a text is narrated, how the reader is constructed, how metaphorical language is used and so on.

AO4

This states that you must show understanding of the way meaning is affected by context. Context is an important term. It refers to all the possible factors that can affect the way a text is read and understood. These will involve issues surrounding the writer/speaker of a text, the reader/hearer of a text, and the text itself.

English language and literature

AO5

This states that you must identify and consider attitudes and values which are shown in speech and writing. Attitudes in speech and writing should not be too difficult to identify, but 'values' is a more difficult term until you are familiar with it. It relates to the beliefs and principles which the producer of a text holds, often assuming that the text receiver holds them too. A useful term to describe a person's or a culture's beliefs and principles is ideology.

Literary and non-literary approaches

War has always been one of the most written about subjects, used by writers as various as Homer, Shakespeare, Wilfred Owen and Winston Churchill. It has been the basis of novels, plays, poems and short stories. In non-literary texts it has been the topic of newspaper and magazine articles; biographies and autobiographies; conversations which have been transcribed and historical writing. We shall be examining a range of types of writing to see how differently the writers approach their subject as well as what they have in common. In particular the poetry of Wilfrid Owen will be set against other types of text relating to war.

First of all we need to explore the problem of what is meant by 'literary' and 'non-literary'. It is difficult, for example to identify Pat Barker's *Regeneration* trilogy. In these three books the author writes about the First World War, basing her account around known historical facts concerning the two famous war poets Wilfred Owen and Siegfried Sassoon. The author traces their relationship with Captain Rivers, an army psychiatrist who worked at Craiglockhart Hospital in Edinburgh where he treated both the young poets. Although a good deal of the book is based on historical fact, much of it relies, as novels do, on the creative imagination of the writer. Inevitably the conversations are invented, although in such a way as to make them true to the known facts, a number of characters are also fabricated.

So is this then a literary work, a novel, or is it a historical work and non-literary? Most people would probably conclude that, despite the historical basis, this is a literary work and considerably fictionalised, but it illustrates the difficulties of categorising work in this way. Historical writing tends to have a built-in bias because of the viewpoints of the writers, who bring their own attitudes and values to the writing, so that for every history book published as factual there will be a historian somewhere who will describe it as fictional.

The shaping of Wilfred Owen's 'Anthem for Doomed Youth'

To illustrate some of the ways of looking at literary and non-literary texts we'll look at one of Owen's most famous war poems.

Anthem for Doomed Youth

What passing-bells for these who die as cattle?
* Only the monstrous anger of the guns.*
* Only the stuttering rifles' rapid rattle*
Can patter out their hasty orisons.
No mockeries for them from prayers or bells,
* Nor any voice of mourning save the choirs, –*
The shrill, demented choirs of wailing shells;
* And bugles calling for them from sad shires.*

What candles may be held to speed them all?
Not in the hands of boys, but in their eyes
Shall shine the holy glimmers of good-byes.
The pallor of girls' brows shall be their pall;
Their flowers the tenderness of silent minds,
And each slow dusk a drawing-down of blinds.

Glossary

orisons prayers
pall cloth spread over a coffin

TASK

Read the poem carefully several times. What kind of lexis or vocabulary does Owen use? Is it the sort of language you associate with poetry? If so, why?

CONSIDER

You may have noticed some of the following points.

(a) Some words are used which we would not normally come across, or only in other contexts, for instance 'orisons', 'passing-bells', 'pall', 'save'.
(b) Phrases containing a word order that is only usually found in poetry are used, for example, 'Nor any', 'Not in …'.
(c) An adjective is used in combination with a noun it would not normally be associated with in 'sad shires'.
(d) Words are used largely for descriptive effect, as in 'monstrous anger', 'shrill, demented choirs' and 'stuttering rifles' rapid rattle'.
(e) Many words have more impact through **alliteration**, as in the last example in **(d)** and 'glimmers of good-byes'.
(f) Words tend to be repeated, as in 'only', 'nor' and 'not'.

We learn from this that words are used in different ways for different purposes. In this case the poet is dealing with the slaughter of a whole generation and he uses heightened words and careful patterning to achieve the level of intensity required. Some of the techniques he uses, such as alliteration, are particularly associated with poetry. However, you will find alliteration in most types of text. Look for instance at the language of advertising where such techniques are also to be found. Those who are writing to persuade us of something, pull out all the stops. Owen is trying to persuade his audience of the terrible death that awaits his generation. Its horror all the more stark because the usual rites of death are absent: a decent burial, tolling church bells, prayers and hymns of farewell.

Other examples in this chapter of pieces of so-called non-literary writing (from newspapers and magazines for instance), will give you the opportunity to reflect further on whether there is any useful distinction to be made between these different kinds of text.

Drafting a text

You will be familiar with the drafting process from your GCSE work and most writers undertake the same process. Very few people can write something that is just what they want at the first attempt. There are many manuscripts available which show the stages poets have gone through before achieving the end result. Interestingly one of the available sets of evidence relates to 'Anthem for Doomed Youth'. There are four drafts of the poem, each of

English language and literature

which has numerous alterations and we know that the final draft was arrived at after Owen had shown the poem to Siegfried Sassoon at Craiglockhart. Pat Barker in *Regeneration* creates the conversation Owen and Sassoon might have had. At the beginning of the conversation Owen had a draft which began, 'What minute-bells for these who die so fast?' Later the conversation goes like this:

> (Sassoon) What draft is this?
>
> 'Lost count', Owen said. 'You did tell me to sweat my guts out.'
>
> 'Did I really? What an inelegant expression. "What passing-bells for those who die as cattle?" I see we got to the slaughterhouse in the end.' Sassoon read through the poem. When he'd finished he didn't immediately comment.
>
> 'It's better isn't it?'
>
> 'Better? It's transformed.' He read it again. 'Though when you look at the sense you do realise you've completely contradicted yourself, don't you? You start by saying there is no consolation, and then you say there is.'
>
> 'Not consolation. Pride in the sacrifice.'
>
> 'Isn't that consolation?'
>
> 'If it is it's justifiable. There's a point beyond which –'
>
> 'I don't see that.'
>
> 'There's a point beyond which you can't press the meaninglessness. Even if the courage is being abused, it's still ...'

We can't look at all the changes that were made here, but it is helpful to examine some of them. The title of the poem was originally 'Anthem for Dead Youth' , the word 'dead' only being changed to 'doomed' in the final draft. The first line of the poem was originally 'What minute-bells for those who die so fast?' 'Minute-bells' changed to 'passing-bells' and 'who die so fast' was altered to 'who die in herds', then 'dumb-dying cattle' before ending up as 'who die as cattle'. The word 'silent' in the penultimate line was only arrived at after the following had been tried and discarded: 'mortal', 'all men's', 'comrades', 'rough men's', 'broken', 'simple', 'frail', 'innocent', 'patient' and 'sweet white'.

ACTIVITY

Why do you think Owen came to his final decisions in the examples given above? Do you agree that he made the right choice?

CONSIDER

We are of course in a guessing game here, but it is worth considering why some words might have been used and then discarded.

(a) The word 'doomed' in the title was actually suggested by Siegfried Sassoon. There is a big difference in the effect of the two words. 'Dead' is a descriptive word but has a much less emotional effect then 'doomed' which suggests that not only did the men die but that fate made it inevitable from the first that they should do so. We assume that this is the desired effect because Owen was trying to make the British public realise that their young men were being slaughtered without a chance of survival. Pat Barker highlights this point when Siegfried

Sassoon says 'I see we got to the slaughterhouse in the end'.

(b) 'Minute-bells' was replaced by 'passing-bells'. The meaning is almost identical so we need to look for the differences in the sound patterns. 'Minute' has a harder and quicker sound than 'passing', with its soft **sibilants**. 'Passing' also has a clearer connection with death, which we often refer to euphemistically as 'passing away'.

(c) 'As cattle' seems much more effective than 'so fast' since it reinforces the idea of young men being doomed and highlights the indignity of their deaths, the lack of humanity in the way they are treated both before and after death and the thoughtlessness which has led to those deaths. The word 'cattle' may be thought more effective than 'herds' because it is a two-syllable word with a final unstressed syllable The sound dies away as you say it – just as the young men do.

(d) The various possible alternatives to 'silent' could each be argued on their merits. They divide roughly into two groups: nouns or noun phrases, such as 'all men's', and adjectives, such as 'innocent'. The former group seem to relate more to the men at the front themselves, the latter to their wives and mothers at home. It seems in the end appropriate that a word from the latter word class should be chosen, since the end of the poem concentrates on the effect of the deaths on the loved ones at home, the powerless, suffering relatives who have no voice.

Language and purpose

Some references have been made above to the author's purposes. In the case of Wilfred Owen we do not have to guess because he wrote a good deal about what he was trying to do. Most famously he wrote 'Above all I am not concerned with poetry. My subject is War and the pity of War. The poetry is in the pity.' However, we have to be careful how we interpret this. Does he really mean that he is not concerned with poetry, or that his concern with poetry is less than his concern with the pity of war?

In view of the drafting process we have already looked at it seems clear that he was very concerned to get the most effective wording in order to fulfil his purpose, to write a poem which would effectively persuade the British public of the enormity of what was happening at the Front. We have to conclude that, although transmitting the pity of war may have been Owen's main aim, it is not possible to separate it completely from his desire to write effective poetry.

If we look at Pat Barker's *Regeneration* from the two points of view of language chosen and the purposes for which it was chosen, we may find some aspects that coincide with Owen's purposes despite the great differences between the two types of text. It should be clear, even from the brief extract given, that Pat Barker is trying to show the importance of the subject-matter of Owen's poetry to both young men. They are presented as entirely absorbed in finding the right words for Owen's purpose. The emphasis on 'slaughter' and 'cattle' comes across very clearly and intimates that Pat Barker is also concerned to make another generation aware of the atrocities of the First World War. She chooses her language just as carefully as Owen, and although she is writing what might be described as a historical novel, she uses language differently.

This extract is dialogue and uses colloquial language and informality, for example, 'Lost count', 'sweat my guts out'. At the same time because of the nature of the discussion which is taking place, the language takes on philosophical dimensions, with references to 'pride', 'sacrifice', consolation' and other abstract words which point to the intellectual basis and higher purposes of Owen's poetry.

The point was made earlier that Pat Barker's book has some of the characteristics of a literary text and some of the characteristics of a non-literary text. What our study so far

English language and literature

English language and literature

suggests is that the distinction is meaningless. What we are doing is looking at texts in order to see how they are constructed, what the authors' purposes are and how, or if, they achieve those purposes. We need to be aware that there are all sorts of different kinds of text but it is not helpful to categorise them as to whether they are literary or not.

The differences between spoken and written language

We have seen from looking at *Regeneration* and 'Anthem for Doomed Youth' that there is a marked difference between informal speech and the heightened language of poetry. Equally there are many differences between written and spoken language.

TASK

1   Look at Chapter 3, pages 21–28 of the English Language section.

CONSIDER

(a)   Written language gives a permanent record; speech does not in many circumstances.

(b)   Speech can be more spontaneous than written language, which can be rewritten and altered before being presented.

(c)   Speech is full of pauses, which do not necessarily occur at clause boundaries, i.e. do not always correspond to punctuation.

(d)   Speech contains a lot of **fillers**, such as 'er' and 'erm'.

(e)   Speakers use markers to invite the listener to share their point of view, for example, 'like', 'you know', 'ain't it'.

(f)   Speech is more repetitive than writing.

(g)   In speech a sentence is often not completed, or is completed with a different grammatical construction from the one that started it.

2   Read the following transcribed extract from a speech entitled *The Naval Sister's Tale*:

In January of 1940 I was called m … I was called up and … but I had to give notice to the Northumberland County Council and I actually went to … Haslar … which is the navy's biggest naval hospital … in … in … Haslar … in … Gosport Hampshire … in … in … in about … April of 1940 … well … soon after that they had the all the people after the … Dunkirk coming in … and about May … or June … May I think and … then … in September I was appointed to … a naval establishment in Largs in … Scotland … and we had an Admiral Spooner in charge … he was later lost at Singapore … and … there were Wrens in this establishment and I was running the sick bay there … sick quarters … after about eighteen months there … I … was … I went up to … I was transferred to … a hospital called Kings Seat in … near Aberdeen … it was a psychiatric hospital which was … taken over for the duration by the Navy … and … again after about four or five months I was due some leave and I went to London … whilst I was there … and … it … a wonderful thing happened to me … I received a telegram to say … appointed to Hospital Ship No 33 … which is called the Chichilinka and … I had to join this ship in Liverpool in … September … of 1942 …

Find as many as you can of the features mentioned above in Task 1 that characterise the spoken word. How effective do you think this extract is as a piece of communication?

> **CONSIDER**
>
> You should have had no difficulty in finding examples of most of the aspects mentioned in **(a)–(g)** above. As far as its effectiveness is concerned, you have to bear in mind that you should not judge it by the same criteria as written text, even though, unlike most speech, it now has a permanent record. Transcribed speech may appear rather less organised and coherent than written communication but bear in mind that two modes are involved here. Speech, which belongs to one mode, has been transferred to another mode but should not be judged as a piece of writing. The hesitations and awkwardness of grammar we notice when speech is transcribed are not a problem when they are experienced in a conversation.

Different ways of telling a story

The point of view

You may wish to refer to the consideration of narrative point of view on pages 138-142 in Chapter 2 of the Literature section. There are, however, many other genres that make use of narrative: poetry, history, biography, autobiography, newspapers, magazines among others. It was pointed out in Chapter 2 that the two most common narrative points of view are the first person and the third person accounts. To illustrate the first person viewpoint from another genre, let's look at Wilfred Owen's 'Strange Meeting':

Strange Meeting

It seemed that out of battle I escaped
Down some profound dull tunnel, long since scooped
Through granites which titanic wars had groined.

Yet also there encumbered sleepers groaned,
Too fast in thought or death to be bestirred.
Then, as I probed them, one sprang up, and stared
With piteous recognition in fixed eyes,
Lifting distressful hands, as if to bless.
And by his smile, I knew that sullen hall, –
By his dead smile, I knew we stood in Hell.

With a thousand pains that vision's face was grained;
Yet no blood reached there from the upper ground,
And no guns thumped, or down the flues made moan.
'Strange friend,' I said, 'here is no cause to mourn.'
'None,' said the other, 'save the undone years,
The hopelessness. Whatever hope is yours,
Was my life also; I went hunting wild
After the wildest beauty in the world.
Which lies not calm in eyes, or braided hair,
But mocks the steady running of the hour,

And if it grieves, grieves richlier than here.
For by my glee might many men have laughed,
And of my weeping something had been left,
Which must die now. I mean the truth untold,
The pity of war, the pity war distilled.
Now men will go content with what we spoiled,
Or, discontent, boil bloody, and be spilled.
They will be swift with swiftness of the tigress.
None will break ranks, though nations trek from progress.
Courage was mine, and I had mystery,
Wisdom was mine, and I had mastery:
To miss the march of this retreating world
Into vain citadels that are not walled.
Then, when much blood had clogged their chariot-wheels,
I would go up and wash them from sweet wells,
Even with truths that lie too deep for taint.
I would have poured my spirit without stint
But not through wounds; not on the cess of war.
Foreheads of men have bled where no wounds were.

I am the enemy you killed, my friend.
I knew you in this dark: for so you frowned
yesterday through me as you jabbed and killed.
I parried; but my hands were loath and cold.
Let us sleep now ...'

ACTIVITY

From whose point of view is the poem written? What effect does this have?

CONSIDER

(a) The poem initially appears to be written from the point of view of the poet, or a **persona** he has assumed. He speaks the opening lines. However, as the poet recognises that he is in hell and has met a dead enemy soldier there, the viewpoint shifts and the words of the other soldier take over. So you can see that a first person narrative doesn't necessarily mean that only one point of view is presented. In this instance the majority of the poem consists of the German soldier's words. We are told relatively little of the first speaker's point of view. He appears to feel that finding himself in hell is not a cause for mourning since he has escaped from battle. Just before the German soldier speaks there is a balance established in the poem between the visible distress on his face on the one hand and on the other hand the absence of guns and bloodshed which the poet associates with the war above ground. The second speaker takes over and expresses with lyrical intensity all that has been lost by his death, for which the poet or persona was responsible. You will have noticed the number of first person pronouns used in the poem. They are particularly insistent where they become part of a larger repeated pattern:

Courage was mine, and I had mystery,
Wisdom was mine, and I had mastery:

(b) The loss of identity is evident here and it is reasonable to assume that the words of the German instil a strong feeling of guilt in the Englishman. We are not told his reaction. There are, however, various pointers, which might lead us to draw conclusions. The fact that the poem has been written by Owen suggests his concern with its subject-matter. Even if he is assuming a persona at the beginning of the poem, he almost certainly strongly identifies with that persona and, as the poet, lets the poem speak for itself. It is also notable that the German soldier speaks of 'The pity of war, the pity war distilled'. Since these words are so close to Owen's own words in describing his poetic intentions, we can feel fairly sure that he identifies with the German. Indeed by putting the words in the mouth of the enemy soldier, Owen is subtly making a point about the general guilt of nations at war but equally about the way in which soldiers of all nations are exploited and dehumanised by war. Therefore by writing as he does Owen skilfully evokes a certain response in the reader. We will almost certainly identify ourselves with the speaker and because the enemy soldier speaks at greater length and speaks last, we identify most closely with him. However, this is really Owen's own comment on war and in the end it is Owen and his viewpoint with which we identify.

Third person narrative

A very different account of war is given in an **obituary**, which appeared in the *Daily Telegraph* on March 18th, 1999. It is the obituary of Captain David Goodwin, a naval officer who took part in the attack by Fairey Swordfish aircraft on the Italian fleet at Taranto in 1940:

Captain David Goodwin, who has died aged 87, was one of the observers who flew on the historic Fleet Air Arm night strike against the Italian battle fleet in its naval base at Taranto on November 11 1940.

The 21 Fairey Swordfish, armed with torpedoes, bombs or flares, were launched from the aircraft carrier *Illustrious* but included aircraft and crews from *Eagle*, of whom Goodwin and his Royal Marine pilot, Captain 'Olly' Patch were one.

Their Swordfish, armed with bombs, was in the first striking force of 12, but became detached from the rest during the flight to the enemy coastline. When they first arrived at the target, they thought 'there was nothing much happening', but they soon found themselves diving down through 'a wonderful Brocks benefit' of tracer and searchlights to bomb cruisers and destroyers in the Mar Piccolo, the inner harbour.

Patch made his escape flying low over the roofs of the town, unmolested except for what he called 'one horrid little man firing at us'. As the tracer screamed past their wings, Goodwin's comment was: 'The saucy so-and-so!'

Glossary

| *a wonderful Brocks benefit* | a spectacular display of lights from the gunfire
Brocks manufacture fireworks |

ACTIVITY

From whose point of view is this passage written? How does it affect our reaction?

CONSIDER

(a) This passage is written in the third person and therefore we might expect it to be objective. We do not even know the name of the person who wrote it; we just think of the author as a reporter.

(b) For the most part it does give an apparently objective viewpoint. We are presented with 'facts', although of course, as is the case with the historical accounts mentioned earlier, the effect is largely dependent on which particular facts are chosen.

(c) Although the narrative here is in the third person, there are some examples of direct speech, which have clearly been selected with care. For instance the casual comments that 'there was nothing much happening' and that there was 'a wonderful Brocks benefit' of tracer fire seem to have been chosen to impress upon the audience the calm and aplomb of our British airmen under fire. Similarly Patch's comment about 'one horrid little man firing at us' is an excellent example of **litotes** or understatement, an example of the British tendency to maintain a stiff upper lip in a crisis.

(d) By choosing facts carefully and by judicious insertion of direct speech the writer hopes to induce a certain response in the reader; it is assumed that we will be proud of a man who has displayed courage and skill and that as a result we shall be proud to be British.

The spoken narrative

You may have noticed that *The Naval Sister's Tale* is an **eyewitness account** of events that occurred during the Second World War. We call something an eyewitness account when it relates actual events as closely as possible. For instance you may be called on by the police to give an eyewitness account of an accident. The naval sister describes as far as possible exactly what happened and what she saw and experienced.

This raises interesting questions in relation to Owen's poetry. We have seen that Owen uses his experiences as a soldier in the First World War to create poetry.

◆ Is he giving eyewitness accounts in his poetry?
◆ If so, in what ways do they differ from the transcribed account you have just looked at?
◆ Is something that has been crafted as valuable as an eyewitness account?

The obvious difference, apart from the fact that it is in spoken English, between *The Naval Sister's Tale* and Owen's poems is that whereas the Sister tells us what happened without any embroidery, Owen uses all the poetic techniques at his disposal in his account. Inevitably these techniques take us away from a bald recounting of events, even though we might argue that they represent a higher kind of truth.

Other aspects of form and structure

Narrative viewpoint is only one aspect of telling a story. There are many other variable aspects in the genres we are looking at. We have already noticed some of the differences in language between poetry and prose.

TASK

What do you think are the differences in form and structure between poetry and prose?

CONSIDER

(a) Prose tends to be structured in complete sentences, whereas poetry is often more concise and **elliptical**.

(b) Prose is divided into paragraphs, poetry into either verse paragraphs or stanzas.

(c) Punctuation is important to the structure of both prose and poetry but in poetry there is great significance in the line as a unit as well as in the overall syntactical unit which often goes beyond the line.

(d) The structure in poetry tends to come through repetition, either of line, **refrain**, individual words or through rhyme. Prose may also structure through repetition within the syntactical unit but does not use repetition so insistently as poetry.

ACTIVITY

Study the two following extracts. The first is from Wilfred Owen's poem 'Exposure', the second from *A Nurse's Story*, which was published in *Harper's Weekly* in June 1864. *A Nurse's Story* gives an account of nursing Union soldiers, that is soldiers from the north fighting during the American Civil War.

Exposure

Our brains ache, in the merciless iced east winds that knive us...
Wearied we keep awake because the night is silent ...
Low, drooping flares confuse our memory of the salient ...
Worried by silence, sentries whisper, curious, nervous,
        But nothing happens.

Watching, we hear the mad gusts tugging on the wire,
Like twitching agonies of men among its brambles.
Northward, incessantly, the flickering gunnery rumbles,
Far off, like a dull rumour of some other war.
        What are we doing here?

The poignant misery of dawn begins to grow ...
We only know war lasts, rain soaks, and clouds sag stormy.
Dawn massing in the east her melancholy army
Attacks once more in ranks on shivering ranks of gray,
        But nothing happens.

A Nurse's Story

It was at Memphis that I saw one of the most affecting scenes in my whole experience as a nurse. Someone came up one day to the hospital and told me that a boat had just come in from Vicksburg, loaded with wounded, in a very suffering condition. I had no-one of my own sex with me at the time, save a young girl, a daughter of one of the wealthiest and once most prominent men of the vicinity – a secessionist by the way.

This girl – Olive Lancaster – of course I cannot give her real name – had left her father's house to nurse wounded Union soldiers, greatly to the disgust of her family, who at once disowned her, not at all, however, to the daunting of the brave girl.

She had been educated in a Northern school, and she told me sometimes of a young Northern cousin, whom she loved very dearly – beyond cousinly limits I fancied – for her cheek took a richer carmine when she talked of him, and her eyelids drooped, as eyelids are not apt to droop for cousins. It was from him more than any other Northern associations she had got those sentiments which banished her from her father's house, and made her a tender and efficient nurse of our loyal defenders. I alone knew how fearfully she watched for his face among the wounded who came to us …

These poor wounded soldiers lay as thickly as they could be put, upon the open deck, and the blood from their wounds had literally drenched the whole floor, so that we could not step without putting our feet in pools of it.

How do these two examples of different genres differ in form and structure in the ways suggested in **(a)**–**(d)** above? Give examples and comment on them.

CONSIDER

(a) The three stanzas of 'Exposure' are matched by the four paragraphs from *A Nurse's Story*. The two pieces form an interesting comparison in that one is telling us that 'nothing happens' while the other one is telling us what does happen. So structurally the three stanzas of the poem tend to build up a picture of suffering, while the three prose paragraphs move on from point to point in a narrative. Although Owen does in fact write in complete sentences here, an interesting structural device is the use of repeated dots. They usually indicate something omitted and, although there is no grammatical omission, they serve to heighten the unnerving sense the poem gives of an uneasy silence. They also draw attention to the importance of the line as a unit, coming as they do at the ends of lines.

(b) Lines as units are also emphasised by the use of rhyme, often in Owen's case the use of half rhyme or pararhyme. There is a good example here in the pararhyme 'silent' and 'salient'. By associating these words through the rhyme Owen is heightening one of the main points the poem makes, that the silent waiting and the suffering resulting from the weather are just as agonising as the 'salient' itself. Both these words are also followed by repeated dots, as discussed above and perhaps also indicating the thoughts which language is inadequate to express. Rhyme is of course one of the ways of structuring through repetition mentioned above. Other examples from 'Exposure' are 'But nothing happens', which adds to the unnerving uncertainty of the soldiers' experience and of course the stanza structure itself.

(c) The structure of the prose passage is very simple and clear. The paragraphs are introduced in ways that link them with the preceding paragraphs. The girl is not referred to by her proper name in the opening paragraph but is named at the beginning of the second paragraph, thus forming a link. The content of the first paragraph, the girl being disowned by her family, is explained in the third paragraph by her 'Northern education', while the closing line of the same paragraph prepares us for what is to come. Note that the final paragraph in the prose passage does not immediately follow on from the other three.

Relation between structure and purpose

One of the questions you need to ask yourself is why the writer chooses a particular form and structure. The reasons for choice of a particular genre are complex, but the ability to write poetry is a gift, which many of us do not have. For those, like Owen, who do, the feeling that they should express themselves in this way is often overwhelming. Most of us, if we wish to make the public aware of something, as clearly both Owen and the nurse do, are most likely to write something for a newspaper or magazine, as the nurse has done. Both forms of writing are persuasive in their different ways. Also the nurse has a narrative to recount, which can be effectively done in prose. Owen is more concerned here with evoking a situation and mood, which he does extremely effectively by using all the poetic techniques at his command.

Relation between language and purpose

It has already been pointed out that one of the aspects you have to consider at AS Level is the way language is used to fulfil the writer's aims.

ACTIVITY

Looking again at 'Exposure' and *A Nurse's Tale* consider the relationship between language and the writer's purposes.

CONSIDER

Exposure

In 'Exposure' Owen makes use of many techniques to make his poem persuasive and therefore effective. This is apparent from the opening line, which makes the audience aware of the cruel effects of the weather. 'Our brains ache' suggests the way the weather even penetrates to the sensitive and well-protected brain. The assonance and metaphor of 'iced east winds that knive us' effectively make us aware of physical suffering. One of the most telling aspects of the poem is the way in which it blurs the distinction between the two enemies, the German army and nature. So the clouds are seen as dawn's 'melancholy army', dressed in the field grey of the Germans. The brambles of the natural world on which we may cut ourselves are compared to the barbed wire on which men died in battle. Long lines with long vowel sounds evoke a sense of time wearily passing, with the more abrupt, short final line bringing us up short with a reminder of the apparent futility of the situation. Owen uses many words which belong to the semantic field of suffering and cruelty: 'merciless', 'agonies', and 'misery' as well as words which suggest fear and unease: 'confuse', 'worried', and 'nervous'. Connections are made between words through pararhyme, not always at the ends of lines. For instance 'wearied' and 'worried' are connected through their similar sounds and remind us of the connection between the physical and mental conditions of the men. All of Owen's techniques are used to make us aware of the suffering entailed in war, the 'pity of war' and its futility.

A Nurse's Story

The prose passage deals with the suffering in the aftermath of battle, Owen's poem with the suffering before action takes place. The emphasis in the prose passage is mainly on Olive Lancaster and her relationship with her cousin, whereas Owen is concerned with the soldiers in general and does not use any proper names. The nurse is concerned to show the heroism of both the soldiers and the nurses and her story works by highlighting the couple's story. She uses emotive adjectives such as 'affecting' and 'suffering' in connection with the general sufferings of the soldiers and gives a blunt and graphic description of the blood, which lay in pools over the floor.

However, her descriptive powers are employed more to describe the emotional life of Olive, 'her cheek took a richer carmine when she talked of him.' Here she is writing in the style of a woman's magazine and of course the wording seems old-fashioned having been written a century and a half ago. 'Carmine' is a more romantic way of saying 'red' and the whole clause is a roundabout and rather artificial way of saying she blushed. Owen's linguistic techniques evoke strong emotion in the reader, without being in the least sentimental, whereas the nurse's use of language seems designed to induce sentiment in the reader; Olive is described as 'a tender and efficient nurse of our loyal defenders' and the men as 'these poor wounded soldiers'. This use of cliché is designed to appeal to stock emotions. The audience's response is therefore a response which does not require thought. In contrast Owen's appeal is much more individually and originally expressed, often extorting a response from his audience, which shocks them into thought and therefore emotion.

In part of the prose passage not printed above, the nurse writes of the appearance of Olive's beloved. Predictably he turns out to be an ideal hero, who when moved 'made no moan' 'though his lips whitened, and drops forced out by agony stood on his forehead'. The idea of the writer having any sympathy with men's human weaknesses in war seems inconceivable, a stark contrast to Owen's sympathy with those weaknesses in an unacceptable situation.

The nurse's purpose seems to be to highlight heroism on the side she sees as the 'good' side in the Civil War. The nurse Olive is portrayed as equally heroic and the subsequent marriage between her and her wounded cousin seems designed to illustrate that the brave deserve the fair.

How attitudes and values are conveyed by language

Since writers' purposes are intimately bound up with their attitudes and values, much of what has been written above about purposes is relevant here as well. However, in order to cover this aspect more fully, we shall look at some further evidence. The following two extracts are taken from Owen's *Mental Cases* and Ernest Hemingway's *A Farewell to Arms*. The poem is about people who have been mentally tortured by war. The prose passage concerns Italians in the First World War being taken and shot by their own battle police:

Mental Cases

These are the men whose minds the Dead have ravished.
Memory fingers in their hair of murders,
Multitudinous murders they once witnessed.
Wading sloughs of flesh these helpless wander,
Treading blood from lungs that had loved laughter.
Always they must see these things and hear them,
Batter of guns and shatter of flying muscles,
Carnage incomparable, and human squander
Rucked too thick for these men's extrication.

Therefore still their eyeballs shrink tormented
Back into their brains, because on their sense
Sunlight seems a blood-smear; night comes blood-black;
Dawn breaks open like a wound that bleeds afresh.
Thus their heads wear this hilarious, hideous,

Awful falseness of set-smiling corpses.
Thus their hands are plucking at each other;
Picking at the rope-knots of their scourging;
Snatching after us who smote them, brother,
Pawing us who dealt them war and madness.

A Farewell to Arms

Two carabinieri took the lieutenant-colonel to the river bank. He walked in the rain, an old man with his hat off, a carabinieri on each side. I did not watch them shoot him but I heard the shots. They were questioning someone else. This officer too was separated from his troops. He was not allowed to make an explanation. He cried when they read the sentence from the pad of paper and cried while they led him off, and they were questioning another when they shot him. They made a point of being intent on questioning the next man while the man who had been questioned before was being shot. In this way there was obviously nothing they could do about it. I did not know whether I should wait to be questioned or make a break now. I was obviously a German in Italian uniform. I saw how their minds worked; if they had minds and if they worked. They were all young men and they were saving their country… We stood in the rain and were taken out one at a time to be questioned and shot. So far they had shot everyone they had questioned. The questioners had the beautiful detachment and devotion to stern justice of men dealing in death without being in any danger of it.

The two passages form an interesting contrast in terms of the ways in which they reveal attitudes and values. Both relate to the same World War and both writers have experienced war for themselves. Hemingway was an ambulance driver on the Italian front and was badly wounded.

ACTIVITY

As a preparation for considering how attitudes and values are revealed, write down the obvious differences between the two passages and any similarities.

CONSIDER

(a) One passage is poetry, the other is prose.
(b) Both passages describe a situation from one person's point of view in which other people are seen suffering.
(c) The attitudes of the writers to their subject matter are very different.
(d) The two passages are written in very different kinds of language.
(e) Their tones are very different.
(f) The sentence structures are more complex in the poem than in the prose passage.

If you look further at the points outlined above you can begin to see how attitudes and values are revealed in the two passages.

(a) It is often the case that language is more heightened and feeling more intensely conveyed in poetry, but not necessarily.
(b) If you have noticed that in both cases a situation is observed and commented on by someone, and that the situation involves suffering, you are beginning to evaluate attitudes.
(c) It is always useful to decide what you think the author's attitude is towards the subject matter being dealt with. Here their attitudes are very different: Owen seems very emotionally involved with the people he is describing and appalled at their plight, while Hemingway seems very detached.

English language and literature

(d)/(e) The language and tone are therefore very different in the two passages. Hemingway's language is plain, terse and economical. He states the situation without any descriptive detail. There is an almost entire absence of adjectives in the passage. However, his tone is not always matter-of-fact and the occasions where he uses irony colour our response to everything he writes. For instance, after describing the actions of the *carabinieri* without comment, he goes on to say 'I was obviously a German in Italian uniform'. If you are not reading carefully this may at first seem confusing. However, on reflection you know that he is not a German in Italian uniform, so his tone here must be ironic as it is when he says 'They were all young men and they were saving their country'. Clearly he means the opposite. Although Hemingway's narrator is not at all emotional here, the implication of the passage is that because he is critical of the *carabinieri* and their destruction of their country, he must have the opposite values. His attitude to the deaths of the soldiers also becomes clear through his choice of detail, for instance the fact that one officer cries and that the executions are arranged conspiratorially so that one soldier is questioned as another dies.

The Owen poem is not at all plain or unadorned in its use of language. There are many descriptive words, including 'purgatorial', 'wicked' and 'blood-black' all of which have ominous connotations, while the word 'hellish', normally an adjective, is used as a noun to indicate the status of these suffering mental patients. All of these words are indicative of the attitude Owen has towards war and its effects. This in turn suggests the kind of values he has, relating to human decency and the importance of our attitudes to our fellow human beings. There is also a strong implication in his war poetry that there are people in authority who are to blame for the atrocities people suffer. The point is made subtly here by the use of the word 'murders', repeated with the addition of the adjective 'multitudinous', to describe the deaths of men in war. The government of the time would not have used such a word and Owen's choice of it suggests that the people who sent these men to their deaths were in fact murderers. The use of the word 'squander' also suggests that those in charge place very little value upon the lives that are lost.

The kind of imagery Owen chooses also shows us how he feels about these men. He writes 'These are the men whose minds the dead have ravished.' In comparing the effect war has had on the minds of these men to the effect of rape on a woman's body and mind, he suggests the strength of his feeling. Owen's values may seem to us the kind of values we would expect people to have, liberal and humane. At the time when he was writing, however, his values were diametrically opposed to the more widely held values of his country. The majority of people had no first-hand experience of the horrors of war and were constantly exposed to government propaganda. This extolled the value of heroism and the glory of giving your life for your country. Owen, on the other hand, was all too aware of what war really entailed and saw it as a futile sacrifice. He clearly felt that the price these 'Mental Cases' had to pay for patriotism was too high. Their continued suffering, which will go on into the foreseeable future, is powerfully brought out in the line 'Dawn breaks open like a wound that bleeds afresh'. Because the image is taken from these men's past experience and the causes of their plight, it is very appropriate and reminds us that the dawn, which to most people brings new hope, is only the herald of another day of misery for these men.

(f) The sentence structures in the prose passage are clear and uncomplicated. Most of the sentences are **compound** rather than **complex**, containing co-ordinate clauses linked by 'and' or 'but'. Very few subordinate clauses are used. This lucidity, in conjunction with the carefully used irony, has the effect of making Hemingway's attitude crystal clear. There is no complex description to detract from the stark horror of what is being enacted before the narrator and there is no need for commentary to make us understand that his values are totally opposed to those of the executioners. His ironic comment on the devotion of these men to justice shows us exactly how he views their actions and therefore what his own, very different view of justice is.

Owen's sentence structures are not all complex, but they are more cluttered by the proliferation of descriptive phrases: 'Batter of guns and shatter of flying muscles,/Carnage incomparable, and human squander …' The first four lines of the second stanza quoted form a complex sentence, made more complex partly through the use of semicolons, so that what might have been three sentences becomes one. This seems to be a result of Owen's desperation to make his audience realise the horrors these men have suffered and are suffering. The cumulative effective of the present participles 'plucking', 'picking', 'snatching' and 'pawing' also has a similar effect. It particularly draws attention to the humiliation of these men who are doomed to spend the rest of their lives in futile gesture.

The importance of context

The context in which any given text is written is very important in shaping its meaning. Without some understanding of the First World War and the particular circumstances in which it was fought, Owen's poetry would mean very little. Not only do we need to know something about trench warfare, the numbers of people who died and so on, but we are also affected in our reading of the poetry by our knowledge of Owen's biographical details. The fact that he bravely spoke out against the atrocities of the war, that he spent time at Craiglockhart Hospital because of the effect the war had had on him, and perhaps above all the fact that he died in action a week before the Armistice in November 1918, all influence our reading of his work. We may even ask ourselves whether Owen would be as famous as he is if he had not died so young.

Owen himself insistently draws our attention to 'the pity of war' and, as mentioned earlier, is apparently more concerned with that than with poetry itself. In other words, Owen is putting context before poetry. Is that how you would see his poetry? Another question arising from the above discussion is whether Owen is a war poet or simply a poet of the First World War. Does the message he puts across apply equally in the twenty-first century? This is something for you to think about, but the fact that his poetry is still being studied would seem to suggest that Owen's poetry has relevance today.

Bear in mind that there is a strong link between context and purpose. A writer's purpose is born out of the circumstances of the writing. This in its turn is strongly linked to attitudes and values and you can easily see that Owen's attitudes are all connected with the situation he found himself in during the war. His values are partly a result of his upbringing and social influences but, as we have seen above, they are also engendered by the particular situation he had to cope with. Conflicting values, Owen's own and those of the army, government and so on, themselves form part of the context in which his work was written. So you need to think of context in terms of all those aspects which form it.

Remember also that you as reader form part of the context. You both construct your own meaning from the text by what you bring to it and you are constructed as a reader by the devices the writer uses to influence you.

English language and literature

English language and literature

TASK

Go back to *Strange Meeting* on page 95 and consider how you are constructed as a reader in the process of responding to this text.

CONSIDER

(a) Owen creates a setting we can empathise with because we have all created our own vision of hell in our minds.

(b) By using direct first-person speech Owen puts the reader in a position where their response is much more personal, as though they are being addressed: 'I am the enemy you killed, my friend.'

(c) The lyrical language which laments the loss of life and potential strikes a chord in the listener who shares the same cultural and spiritual values as Owen.

(d) Owen appeals to a common sense of guilt, which is also something partly cultural and partly religious.

(e) The vision of a finer world, which might have been ours makes us share Owen's sense of poignancy and regret.

Gender

The scene of battle was entirely a man's world during the First World War. You may therefore feel, especially if you are female, that this topic of study is in some ways limited. Where do women fit in and how do they react? Although they were not at the Front, except in a nursing capacity, they were of course deeply concerned in their capacities as wives, mothers, sisters and so on of the fighting force. Owen draws attention to their silent suffering in *Anthem for Doomed Youth*. R C Sherriff in *Journey's End* writes about the woman who is sister to one of his characters, and potential wife to another, as though she would certainly be incapable of understanding the realities of life at the Front, and should be kept in ignorance of them. A woman's perspective is presented by May Wedderburn Cannan in *Lamplight* and Elinor Jenkins in *Dulce et Decorum?* The effect of the death of a loved one on the woman at home is very different in these two instances and an interesting comparison could be made between them.

Women played a much more important part in the Second World War, as suggested by *The Naval Sister's Tale*. It is interesting to note that the role of women in war changed very little between the time of the American Civil War and the First World War. Since that time women have come into their own as writers about war, Pat Barker's *Regeneration* trilogy being an outstanding example. Susan Hill also wrote a very successful novel about the First World War, *Strange Meeting*, proving the amazing power of the imagination to create what has never been experienced.

You could usefully compare texts written by women and men to analyse their portrayal of war and how far they appear to present it from different perspectives. A female poet who presents very much a woman's perspective on war is Jessie Pope. For instance in *Socks,* she takes on the **persona** of a woman knitting socks at home while the men are away fighting. She glibly assumes that the man in her thoughts will 'come out on top, somehow'. This makes a stark comparison with the portrayals of what's going on at the front through the vivid imaginations of later writers such as Hill and Barker.

TECHNICAL TERMS

alliteration   repeated consonant sounds at the beginnings of words

complex clause   a main clause with subordinate parts

compound clause   mixture of parts to make a whole clause

co-ordinate clause   equal parts of a whole or compound clauses making a sentence

eyewitness account   an account of something seen by the person who recounts it

fillers   sounds that fill up pauses in speech

litotes   deliberate understatement

obituary   a review of the life of a dead person

persona   a mechanism whereby an author takes on another identity for the purposes of his or her writing

salient   stands out as important

sibilants   the use of repeated 's' sounds in words

stanzas   the verses into which poems are often divided

4 | The changing language of literature

In this chapter we shall be comparing *Alice's Adventures in Wonderland* by Lewis Carroll and *The BFG* by Roald Dahl. 'Alice' (as it will from now on be referred to) was published in 1865, *The BFG* in 1982. In more than a century we should expect to find considerable changes: in the use of language; in the society depicted; in attitudes and values, particularly perhaps in the relationships between adults and children, always a vital aspect in relation to children's literature.

The stories
Let's start by summarising these two stories.

'Alice'
The heroine gets tired of sitting with her sister on a bank and, seeing a white rabbit with a waistcoat and pocket-watch, follows it down a rabbit-hole. She seems to fall a very long way down the hole, eventually arriving in a room which has a door onto a lovely garden. In order to get into the garden Alice has to make herself smaller and a good deal of the story revolves around changes of size. In the course of her adventures Alice meets many strange people, such as the Duchess for whom everything has a moral and whose baby seems to change into a pig. The people and animals she meets seem to have little or no clear connection with one another and the geography of the adventures is very unclear. The animal characters, such as the March Hare and the Dormouse that Alice meets at the Mad Hatter's tea party, speak like humans. Eventually Alice finds her way into the lovely garden and discovers it is peopled with playing cards, all under the domination of the Queen of Hearts, who constantly shouts 'Off with his (or her) head'. Alice plays a game of croquet with live flamingos as mallets and hedgehogs for balls. The climax of this part of the book is the trial of the Knave of Hearts for stealing tarts. When Alice contradicts the Queen who orders her head to be cut off Alice sends the whole pack of cards flying and wakes up from her dream.

English language and literature

The BFG

This story starts with Sophie, the heroine, lying awake in the dormitory of the orphanage where she lives. She looks out of the window and sees a curious tall, thin, black figure. He mysteriously takes something from a glass jar and puts it into a kind of trumpet, then blows it into the bedroom of some children opposite. Next he takes Sophie away by force to his own land. Sophie discovers this is the land of giants, but whereas the Big Friendly Giant has taken her (because she has seen him and that is forbidden), the other giants are huge, cruel, child-eating monsters. Sophie discovers that the BFG collects dreams in glass jars and blows them into children's heads and he lives on the foul-tasting vegetable snozzcumber. Sophie is appalled at the deaths of so many innocent children to feed the giants, so she and the BFG devise a plan to save them. This involves the BFG in creating a very special dream/nightmare to be transmitted to the Queen of England, alerting her to the terrible things that are happening and providing proof in the form of Sophie, who is sitting on her windowsill when she wakes up. All works out as planned and once the Queen has been convinced, nine helicopters are sent to the giants' land, one to transport each of the giants back to an enormous pit where they are kept and fed on disgusting snozzcumbers. Sophie is rescued from the cruel orphanage and the BFG lives happily, writing a very popular book about his adventures called *The BFG*.

TASK

Write down all the points of comparison and contrast you can find from reading the summaries above. If you already know the stories you will be able to give a fuller response.

CONSIDER

(a) The heroine in each case is a girl who meets a strange character such as would not be encountered in the real world.

(b) A series of adventures results, but you may gather even from the brief synopsis that the events in 'Alice' are random and not in an ordered sequence. In *The BFG*, however, the plot is clearly developed; Sophie devises a plan to save the children who are being eaten by the giants and carries it through.

(c) In some ways 'Alice' is more clearly constructed than *The BFG*. It has a framework in the dream with which it begins and ends and this partially explains the story. However *The BFG* starts with something unreal and finally merges into reality.

(d) Both stories involve sleep and waking. Alice has a dream and awakens from it at the end, returning to the real world. Sophie is wide-awake in bed at the beginning and carries her extraordinary adventure back into her real world at the end. Lewis Carroll makes a much clearer distinction between the real world and the dream world.

(e) *The BFG* has a clear moral; Sophie is appalled by the giants' eating of children and puts an end to it. 'Alice' is much less clear in this respect. Many of the things people do seem equally bad in theory, such as the Queen's constant orders to execute people, but since they never actually come to anything this doesn't seem to matter very much.

(f) Sophie's experiences in the human world are not happy. She has been unkindly treated and the BFG offers an attractive alternative. Alice, on the other hand, has a kind and caring sister, but is treated with at best indifference and often with rudeness in the dream world.

(g) Both stories are set in locations that do not exist in the real world.

Historical context

We might expect the differences between the two stories to relate largely to the time in which they are set, so it is helpful to examine the context. We probably all have some idea of what life was like for children such as Alice in the Victorian age. The image that is projected is one of a society where children were seen and not heard. Although this is clearly a generalisation there is a good deal of truth in it. The Victorian middle classes thought of themselves as very upright and moral, they went to church regularly and brought their children up to follow in their footsteps. Their strict ideas meant that many children had little spontaneous enjoyment in their lives. However, it is clear that there were many exceptions to this rule. The story of 'Alice' originated from a boat trip Lewis Carroll went on with Alice Liddell, and her sisters. Alice was the daughter of the Dean of Christ Church in Oxford, Henry George Liddell. They were obviously brought up in a much more enlightened way than many of their contemporaries. Whereas most Victorian children's books were much more concerned with presenting a moral, and with suggesting that any child who does not follow the moral path is preparing themselves for damnation, 'Alice' was a refreshing change when it was published in 1865, which largely accounts for its great popularity.

Interestingly, as we have noted above, it is the late twentieth century story which points a moral, not the Victorian one. It is Sophie who is cruelly treated and needs to be rescued, whereas Alice's older sister, having listened to Alice's account of her dream and the adventures in Wonderland, falls into a kind of dream herself:

> Lastly, she pictured to herself how this same little sister of hers would, in the after-time, be herself a grown woman; and how she would keep, through all her riper years, the simple and loving heart of her childhood: and how she would gather about her other little children, and make their eyes bright and eager with many a strange tale, perhaps even with the dream of Wonderland of long ago …

A simple, loving family relationship is brought out here, very different from the situation of Sophie, orphaned and neglected. All this suggests that we should try not to approach texts with too many preconceived ideas and that we should be ready to test our ideas to find out how far they are valid.

In the last part of 'Alice', which gives the sister's reactions, there is also a plausible explanation for the things that Alice has dreamed:

> So she sat on, with closed eyes, and half believed herself in Wonderland, though she knew she had but to open them again, and all would change to dull reality – the grass would be only rustling in the wind, and the pool rippling to the waving of the reeds – the rattling teacups would change to tinkling sheep-bells, and the Queen's shrill cries to the voice of the shepherd boy – and the sneeze of the baby, the shriek of the Gryphon, and all the other queer noises, would change (she knew) to the confused clamour of the busy farm-yard – while the lowing of the cattle in the distance would take the place of the Mock Turtle's heavy sobs.

We might perhaps feel that this is appropriate for a Victorian story, suggesting that everything can be explained. *The BFG* is very different, because from the beginning Sophie is wide awake and, although at first the BFG insists that Sophie has to be snatched because she has seen him and no child is allowed to do so, in the end he comes to live in England and assumes a place in society. The strangeness of the story is blended into reality. Roald Dahl seems to suggest that some aspects of life cannot be explained easily and that an element of fantasy is necessary for all of us. It may be argued that Lewis Carroll would agree with this view but he is more careful to draw the boundaries around the fantasy than Roald Dahl.

Authority figures

One of the most interesting aspects of social context is the authors' portrayal of authority figures. The only authority figure in Alice's real world is, as we have seen, her sister, who is portrayed as protective and caring. In Sophie's world there are no caring authority figures:

> **You got punished if you were caught out of bed after lights out. Even if you said you had to go to the lavatory, that was not accepted as an excuse and they punished you just the same.**

Again, paradoxically, this seems more like the sort of situation you would expect to come across in Dickens rather than in a late twentieth century story. Authority figures in Dahl are often oppressive and frightening. This is true also for Alice, in the world of dream, exemplified by the Queen of Hearts but also by the White Rabbit, who calls imperiously on Mary Ann to fetch him his gloves. Alice comments at one point:

> 'Everybody says 'come on' here … I never was so ordered about in all my life, never!'

You will notice also how much rudeness there is in the behaviour of the Wonderland characters:

> 'You!' said the Caterpillar contemptuously. 'Who are *you*?'
> 'You can draw water out of a water-well,' said the Hatter; 'so I should think you could draw treacle out of a treacle-well – eh, stupid?'

The BFG can also be rude on occasion:

> **'You are once again gobblefunking!' the Giant shouted. 'Don't do it! This is a serious and snitching subject.'**

And the child-eating giants are also extremely rude:

> **'Just this once,' the Bloodbottler said, 'I is going to taste these rotsome eats of yours. But I is warning you that if it is filthsome, I is smashing it over your sludgy little head'**

No doubt the rudeness of the Wonderland characters was one of the aspects that was most appealing to the children who read it at the time, because for children to be rude was much less acceptable in Victorian times than now. Children still love rudeness in books, largely because it is frowned on by authority figures, but of course we are much more tolerant in what we allow children to say nowadays.

ACTIVITY

Read the following two passages. The first describes the first meeting of the Queen of England and the BFG. The second is from the description of the croquet match in 'Alice':

Text 1

Considering she was meeting a giant for the first time in her life, the Queen remained astonishingly self-composed. 'We are very pleased to meet you,' she said …
'Oh, Majester!!' cried the BFG. 'Oh Queen! Oh Monacher! Oh, Golden Sovereign! Oh, Ruler! Oh, Ruler of Straight Lines! Oh, Sultana! I is come here with my little friend Sophie…to give you a …' The BFG

hesitated, searching for the word.

'To give me what?' the Queen said.

'A sistance,' the BFG said, beaming.

The Queen looked puzzled.

'He sometimes speaks a bit funny, Your Majesty,' Sophie said. 'He never went to school.'

'Then we must send him to school,' the Queen said. 'We have some very good schools in this country.'

'I has great secrets to tell Your Majester,' the BFG said.

'I should be delighted to hear them,' the Queen said. 'But not in my dressing-gown.'

Text 2

'Now, I give you fair warning,' shouted the Queen, stamping on the ground as she spoke; 'either you or your head must be off, and that in about half no time! Take your choice!'

The Duchess took her choice, and was gone in a moment.

'Let's go on with the game,' the Queen said to Alice; and Alice was too much frightened to say a word, but slowly followed her back to the croquet-ground …

All the time they were playing the Queen never left off quarrelling with the other players, and shouting 'Off with his head!' or 'Off with her head!' Those whom she sentenced were taken into custody by the soldiers, who of course had to leave off being arches to do this, so that by the end of half an hour or so there were no arches left, and all the players, except the King, the Queen, and Alice, were in custody and under sentence of execution.

What do you find interesting about the ways in which the two passages deal with the concept of authority?

CONSIDER

(a) In Text 1 some of the BFG's repeated exclamations to the Queen are ludicrously funny, and these suggest that the author speaks with tongue in cheek and the apparent reverence for majesty is probably partly making fun of it. The relationship between the three characters here is interesting in that the BFG, at first a frightening and powerful figure, becomes subordinate and confiding. Sophie, who was at first the victim, now shows her superior education and speaks in a forthright way to the Queen, respectful but not subservient. The Queen herself is clearly in command and plans to organise the giant's education, but not until she has got dressed in a way that will be suitable to her position. She is polite but firm.

(b) In Text 2 the Queen in 'Alice' is never polite; she is rude, peremptory and impetuous. The way in which this causes disorder is shown through the effect on the game of croquet: not only is the number of players reduced, but the cards who formed the arches have to do their job of arresting those who have forfeited the Queen's good opinion and thus the game becomes pointless. The futility of it is underlined a little further on in the book when the King pardons all those under sentence.

(c) It is interesting to speculate what the authors intend by these representations of people in authority. Perhaps, although 'Alice' has no overt moral, the episode shows us that excessiveness rudeness and thoughtless actions are counterproductive. *The BFG* on the other hand illustrates the commonsense of the Queen and the importance of authority being backed up by intelligence and a capacity to take into account the views of others.

English language and literature

English language and literature

The audience

So what kind of an audience or readership were Lewis Carroll and Roald Dahl writing for? Some of you may have read Roald Dahl's books yourself when you were a child. *The BFG* is always classified as a children's book and will probably appeal to most children between the ages of six and eleven.

It is much harder to decide on the readership of *Alice in Wonderland*. Although it was certainly written as a children's book and with the Liddell children specifically in mind, it has become a classic and one of those books which is read at least as much by adults as by children.

ACTIVITY

Why do you think it is less clear whether *Alice in Wonderland* is a children's book than whether *The BFG* is?

CONSIDER

(a) The main reason why 'Alice' seems to be regarded differently from many children's books is probably because of its complexity. It is the kind of text which people can interpret in a variety of different ways, philosophical, sexual, political and social as well as literary. Is it just a dream in which the world appears a topsy-turvy place, only to be restored to its normal orderliness when the dream is over? Or is it, on the other hand, a mirror of the real world, indicating that the real world itself is in fact anarchic and disordered? Some readers have seen sexual connotations in Alice falling down the rabbit hole, and the endless transformations that take place in the book can themselves be interpreted in a number of different ways. For instance, Alice starts off a certain size but from the point where she first drinks from the bottle in the room opening into the garden, her size varies until the point where she is about to wake from her dream, 'she had grown to her full size by this time.' Lewis Carroll constantly draws attention to Alice's changing size and the confusion it causes. This may possibly be a comment on how difficult it is to be certain of your own identity because of the effect of life's changing circumstances. Because of the complexity of the text, critics are constantly searching for new things in it.

(b) *The BFG* appears somewhat more straightforwardly to appeal to an audience of children. The story is clearly and simply developed, with plenty of action, chapters that end on cliff hangers, an appealing and sympathetic central character (and one who has the normal defects of all human beings; for instance she wears thick-lensed glasses) and funny and inventive language. Both books reveal a good deal about their authors' attitudes and values, but there is little to suggest a deeper hidden meaning in *The BFG*.

Language

We should expect to find rather different language used in the two books because of the different periods when they were written.

TASK

1   What differences would you expect to find between the types of language used in the two books?

CONSIDER

In the older book:
- ◆ language might be more formal
- ◆ paragraphs might be longer
- ◆ sentence structures might be longer and more complex

♦ vocabulary might be more demanding, more **latinate**
♦ semantic fields might relate to the religious and the moral.

In order to test these points, we need to look at typical passages from the two books.

2 Read the following passages, the first from 'Alice', the second from *The BFG*. Analyse the language used to test the points made above:

Text 1

'And yet what a dear little puppy it was!' said Alice, as she leant against a buttercup to rest herself, and fanned herself with one of the leaves: 'I should have liked teaching it tricks very much, if – if I'd only been the right size to do it! Oh dear! I'd nearly forgotten that I've got to grow up again! Let me see – how is it to be managed? I suppose I ought to eat or drink something or other; but the great question is, what?'

 The great question certainly was, what? Alice looked all round her at the flowers and the blades of grass, but she could not see anything that looked like the right thing to eat or drink under the circumstances. There was a large mushroom growing near her, about the same height as herself; and when she had looked under it, and on both sides of it, it occurred to her that she might as well look and see what was on top of it.

Text 2

The Big Friendly Giant was seated at the great table in his cave and he was doing his homework.
 Sophie sat cross-legged on the table top near by, watching him at work. …
 'But can you really and truly tell what sort of a dream it's going to be simply by listening to it?' Sophie asked.
 'I can,' the BFG said, not looking up.
 'But how? Is it by the way it hums and buzzes?'
 'You is less or more right,' the BFG said. 'Every dream in the world is making a different sort of buzzy-hum music. And these grand swashboggling ears of mine is able to read that music.' …
 'Human beans is having their own music, right or left?'
 'Right,' Sophie said. 'Lots of music.'
 'And sometimes human beans is very overcome when they is hearing wonderous music. They is getting shivers down their spindels. Right or left?'
 'Right,' Sophie said.
'So the music is saying something to them. It is sending a message. I do not think the human beans is knowing what that message is, but they is loving it just the same.'
 'That's about right,' Sophie said.
 'But because of these jumpsquiffling ears of mine,' the BFG said, 'I is not only able to hear the music that dreams is making but I is understanding it also.'

CONSIDER

(a) It may surprise you to notice that the register of the passage from 'Alice' is not very formal. Alice talks to herself using ellipsis and starts a sentence with 'And'. Lewis Carroll makes the whole passage more informal by letting the reader see into Alice's mind as she talks aloud. At times, however, her language may seem a little stilted to the twenty-first century reader, for example, 'Let me see – how is it to be managed?' In the narrative part of the passage, phrases such as 'under the circumstances' and 'it occurred to her' are quite formal.

(b) The passage from *The BFG* is less formal, with Sophie's language being more childlike than

Alice's, 'But can you really and truly tell …' And of course the coined words with which the book abounds make the whole passage seem much less formal. We shall consider those in more detail later.

(c) The whole passage from Alice is two paragraphs; they are much longer than the paragraphs in *The BFG*, although that is largely explained here by the fact that it is a dialogue.

(d) Neither passage uses very complex sentence structures. The sentences in 'Alice' are on the whole longer but they are largely made up of co-ordinate clauses, linked by 'and' and 'but' rather than of subordinate clauses. This is also true of *The BFG*, which tends also to join two clauses with 'but' and start sentences with 'And'.

(e) The vocabulary in 'Alice' is not complex, the most obvious latinate words being 'circumstances' and 'occurred'. It might be said that the vocabulary in *The BFG* is more demanding because there are so many words we do not know the meaning of, although it can be argued that it is not difficult to work out their meaning from the context.

(f) The only obvious semantic field in the first passage is the natural world, while in the second passage there are semantic fields of dreams and music. Neither passage makes any reference to morality.

Creating context

We noted earlier that both stories involve a young girl meeting characters we would not expect to find in the real world. This is one aspect of the ways in which the two authors create context in order to establish an imagined world. How do they do this?

TASK

Write down as many ways as you can think of used by either author to create their imagined world.

CONSIDER

The BFG

(a) Roald Dahl uses non-standard English for the BFG.
(b) He also coins many words to give the BFG reality as a non-human being.
(c) He locates the BFG's home in an area that is not in the atlas.
(d) He gives him a non-human physical shape.
(e) His food, habits and view of life are very different from ours.

Alice

(f) Lewis Carroll uses a setting with many imaginary features.
(g) He uses various kinds of **metamorphoses** to suggest the unreality of the situation.
(h) He allows animals to talk.
(i) He sets his story in the framework of a dream.
(j) He uses language in nonsensical ways.

You may have thought of points that are not on this list, but these cover the main areas. We now need to look at some of these areas in more detail to see how effectively they are used.

Aspects of the use of language

We have noted that both authors use language in inventive and interesting ways. Let's look first at the language of 'Alice' to see how it varies from what we are used to. You will have noticed that the passage we looked at earlier for language use contained no unusual features. That is because those features only come into play when Alice is interacting with the Wonderland creatures. This is well illustrated by the fact that when Alice tries to remember standard Victorian rhymes they come out very differently from what she is used to. So:

How doth the little busy bee
Improve the shining hour ...

becomes:

How doth the little crocodile
Improve his shining tail ...

The rhyme 'You are old, Father William' also becomes altered (metamorphosed). We obviously ask ourselves why this is so and there are many possible answers. One may be that in the world of dream everyday things are always altered, possibly reflecting the subconscious mind and suggesting that the world is a much more complex and disorderly place than we believe when we are awake.

Lewis Carroll often uses words in a punning way, as when he entitles Chapter 4 'The Rabbit sends in a little Bill'. The sentence as it stands immediately suggests payment for something, whereas in this instance Bill is a lizard who is sent down a chimney by the White Rabbit. This is amusing but also has the effect of making us examine language more carefully so that we are less inclined to take it at face value. The confusing nature of life is constantly mirrored in the language used, as Alice finds to her cost. Earlier a passage was quoted concerning a treacle-well. Following on from a discussion of whether you can draw treacle from a treacle-well, the Dormouse uses the word 'draw' in another sense, confusing Alice greatly:

'They were learning to draw,' the Dormouse went on, yawning and rubbing its eyes, for it was getting very sleepy; 'and they drew all manner of things – everything that begins with an M – '

The Dormouse goes on to comment on the phrase 'much of a muchness' and asks Alice whether she ever saw 'a drawing of a muchness?' The word processor on which this is being typed has underlined 'muchness' as a non-word, and yet it is a word we frequently use in the above collocation. As a noun, however, we would probably find it difficult to define and Lewis Carroll brings out such oddities in the language throughout the book. They highlight the problem of communication and the extent to which meaning is created by the reader or listener and may differ quite radically from the meaning intended by the speaker. In this, as in many other ways, 'Alice' may be regarded as a curiously **post-modern** novel.

Alice constantly gets into difficulty in trying to communicate with other characters in

English language and literature

Wonderland. One instance of this is in conversation with the Mad Hatter who asks her 'Why is a raven like a writing-desk?':

> 'Come, we shall have some fun now!' thought Alice. 'I'm glad they've begun asking riddles. – I believe I can guess that,' she added aloud.
> 'Do you mean that you think you can find out the answer to it? asked the March Hare.
> 'Exactly so,' said Alice.
> 'Then you should say what you mean,' the March Hare went on.
> 'I do,' Alice hastily replied; 'at least – at least I mean what I say – that's the same thing, you know.'
> 'Not the same thing a bit,' said the Hatter. 'You might just as well say that 'I see what I eat' is the same thing as 'I eat what I see'!'

Alice has an interest in riddles like most children, but she never discovers why a raven is like a writing-desk. The March Hare's pedantry leads her away from the topic to the question of how far you can interchange object and subject in a sentence without changing the meaning. It soon becomes clear that in most instances you can't, even though the proposition Alice started out with was perfectly clear. This illustrates the importance of grammatical structure and the need for us all to use the same structure in order to understand what other people are saying to us. We might conclude that since the Mad Hatter and the March Hare are, as their names suggest, somewhat mad, we cannot trust what they say, but we would have to agree that they are largely right in this instance.

A similar point is illustrated by the BFG's idiosyncratic way of speaking. He breaks what we would see as the grammatical rules of standard English and invents many words. However, because he does not move fundamentally away from the basic grammatical structure that we all use, we are perfectly well able to understand what he says. An interesting parallel with *The BFG*'s word coinage can be found in Lewis Carroll's *Through the Looking-Glass*, which includes the nonsense poem 'The Jabberwocky'. The poem begins:

> 'Twas brillig and the slithy toves
> Did gyre and gimble in the wabe;
> All mimsy were the borogoves,
> And the mome raths outgrabe.

Here we can see that there is a coherent grammatical structure and we can decide which word class each of the words belongs to, although we are still unable to understand the passage because so many of the open word classes, nouns, adjectives and verbs are made up. *The BFG* uses coined words more selectively so that there is always enough in the context to enable us to get the gist of the meaning.

In *The BFG*, the oddities of language use are all confined to the BFG himself and serve to define him as a non-human being or 'bean' as he would say. He and Sophie are contrasted in that Sophie is educated, whereas the BFG is not. This is effectively brought out by his non-standard English, one prominent feature of which is his tendency to match a first person pronoun with a **third person verb**, 'So what I is trying to explain to you ...' The other major feature that makes the BFG's language unique is Dahl's own coinages, as mentioned above. They are well illustrated in the passage given earlier concerning dreams and music: 'buzzy-hum', 'swashboggling', 'human beans', 'spindels' and 'jumpsquiffling'. It is interesting to note that the BFG, although he uses many words that are not in the dictionary, has the same **morphological** patterns as we would expect in English. We have seen this also in 'The Jabberwocky' above. 'Swashboggling' is clearly an adjective and suggests the related word 'swashbuckling' to us. As far as meaning is concerned we have to work out our own from the context, which is not too difficult. We may come up with slightly different meanings, but as has already been pointed out we each create our own meaning for thc text we read anyway. As in the case of 'swashboggling', most of Dahl's coinages have some basis we recognise in English; 'spindels' is similar to the word 'spine' and the context of music sending shivers down the 'spindels' makes it easy for us to interpret.

An interesting use of language is the BFG's constant question to Sophie 'Right or left?' where the context clearly suggests 'Right or wrong?' Lewis Carroll illustrates here how we tend to use patterns in language, many of which use the same word in different contexts. The consequent confusion of the BFG is amusing and also of course imitative of a child's learning patterns. Children often pick up a pattern from one context and carry it over into another where it does not apply. Another entertaining use of language by the BFG is the substitution of syllables in a word to create a new one; so 'bloodcurdling' becomes 'curdbloodling' and 'hunky-dory' becomes 'dory-hunky'.

TASK

Note down what you think are the authors' purposes in using language as they do.

CONSIDER

(a) Both books entertain through language.
(b) Both authors create vivid and unique characters through use of original language.
(c) The language makes the contexts also excitingly different.
(d) There is an educational effect in making children think about word patterns and sounds and enjoy their own experiments with language.

ACTIVITY

Choose a passage containing original use of language from each book. Analyse the two passages to find out exactly how the author makes use of English to create his effects. What are the differences and similarities in the authors' uses of language? What purposes do you think the authors have in using language as they do?

Language change or cultural change?

Sometimes what appears to be language change can be more accurately described as cultural change.

TASK

Read the following two passages, the first from 'Alice', the second from *The BFG* and make a list of all the aspects which enable you to tell that one story is Victorian and one twentieth century. In the first passage Alice is feeling confused about her own identity because of her frequent changes of size:

'I'm sure I'm not Ada,' she said, 'for her hair goes in such long ringlets, and mine doesn't go in ringlets at all; and I'm sure I can't be Mabel, for I know all sorts of things, and she, oh! she knows such a very little! Besides, she's she, and I'm I, and – oh dear, how puzzling it all is! I'll try if I know all the things I used to know. Let me see: four times five is twelve ... oh dear! I shall never get to twenty at that rate! However, the Multiplication Table doesn't signify: let's try Geography.

The second passage is taken from towards the end of *The BFG*, where they are organising helicopters to transport the child-eating giants to England:

The BFG looked down from his lofty perch and said, this time to the Head of the Air Force, 'You is having bellypoppers, is you not?'

'Is he being rude?' the Head of the Air Force said.

'He means helicopters,' Sophie told him.

'Then why doesn't he say so? Of course we have helicopters.'

'Whoppsy big bellypoppers?' asked the BFG.

'Very big ones,' the Head of the Air Force said proudly. 'But no helicopter is big enough to get a giant like that inside it.'

'You do not put him inside,' the BFG said. 'You sling him underneath the belly of your bellypopper and carry him like a porteedo.'

'Like a what?' said the Head of the Air Force.

''Like a torpedo,' Sophie said.

'Could you do that, Air Marshal?' the Queen asked.

'Well, I suppose we could,' the Head of the Air Force admitted grudgingly.

'Then get cracking!' the Queen said...

CONSIDER

Alice

(a) The names Ada and Mabel are old-fashioned and suggest an earlier age, as do ringlets.

(b) Alice says 'for' where a modern child would almost certainly say 'because'.

(c) The correct grammar of 'I'm I' would probably have become the colloquial 'I'm me'.

(d) 'I'll try if' would become something like 'I'll see whether'.

(e) 'Multiplication Table' would become 'times tables'.

The BFG

(f) The language is altogether more informal; the grown-ups speak rather like children would.

(g) The BFG is characterised by some formality, for example, he says 'do not' rather than 'don't';

(h) There is a mixture of colloquial words, 'sling' and 'belly' and more formal phrases, 'lofty perch'.

(i) The question 'Like a what?' would have been considered very rude at the time when 'Alice' was written.

So overall we notice that the differences between the two passages in terms of style and grammar are not great. Some of them are cultural differences, related to names and fashions. Some of them are grammatical, but they are minor differences, such as the use of adverbs and the adoption of forms that are ungrammatical in standard English but acceptable in speech. The formality of the basic narrative of *The BFG* emerges here, in contrast to the more informal dialogue.

The clash between human and non-human cultures

We have noted that both books involve little girls in communication with different types of people from other worlds. You can usefully explore the ways in which the girls and the non-humans interact. The following passage from *The BFG* shows Sophie and the BFG misunderstanding one another because of the differences between them:

The Giant picked up the trembling Sophie with one hand and carried her across the cave and put her on the table.

Now he really is going to eat me, Sophie thought …

'I is hungry!' the Giant boomed.

'P… please don't eat me,' Sophie stammered.

The Giant let out a bellow of laughter. 'Just because I is a giant, you think I is a man-gobbling cannybull!' he shouted. 'You is about right! Giants is all cannybully and murderful! And they does gobble up human beans! … Every night Bonecruncher is galloping off to Turkey to gobble Turks…He says Turks from Turkey is tasting of turkey … Greeks from Greece is all tasting greasy.'

'I imagine that's possible too,' Sophie said. She was wondering with a bit of a tremble what all this talk about eating people was leading up to. Whatever happened, she simply must play along with this peculiar giant and smile at his jokes.

But were they jokes? Perhaps the great brute was just working up an appetite by talking about food.

In some ways the situation described here is somewhat reminiscent of a kidnapping in the human world, but the horror of that for children is offset by the humorous use of language and the awareness that this is a fantasy. Sophie does not know how to behave in this situation and thinks desperately of strategies to cope, such as agreeing with the giant, 'I imagine that's possible too.' Her language is carefully chosen to be non-committal and not to give offence. You will probably notice that Sophie soon becomes friendly with the BFG, although she describes him here in the early stages of their acquaintance with the phrase 'the great brute', which shows no fellow feeling for him at all. Later on in the book, however, she comes to feel very differently about him. In a similar way you read that people who are kidnapped often come after a period of time to have compassion for, and understanding of their kidnappers.

One of the strategies Roald Dahl uses to enable him to write about man-eating giants without frightening his audience is to make constant jokes. It is impossible for children to take the idea of man-eating giants seriously in the light of the BFG's comments about how people from different areas taste, the Panamanians of hats, the Welsh of whales and so on. Of course we need to distinguish between the two audiences, the audience of children reading or listening to the book and Sophie as the BFG's audience. She is not so sure whether or not these are jokes and how she should react to them. Like most child heroines, she behaves with great bravery and commonsense, something children's authors tend to suggest is often lacking in the adult world. The writer shows us Sophie's reactions through her words and through what is going on in her mind. She is careful in turn taking, uses **phatic** phrases to placate the BFG and asks questions to keep him talking. Even though she is feeling desperate she knows she must 'play along with this peculiar giant and smile at his jokes.' Through her astute mixture of conversational strategies and behaviour, she gradually comes to know and trust her captor, enabling her to work with him to defeat evil, as all heroines should, in the form of the 'cannybull' giants.

The following passage from 'Alice' also illustrates a clash of cultures. Alice is in the Duchess's kitchen and has just commented that she didn't know cats could grin:

'You don't know much,' said the Duchess; 'and that's a fact.'

Alice did not at all like the tone of this remark, and thought it would be as well to introduce some other subject of conversation. While she was trying to fix on one, the cook took the cauldron of soup off the fire, and at once set to work throwing everything within her reach at the Duchess and the baby – the fire-irons came first; then followed a shower of saucepans, plates, and dishes. The Duchess took no notice of them even when they hit her; and the baby was howling so much already, that it was quite impossible to say whether the blows hurt it or not.

English language and literature

English language and literature

'Oh, *please* mind what you're doing!' cried Alice, jumping up and down in an agony of terror. 'Oh, there goes his *precious* nose', as an unusually large saucepan flew close by it, and very nearly carried it off.

'If everybody minded their own business,' the Duchess said in a hoarse growl, 'the world would go round a deal faster than it does.'

'Which would not be an advantage,' said Alice, who felt glad to get an opportunity of showing off a little of her knowledge.

Alice is in many ways in a more difficult situation than Sophie since she meets many odd 'people' and never has time to consolidate a relationship with any of them. The Duchess is one of the rudest and most uncompromising of the characters she meets as this passage shows. Alice and Sophie are both feisty characters but Alice is perhaps more opinionated and dislikes being contradicted as you can see from the end of the passage above. The scene depicted is an excellent example of the topsy-turvy world of Wonderland. All the accepted values of Lewis Carroll's world are turned upside down. The Duchess is in the kitchen with a baby and instead of being elegant and refined she is rude and short in tone. The cook, much below the Duchess in the normal social hierarchy, is throwing kitchen utensils at the Duchess. The baby would usually be a precious, pampered person in the family unit and is being threatened by the missiles. The situation is so extreme that Alice is 'in an agony of terror'. Alice is much less conciliatory in her responses than Sophie, but then she is less threatened. She appeals to the Duchess and when that fails, contradicts her. Narrative plays a large part here in comparison with conversation. Aspects of the narrative warn us not to take the situation too seriously. As with *The BFG* there are two audiences, we are able to read the tone of the narrative and take an objective view and Alice, is the audience within the story and cannot be objective. When we read that the Duchess took no notice of the pans even when they hit her and that it was impossible to tell whether the baby was hurt or not, our anxiety is allayed, as it is of course by the total context, particularly when we learn a little later that the baby turns into a pig.

ACTIVITY

In a group of three or four discuss the two societies depicted in *The BFG* and 'Alice'. What are their characteristics? How frightening do they seem to the two girls and how do they cope with the situation? Discuss the literary and linguistic strategies used by the two authors to present the situations.

ACTIVITY

What do you think the two authors are trying to say by showing a clash between two cultures?

CONSIDER

There are many possible answers to this question, but an important aspect is the clash between a child and others. The 'others' therefore may represent adults, the group children of necessity have to battle with as they grow up. They may seem to children at times to be like giants and they often seem to be utterly contradictory and impossible to please, as the creatures Alice meets seem to her. The various strategies the girls use in dealing with these 'people' are the strategies children use in real life in dealing with grown-ups: phatic communication, conciliation, questioning, rudeness and so on. Certainly 'Alice' may well be seen as its author's metaphor for the world in which he finds himself and there may be some thing of this for Roald Dahl in *The BFG*.

Gender

There is not space here to consider the issue of gender fully, but it is a relevant one to both books. In the light of your study of gender issues in language and literature, you might like to consider their relation to 'Alice' and *The BFG*. Why do you think that the male authors chose girls as their heroines? How are female characters presented in the two books? Is there a noticeable difference between the depiction of gender in 'Alice', a mid-nineteenth century novel, and *The BFG*, a late twentieth century one?

TECHNICAL TERMS

latinate   derived from a Latin root

metamorphosis   process of transforming from one form into another through magic or by natural development

morphology   the study of the structure of words

phatic   utterances used to exchange sociable pleasantries as opposed to conveying meaning

post-modern   post-modern writers react against traditional views of form and question the possibility of attaching any definitive meaning to a text. The key word to post modernism is 'experimental'

third person verb   one which is used with 'he', 'she', 'it' or 'they'

English language and literature

English literature

1 | Introduction

This chapter will introduce you to AS Level English Literature, defining key terms and setting out the Assessment Objectives for the course. A variety of texts will be used to illustrate ways to respond to the objectives.

One of the main aims of an Advanced Level English Literature course is to familiarise students with some of the wealth of texts written in the English language. As a student of English Literature one of your main aims should be to respond with enjoyment and enthusiasm to your texts. Such a response will improve your marks in the examination provided that you demonstrate clear evidence of the skills needed at AS Level. In order to understand the skills required, you will need to study the Assessment Objectives for your course.

Assessment Objectives for AS English Literature

The Assessment Objectives have always been one of the most important aspects of any syllabus. Each Assessment Objective specifies one area or aspect of literary response which your answer must aim to fulfil and by which the examiner will measure your achievement. It is a way of telling you what you should be aiming for and what the examiner will be looking for in your answer.

The changes to the AS and A Level specifications which will be taught for the first time from September 2000 involve new Assessment Objectives which we shall consider in detail and which are common to all three Examination Boards. They are not essentially different from the GCSE English Literature Assessment Objectives, but they will be much more precisely targeted in the new specifications and it is especially important that you are fully aware of them.

At GCSE you were expected to:

◆ respond to texts with understanding, writing clearly and appropriately
◆ explore the ways in which writers made their work effective through their use of language and choice of form
◆ make comparisons between texts
◆ have some understanding of the social, cultural and historical contexts in which texts were written.

For the new AS Level, a set of five Assessment Objectives has been developed. We shall

English literature

English literature

look at these in two ways: first to define and explore their implications and then to see how they relate to specific texts and questions.

AO1

The first of the new Assessment Objectives for AS requires the candidate to:
- communicate clearly the knowledge, understanding and insight appropriate to literary study, using appropriate terminology and accurate and coherent written expression.

This Objective emphasises the importance of the way in which you present your material. There is little value in having profound insights about the texts you are studying unless you are able to express them clearly to the examiner. If you feel you have any basic problems with such matters as spelling, punctuation or grammar, you should look for ways to overcome those problems as soon as possible. You may need to talk to your teacher about extra practice or look for one of the many books available now that will give you practical advice. You may find one or more of the following helpful:

How English Works, Michael Swan and Catherine Walker, Oxford
Discover Grammar, David Crystal, Longman
Exercises in Punctuation Revised Edition, John Trevaskis Collins
Spell it Yourself!, G T Hawker, Oxford
Spelling Guide, Collins Gem

Otherwise your knowledge and understanding of the text will go unrecognised because you are not able to convey your meaning clearly.

Clarity is important but to obtain the higher grades you need to show that you have a wide vocabulary and that you are able to use the specialist terms required for discussing literary texts. You will need to familiarise yourself with terms such as **narrator**, **point of view**, **theme**, **metaphor**, **symbol**, and **tone**. These will all be discussed more fully later in the book, but it is a good idea to prepare for that by doing some work on your own.

ACTIVITY

Choose some or all of the critical terms given below, taking note of the definitions beside them. Try to find your own examples of them from texts you have already studied, books you have read for pleasure, or the texts you are now starting to study for AS. When you have found an example, try to say why it does, or does not work to make the writing effective. We will be looking at this important aspect in a lot more detail later.

narrator   the person who tells the story whether in poetry, prose or drama.

point of view   the narrator tells the story, but how do they tell it? You need to consider whether the story is being told in the first person, that is using 'I' or 'We', in the second person, using 'you', or in the third person, using 'he, she or it'. Most importantly you need to decide what different effects these points of view have on you, the reader. Remember that the narrator may not present the viewpoint of the writer.

theme   most texts are based around particular ideas. While *Othello*, for instance, has jealousy as a central theme, *Romeo and Juliet* deals with love and death, the two great themes of literature. However works may have a number of themes and *Othello* is also concerned with love and death since love leads to jealousy and jealousy to death.

metaphor   you will be familiar with this, particularly from your study of poetry at GCSE. It is the use of language to make a comparison, for example when Richard II describes England as 'This royal throne of kings'. There are a number of other specific terms relating to imagery which we shall consider later.

symbol   this is one kind of image, where a lot more meaning is attached to the thing described than the simple word would seem to express. So the cross is a Christian symbol and the swastika was a symbol of Nazi Germany. The rose is often used symbolically in literature, linking the flower with various aspects of love.

tone   this relates to the tone of voice evident in the writing. The tone may be humorous, sarcastic, angry, pleading, threatening and so on. For instance in Willy Russell's *Educating Rita*, when Rita enters and immediately tells Frank 'It's that stupid bleedin' handle on the door. You wanna get it fixed!' her tone is forthright, blunt and rude.

These definitions will be discussed in more detail in the next chapter.

The criteria the examiners give for achieving the top marks for the first Assessment Objective for AS are:

◆ technically accurate style
◆ accurate use of an appropriate critical vocabulary.

Not only is the appropriate vocabulary vital for expressing your meaning; it is also vital for an accurate interpretation of the questions you will be asked. Words such as those defined above are used in the phrasing of questions and your ability to answer the question depends on your ability to understand them.

AO2

The second Assessment Objective requires you to:

◆ respond with knowledge and understanding to literary texts of different types and periods.

This is a most basic and crucial requirement. The nature of the course, which requires you to study drama, poetry, prose (including one pre-twentieth century text) and a Shakespeare play, ensures that you have looked at 'texts of different types and periods'. This Objective assesses how well you know your text and what your level of understanding is.

Levels of reading

Take for instance a novel. You may read it once and have a fair idea of the plot and what sort of people the characters are. On a second reading you may begin to see how one aspect of the text relates to another; you may begin to distinguish the use of **motifs** and **symbols** and to see the overall shape of the plot. It is only on the second and subsequent readings that the full complexity and subtlety of a text will begin to become clear. You need therefore to approach your studies with some enthusiasm for reading and an understanding that you will need to read texts many times in order to get the most out of them.

This is equally true of poetry. In fact students often find that a first reading of a poem can leave them feeling very unsure of what it is about. You may have to read it two or three times just to get an idea of what is going on and then again to notice how the poet has used their skills to obtain particular effects.

English literature

English literature

ACTIVITY

Read the following short poem by William Blake:

The Sick Rose
O Rose, thou art sick!
The invisible worm
That flies in the night,
In the howling storm
Has found out thy bed
Of crimson joy,
And his dark secret love
Does thy life destroy.

On your own or in pairs, try to work out what the poem is really saying, and what are the clues that led you to your conclusion. How has the poet used imagery here?

CONSIDER

(a) At first reading this may seem to be about the way in which a canker worm destroys a rose. Most poems work on at least two levels: the literal and the metaphorical. A canker worm can literally destroy a flower and you might at first think that this is simply what the poet is saying. It may only be on a second or subsequent reading that you realise the poet is really writing about a sexual relationship and the way in which the woman's life is invaded and destroyed by it. The whole poem consists of an extended metaphor which requires close attention. The rose becomes the woman and the 'invisible worm' that destroys her life may be a sexual relationship and its effects, which are deep-seated but not outwardly visible.

(b) The rose is personified when the poet describes it as 'sick' and the idea of sickness also runs through the poem, with the reference to a 'bed' of sickness and the idea of destruction. You might wonder also why the poet uses the phrase 'crimson joy' and what the significance is of the reference to night and storm. Some ways of looking at the poem are suggested here, but there are other ones that may be just as valid. The poem may mean something quite different to you.

Your 'knowledge' of a text then will lead on to 'understanding'.

Texts of different 'types' refers to the different 'genres' which you need to study in order to fulfil the requirements of the Objective. We shall be looking much more closely at 'genre' later on, but basically 'genre' means a literary type or class. The different genres you will be studying are the novel, drama, poetry and so on. There are also sub-genres, in so far as 'drama' may relate to the genre of comedy, tragedy or tragi-comedy, for instance. When you look at a poem you will find it easier to understand if you know whether it is a narrative poem or an ode, a ballad or a sonnet. The novel you are reading may be a novel of classical realism or a detective novel.

AO3

The third Assessment Objective requires candidates to:

◆ show detailed understanding of the ways in which writers' choices of form, structure and language shape meanings.

This is something that has always been fundamental to the study of literature at Advanced Level. You should be familiar with this requirement from some of your GCSE studies, but at

AS, and then A Level, you are expected to look at the texts with greater subtlety and in greater depth. You need to learn how to look at texts in order to get the best out of them. This involves being aware that a literary text is a **construct**.

The creation of text: developing your critical skills

A construct is something that has been created by the author and is not 'real', although of course it creates the illusion of reality. The characters we meet in a novel may seem to us very real, but when you are writing about them you should not write as if you believed in their existence as real people. Speculation about what they might have done in situations other than those actually described in the novel is pointless. Penelope Lively illustrates this point very effectively in her autobiography *Oleander Jacaranda*. She describes how she and her governess, Lucy, read *Nicholas Nickleby* together:

> We discussed exactly what we would do to the Squeers family if we got the chance. If we could take Smike in we would feed him up with Lucy's porridge and he would have the small spare room. We responded as though to an account of things happening to people we knew, with the intensity of personal involvement.

If you can become as interested and involved in your texts as Penelope and Lucy, that is excellent, but you always need to be aware that you are a critic as well as a reader, analysing and passing literary judgements on the characters and that that is what the examiner is expecting you to do. This does not mean that the texts are not about real life, or that you don't receive illumination about life from your reading. You do. As a reader you are actively involved in interpreting and creating the meaning of the text as you read it, but as a critic you also play a detached role, looking at the construct objectively.

Form

The third Assessment Objective requires you to think about the reasons why writers choose the forms they do. You might for instance ask yourself why, within the broader context, Shakespeare chose the drama as his primary form and what effect that has on what he is trying to say. The choice of form within the broad outline is also important. Why does Shakespeare use a **masque** within *The Tempest*, or a **play within the play** in *Hamlet*, both using very different language from that which we find in the rest of the play? These are the sorts of questions you need to be asking yourself as you progress in your studies.

Structure

Similarly you need to look at the structure of the texts you are reading. Is the novel you are reading a **linear narrative**, like Jane Austen's *Pride and Prejudice*, or a **non-linear narrative**, like *The Handmaid's Tale* by Margaret Atwood? There is an infinite variety of methods of constructing a work of literature. Tom Stoppard, for instance, in *Rosencrantz and Guildenstern are Dead* incorporates sections of Shakespeare's *Hamlet* into his play making use of '**intertextuality**' (another useful literary term), while Arthur Miller in *Death of a Salesman*, has devised a stage setting which allows the past to co-exist with the present.

English literature

Language

The third Assessment Objective also requires you to understand how language shapes meaning. You should be used to looking at language with a view to assessing how different types of language are used for different purposes. Language shapes meaning by its tone, so that you need to be constantly listening for different tones: sarcastic, angry, pleading, bullying and so on. If you studied *Macbeth* at GCSE, you will be familiar with the famous speech Macbeth makes when he realises that defeat is at hand:

> *Tomorrow, and tomorrow, and tomorrow,*
> *Creeps in this petty pace from day to day,*
> *To the last syllable of recorded time;*
> *And all our yesterdays have lighted fools*
> *The way to dusty death.*

His tone here is hopeless and fatalistic, whereas at the other end of the spectrum is the ecstatic tone of Romeo's words on first seeing Juliet and falling in love:

> *O, she doth teach the torches to burn bright!*
> *It seems she hangs upon the cheek of night*
> *As a rich jewel in an Ethiop's ear –*

As these passages also illustrate, you will constantly need to be assessing the effect of different types of imagery and stylistic features and noticing how differently language is used in different historical periods. You should already be familiar with some of the plays of Shakespeare and have some idea of the kind of language and imagery he uses. You are perhaps aware that he tends to use what is called **iterative imagery**, that is: image patterns that work through repetition throughout the play. So, in *Macbeth* there is a lot of imagery relating to blood and sleep and in *Romeo and Juliet*, much reference to the stars and light and darkness.

TASK

Look again at the two quotations given above. Try to analyse the language and imagery used here. What is being compared with what? Are the comparisons effective? What kind of language does Shakespeare use?

CONSIDER

(a) You will probably have noticed that, in the passage from *Macbeth*, the language Shakespeare uses is centred around the theme of time. He compares the movement of time with that of a person creeping slowly along. The sense of inevitability about the movement of time is suggested by the repetition of 'tomorrow' and 'day'. Time is also seen as a light which shows us our way yet only leads to death. The despairing tone of the passage comes partly from the stressed syllables at the ends of lines, 'day' and 'death' and also from the repeated consonant sounds in 'day to day' and 'dusty death'. The technical name for this is **alliteration**, a familiar term from GCSE.

(b) The lines from *Romeo and Juliet* obviously have a completely different feel, because they concern love, not death. Romeo's excitement is shown through the exclamatory opening line and Juliet's beauty is seen in terms of light and jewellery. Her beauty set against the background of night is compared to a jewel perfectly set off against dark skin. This brings out the sense of contrast. The radiant effect of Juliet's beauty is also well brought out by the opening line with its repeated 't' and 'b' sounds and by the idea that she can teach the torches because she is brighter than they are.

Obviously the language of a novel will be very different from that of poetry or drama, although they have some common features. The novel is primarily a **prose** form, although there are plenty of narratives in verse. The form of drama varies. It was largely written in verse in Shakespeare's age, but is primarily a prose form in the twentieth century. One of the features which is often common to both the novel and drama is dialogue.

ACTIVITY

Read the following dialogue from *I'm the King of the Castle*, a novel by Susan Hill. It takes place between two boys, Kingshaw and Hooper, who have been brought together by the relationship between their parents, but who have a deep dislike of one another:

'Going somewhere?'
'Get lost, Hooper.'
'Where's the key? Look, this isn't your house, you know, who do you think you are, going around locking doors?'
'Stuff it.'
'You can't come in here any more unless I say so.'
Kingshaw put down the small box he was carrying, wearily. Hooper was very childish.
'You needn't think I'm going away, either. I can stay here all day. All night as well, if I like. I can stay here forever. This is my house.'
'Why don't you grow up?'
'I want to know what's in here.'
'Nothing.'
'That means something. You'd better tell me.'
'Shut up.'

Although of course you can only study the form, structure and language of a novel fully if you have the whole text, you can learn a lot just from looking at an extract. In this case, what has Susan Hill been able to reveal about her characters through the use of dialogue and language? What difference does it make that she chooses to reveal the two boys through what they say rather than by describing them? She does use a little description here. What does that add? Does her writing here enable you to work out what sort of relationship exists between Kingshaw and Hooper?

CONSIDER

(a) Susan Hill makes her characters seem real because she gives them **colloquial language** of the type you would expect boys of their age and social class to use (they are ten or eleven), such as 'Stuff it' and 'Get lost'. It is made clear that a power struggle is going on between the two boys by Hooper's comment 'You needn't think I'm going away, either...' He is determined and prepared to wait as long as is necessary to gain his objective.

(b) That Hooper probably has the upper hand is suggested by the use of the adverb 'wearily' to describe Kingshaw putting down the box. Here we have an extra clue from the author, which is not given through the dialogue itself. This of course is something that novelists can do more easily than dramatists. A dramatist could only have used the word 'wearily' as a stage direction

English literature

whereas the novelist can as it were include the stage directions within the passage. The fact that Hooper says more than Kingshaw, who mainly relies on abuse to defend himself, also suggests that Hooper is winning in the power struggle. It is almost always the case that revealing character through people's own words is more effective than simply describing them, because it is much more immediate and brings you a lot closer to their thoughts.

AO4

The fourth Assessment Objective asks you to:
◆ articulate independent opinions and judgements, informed by different interpretations of literary texts by other readers.

This is a skill that has not previously been required in the precise way that is expected in the new AS Level. Examiners have always thought it helpful that candidates should have some awareness of other people's critical opinions of set texts, but candidates have often gone into the examination with only one view or interpretation of the text in their minds. This is no longer encouraged. In what is often referred to as the post-modern age, it is vitally important to be aware of the vast range of approaches different people have to the interpretation of literature.

This way of looking at things is underpinned by a belief that a text has no fixed meaning but that the meaning is something that comes to light in the interaction between reader and text. In other words, a text has as many meanings as there are readers. We all need to be aware that, as readers, we contribute to the formation of a meaning for a text as a result of our individual, background, upbringing and culture. You will already be aware that your fellow students have their own individual views on the texts you have studied. As long as they are views based on the evidence of the text, they are all valid.

Although there are as many views on a text as there are readers, there are also groups of readers who have broadly similar views on certain aspects of life, which therefore tend to inform their views of literature. For instance, feminists will tend to have one view of literature, as will Marxists will have another. The important thing is not to think that your own view is the only one. Your own view is of course important, and it is particularly important for you to form your own view of literature rather than to base it on someone else's view, however persuasive their arguments may be. Note the importance of the word 'independent' in the Assessment Objective. Your own response to a text is what the examiner primarily wishes to see, but it needs to be presented in such a way as to show that you are aware of other views as well.

Over-reliance on other people's critical views is not looked on favourably by examiners. One of the problems is that, however good the original comment may be, it was rarely formulated in response to the critical task or question that you are responding to. Students often try to twist material acquired from such guides or given to them by their teachers to make it fit the question or task they have before them. In the end, however, you have to think for yourself. Although there is a body of knowledge to be acquired in the study of English Literature, it is mainly a skills-based discipline that cannot be successfully accomplished simply by absorbing and re-presenting what other people have written.

AO5

The final Assessment Objective asks candidates to:
◆ show understanding of the contexts in which literary texts are written and understood.

Although reference has been made to context in syllabuses in the past, questions have not previously targeted this aspect as they will do from now on. It is probably the most challenging of the changes in the new specifications to come to terms with.

Aspects of context: the relation of a part to the whole in a text

You will probably already be familiar with the process of looking at different aspects of a text and then seeing how the different parts relate to each other. At AS Level this way of looking at how the part relates to the whole may in some questions be all that is required of you to fulfil the contextual requirement.

Other relevant aspects of context

It will obviously be helpful, however, if you look at your set texts, and especially those which target this particular Assessment Objective, in terms of a variety of types of context:

◆ the historical and cultural background
◆ the writer's biography and their other works
◆ the literary context and the language context.

To understand the literary context you could look at the period in which the work was written, establish what influenced the writers of the time and whether they belonged to a particular literary group. For instance if you are studying Keats, it might help to know that he is sometimes described as a Romantic poet and is identified with a group of writers who shared some common views and aspirations. You need to acquaint yourself with these shared features and understand how they are revealed in the work of the particular writer you are studying.

The language context is also important. To use an example from the Romantic poets, two of the most famous of that group, Wordsworth and Coleridge, worked together on a plan to try to write poetry in a language that was closer to the language of ordinary people than had been the case in the earlier years of the eighteenth century.

ACTIVITY

Often a good starting-point for the study of context is finding out more about the writer of a given text. Choose one of the authors whose work you are studying and find out what you can about their life and background. If you are studying a modern writer, on whom not much has been written, one of the best sources of information is the Internet. Remember, however, that the reproduction of material of this kind in essays must always be made relevant to the text and the specific task, not just introduced for its own sake.

All of these Assessment Objectives and the demands they make of you will be looked at in detail in the following chapters.

TECHNICAL TERMS

alliteration   the use of repeated consonants at the beginnings of words and stressed syllables

colloquial language   the informal vocabulary used in everyday conversation

construct   is a post-modern word. It is a literary structure created by the writer; either the whole – as in a novel or a play, or part – as in a character

English literature

English literature

intertextuality   the relationship of one text to another, through linguistic echoes or similarities in theme or meaning

iterative imagery   the use of recurring images throughout a text

linear narrative   one where events are largely told in chronological order

masque   a form of entertainment popular in the sixteenth and seventeenth centuries which combined song, drama, music and dance in a poetic form. The actors presented a kind of pageant to celebrate festive occasions, often representing figures from mythology or figures that stood for a particular quality

metaphor   a comparison where one thing is described in terms of another, without using the words 'as' or 'like'

motif   a dominant idea or theme in a work of literarture, expressed through a recurring image

narrator   the voice which tells the story

non-linear narrative   a story which is not told in chronological order. It may shift between past and present, making use of flashbacks and other devices to tell the tale

play within the play   a short play which exists within the structure of the play as a whole, like the 'mouse-trap' play in *Hamlet*

point of view   the angle from which the events of a novel or subject-matter of a poem are seen. This may be the point of view of the writer or that of a created character, or both.

symbol   an image which acquires a significance beyond what would normally be attributed to it, like the Cross for Christianity, or a rose for beauty. Actions and gestures can also be symbolic

theme   one of the ideas on which a work is based

tone   the mood created which may be humourous, serious, sarcastic, and so on

2 | Studying a novel

This chapter looks at the 'novel' genre and examines the ways in which authors make their work effective. Aspects of narrative perspective, presentation of plot, themes, characters, use of language and establishment of mood and setting are all examined. Examples are given from a wide range of novels ranging from the eighteenth to the twentieth century.

At AS Level you will study one prose text, usually a novel, although it could be a set of short stories. The same techniques of analysis can be applied to both genres, the main difference between the novel and the short story being one of scale.

The new AS course will either offer you a choice of novels written at different periods (from the eighteenth century to the present day), or your choice may be restricted to novels from a particular period, such as the second half of the twentieth century. You will probably have studied one or two novels during your GCSE course, so you should have some idea of how to approach one.

How to look at a novel

Although there are striking differences even between novels written during the same period, there are certain common ways of approaching them. So, whichever novel you happen to be studying, you need to think in terms of the following:

- narrative viewpoint
- character
- theme
- setting
- style
- plot and structure.

English literature

Narrative viewpoint

First person narrative

One of the first things you should try to establish when you are reading a novel is the viewpoint from which it is told. As a reader you are very much influenced, sometimes unconsciously, by the narrator. The novelist controls narrative technique to interest you in the story and to attempt to control your responses. So, where the first person narrative is used, as in Charlotte Brontë's *Jane Eyre*, the child's description of the privations of life at Lowood school generates a sympathetic response in the reader. A subtle use of this occurs when Jane describes a winter evening at school:

> Probably, if I had lately left a good home and kind parents, this would have been the hour when I should most keenly have regretted the separation: that wind would then have saddened my heart: this obscure chaos would have disturbed my peace.

The very matter-of-fact tone of the narrative here may at first prevent us from being aware that Brontë is manipulating our emotions through her narrator, Jane. In reality the reasons Jane gives for considering herself better off than others in the same situation only serve to reinforce her friendless situation, therefore making us sympathise with her. While much of the pleasure of reading a novel depends on just this tendency of the reader to side with the point of view of one or more of the characters, alert readers should be conscious of the ways in which the novelist is working to obtain particular responses from them.

The omniscient narrator

The most common type of narrative method in the novel of **classical realism** is that of the **omniscient narrator**. Classical realism refers to the method employed by many nineteenth-century novelists, who attempted to depict people and events realistically. The omniscient narrator is one who knows everything about his or her characters and who tends to write with more detachment than the first person narrator. There is however a wide variety of approaches within this category. George Eliot, for example, in *The Mill on the Floss*, despite writing the novel almost entirely from the viewpoint of the omniscient narrator, makes the reader aware of her own presence using the first person 'I' from time to time in the course of the novel. Other Victorian writers similarly made their readers aware of the presence of the narrator. However, Henry James, a late nineteenth-century writer, protested that this was not acceptable. He felt a writer should be sufficiently detached to be able to persuade the reader of the 'truth' of the events described.

Narrator as persona

Although the narrator and the novelist often seem to be one and the same, you should not assume that they are necessarily synonymous. For example, in Thackeray's *Vanity Fair*, the author takes on a **persona** to fulfil the role of narrator. In a prefatory note to his novel, entitled *Before the Curtain*, Thackeray assumes the role of Manager of the Performance and his characters are described as 'puppets' manipulated by the Manager. The narrator constantly intervenes in the novel, he describes himself and imagines a stereotypical reader named Jones. Sometimes he guesses how Jones would react to particular aspects of the novel. This Manager—narrator is clearly not the same as Thackeray himself.

ACTIVITY

Look at the following extracts and try to identify the narrative viewpoint of each. Write brief notes on any aspect of interest relating to the narrative viewpoint.

Text 1

I have a great deal of difficulty in beginning to write my portion of these pages, for I know I am not clever. I always knew that. I can remember, when I was a very little girl indeed, I used to say to my doll, when we were alone together, 'Now, Dolly, I am not clever, you know very well, and you must be patient with me, like a dear!'

Text 2

No one who had ever seen Catherine Morland in her infancy, would have supposed her born to be an heroine. Her situation in life, the character of her father and mother, her own person and disposition, were all equally against her.

Text 3

Except for the Marabar Caves – and they are twenty miles off – the city of Chandrapore presents nothing extraordinary. Edged rather than washed by the river Ganges, it trails for a couple of miles along the bank, scarcely distinguishable from the rubbish it deposits so freely.

CONSIDER

(a) The first extract is from *Bleak House* by Charles Dickens. The novel has two narrators. Esther Summerson is the one who speaks here. You will have identified that this is a first person narrative, apparently written by someone very humble and unassuming. This means that you have to read between the lines, since you have only her word for it that she is not clever.

(b) The second extract is the opening of Jane Austen's *Northanger Abbey*. The viewpoint here is that of the omniscient narrator, although it may seem to have something in common with the previous extract. Whereas Esther disclaimed any particular merit for herself, Jane Austen oddly (for the time in which she was writing) suggests that her heroine does not have the qualities we might expect of a heroine.

(c) The third extract is the opening of E M Forster's *A Passage to India*. It is also from the viewpoint of the omniscient author and, unlike the other two, begins by concentrating on the surroundings of the novel rather than its characters.

The epistolary form

An epistolary novel is one that is written in the form of letters. Some novels are written entirely in this format, while others make some use of letters. An interesting example of the latter is Mary Shelley's *Frankenstein* in which Frankenstein dabbles in the more obscure areas of science and discovers a way to create a creature who is apparently galvanised into life by an electrical charge. The novel, however, does not begin with Frankenstein's story at all. It opens with a series of letters from Walton, a ship's captain who meets Frankenstein in the frozen arctic wastes as the latter is pursuing the creature he has created. At this point the events of the novel are nearly at a close. The letters are used as a device to make Frankenstein's relating of his story to Walton seem plausible. Through the use of a number of

English literature

first person narratives, Shelley creates an effective structure for her novel. Walton's letters give way to Frankenstein's story, which in turn gives way to the creature's story at the heart of the novel. This then leads on to a further narration by Frankenstein, the novel concluding in the words of Walton, interspersed with those of the creature. The narrative structure functions rather like that of a Russian doll, the outside layers can be removed to reveal a further layer beneath. This method enables Mary Shelley to manipulate the reader's responses as they are presented with the first person accounts of a variety of characters. These multiple perspectives may seem confusing but they enable the reader to have a more rounded view of the characters than could be obtained from a single first person viewpoint, but without sacrificing the immediacy that comes with the use of 'I' and 'we'.

The narrative viewpoint through two voices simultaneously

We have seen that a novel may present a shifting narrative viewpoint. It may also present two discrepant viewpoints simultaneously. A good example of this is Kazuo Ishiguro's *The Remains of the Day*, which is narrated by the central character Stevens, a man who has devoted his life to being a butler. During the course of a journey to the West Country to see a former colleague, he narrates the story of his life, concentrating on the 1930s at Darlington Hall. As he speaks the reader becomes increasingly aware of the discrepancy between Stevens's view of himself and a quite different view which is simultaneously being presented by Ishiguro. This is achieved to a great extent by Stevens's **idiolect**, which characterises him as formal, emotionally repressed and locked in the past, as when he says to his dying father:

> 'I'm glad Father is feeling so much better.'

He distances himself by using the impersonal third person 'Father' instead of addressing his father directly. Such behaviour contrasts markedly with the open language and manner of his colleague, Miss Kenton, the housekeeper at Darlington Hall. It is clear to the reader that she loves Stevens. However he is blind to her love and determinedly represses any personal emotions. We are constantly aware of Miss Kenton's feelings through Stevens's account of her words and actions, although he repeatedly misinterprets them.

TASK

Read the following extract from the opening chapter of *The Remains of the Day*. Stevens has been trying to run Darlington Hall with too few staff and has consequently put together a faulty staff plan. Having been offered the use of his employer's car for a few days' holiday he conceives the idea of going to the West Country to visit and try to enlist the help of an old employee, Miss Kenton, partly prompted by a letter he has received from her. Make notes on your answers to the following questions.

1   From whose point of view is this narrated? Is it Stevens's or is it Ishiguro's, or both?
2   Are there any signs that the author and Stevens do not have entirely coinciding views?

You may be amazed that such an obvious shortcoming to a staff plan should have continued to escape my notice, but then you will agree that such is often the way with matters one has given abiding thought to over a period of time; one is not struck by the truth until prompted quite accidentally by some external event. So it was in this instance; that is to say, my receiving the letter from Miss Kenton, containing as it did … an unmistakable nostalgia for Darlington Hall, and – I am quite sure of this – distinct hints of her desire to return here, obliged me to see my staff plan afresh.

Only then did it strike me that there was indeed a role that a further staff member could crucially play

here; that it was that, in fact, this very shortage that had been at the heart of all my recent troubles.

CONSIDER

(a) One of the interesting factors that probably immediately strikes you is the way Stevens addresses the reader or narratee (a kind of ideal reader the narrator has in mind when narrating his story) as though speaking personally to us. This helps to create a sense of intimacy between speaker and reader, despite the formal use of 'one', and may throw us off our guard.

(b) However, you probably also notice that Stevens seems to protest too much, 'I am quite sure of this', which makes us suspect he may be reading too much into the letter. This is turn suggests that he has a particular interest in Miss Kenton. The reader wonders what it is, whether it is a romantic interest, and therefore is led to doubt how adequate an observer Stevens is. Thus the novelist cleverly undermines Stevens and creates irony without ever having to intervene as a separate person and address the reader directly. There is much more that can be said about the passage. You may have quite different points to make.

Unusual ways of presenting the viewpoint

One of the most interesting examples of an unusual narrative viewpoint occurs in Kate Atkinson's *Behind the Scenes at the Museum*. The whole story is seen from the perspective of one female character, who, at the beginning of the book, describes her own conception. The embryonic narrator exults in her own consciousness and is aware of all the thoughts of her mother and the circumstances of her birth although she has only just been conceived:

I exist! I am conceived to the chimes of midnight on the clock on the mantelpiece in the room

across the hall. The clock once belonged to my great-grandmother… sand its tired chime

counts me into the world. I'm begun on the first stroke and finished on the last when my father

rolls off my mother and is plunged into a dreamless sleep, thanks to the five pints of John

Smith's Best Bitter he has drunk in the Punch Bowl with his friends, Walter and Bernard Belling.

The effect of telling the story from this viewpoint is to make the first person narrator also an omniscient narrator. There is also a strongly humorous tone which is evoked by the embryo's awareness of the undignified details of her own conception.

ACTIVITY

Read the two extracts below. The first is from *The Color Purple*, a modern epistolary novel and describes how Celie, a black girl in the early years of the twentieth century in the southern states of America, has been raped by the man she believes to be her father.

She (Celie's mother) went to visit her sister doctor over Macon. Left me to see after the others. He

never had a kine word to say to me. Just say You gonna do what your mammy wouldn't. First he put his thing up against

my hip and sort of wiggle it around. Then he grab hold my titties. Then he push his thing

inside my pussy. When that hurt, I cry. He start to choke me, saying You better shut up and git used to it.

English literature

English literature

The second extract is from E M Forster's *A Passage to India.* The Collector referred to here is one of the officials of the British Raj in India. One of the central characters, Adela, an English girl, has gone out to India to marry an Englishman, Ronnie. However, she becomes friendly with an Indian, Aziz, who offers to take a group on an expedition to the Marabar caves. An incident occurs and Adela claims to have been assaulted by Aziz. Here the Collector, Mr Turton, breaks the news to Fielding, an English friend of Aziz:

The Collector could not speak at first. His face was white, fanatical, and rather beautiful – the expression that all English faces were to wear at Chandrapore for many days. Always brave and unselfish, he was now fused by some white and generous heat; he would have killed himself, obviously, if he had thought it right to do so. He spoke at last, 'The worst thing in my whole career has happened,' he said. 'Miss Quested has been insulted in one of the Marabar caves.'

'Oh no, oh no, no,' gasped the other, (Fielding) feeling sickish.

'She escaped – by God's grace.'

'Oh no, no, but not Aziz… not Aziz'

He nodded.

'Absolutely impossible, grotesque.'

'I called you to preserve you from the odium that would attach to you if you were seen accompanying him to the Police Station,' said Turton, paying no attention to his protest, indeed scarcely hearing it.

Working on your own or in pairs, examine the two passages to work out from whose point of view the two situations are seen.

1   How do the points of view affect your reaction?
2   How are the differing viewpoints reflected in the language?
3   What factors do you think influenced the writers' choices of viewpoint?

CONSIDER

(a) The first passage presents the rape from Celie's point of view, in a detached way and without analysis. This has a very powerful effect, as does the fact that the language used is concise and graphic, showing us Celie's background and her powerless position in society.

(b) The second passage, on the other hand, gives a more detached, third person viewpoint and does not involve Adela herself. We may not be inclined to accept the truth of the assault, partly because Fielding, a white man, argues vehemently against the possibility, but also because Forster introduces an ironic tone in describing Turton as 'fused by some white and generous heat …'.

(c) There is an interesting contrast of language, the first passage using such childish words as 'titties' and 'pussy', while the second refers to the assault in a veiled way in saying that Adela has been 'insulted'. One of the reasons for this is that *The Color Purple* was published in 1983, while *A Passage to India* was published in 1924. The more explicit language that is acceptable to us now would not have been tolerated in the 1920s. However, in both instances there are more complex reasons for the choice of language. Turton's **euphemistic** language is symptomatic of his inability to see the truth of what has happened and to describe something as it actually is. On the contrary Celie, because she has had no formal education, is only able to describe things in the most basic, childish, inexact way. She is a child who has been brutally subjected to an adult experience.

Your understanding of point of view in a novel will be targeted by AO3 which looks at 'form, structure and language'.

Approaching character in the novel

'Flat' and 'round' characters

An early twentieth century critic and novelist, E M Forster, who wrote *A Passage to India*, categorised characters as 'flat' or 'round'. By 'flat' characters he meant the kind who are not fully developed and do not develop in the course of the novel, often being identified by a single characteristic or one repeated phrase. 'Round' characters are more fully realised, so that you may tend to see them as more 'real' than 'flat' characters. However, you need to bear in mind, as suggested earlier, that they are still literary constructs not real people. One of the aspects that sometimes reminds us the characters we are reading about are fictional constructs rather than living people, is the names they are given. For instance in Brontë's *Wuthering Heights* we come across Heathcliff and Hareton, names which alert us to the characters' relationship with a particular locality (see also 'setting' below). Dickens often uses odd names for his 'flat' characters, such as 'Guppy', 'Jellyby' or 'Snagsby', which also help to distance them from reality. If you train yourself to notice these things you will constantly be reminded of your comparatively detached position as an onlooker regarding a created world.

The complexity of 'round' characters

Nevertheless, the greater complexity of 'round' characters is striking. They interact with other characters and they therefore grow and develop during the course of the novel. This development is inseparable from the action of the novel, since it is through events and experiences and the way people react to them, that change takes place. A good example of a character who grows and develops is Dora Greenfield, the central character in Iris Murdoch's *The Bell*. At the beginning of the novel she is having marital difficulties; her relationship with her husband Paul, is characterised by fear and guilt. The change occurs largely through her experiences when staying in a lay Church of England community. By the end of the novel she has confronted her inner self, reconciled her contradictions and started to plan a future for herself.

TASK

Read the following two passages from *The Bell*. The first passage is the opening of the novel, while the second comes very near the end. By the time of the second passage, Dora has left Paul for good and decided to study to become a teacher. On her last night before setting off to college, she is alone in the lay community and takes a boat out on the lake.

Text 1

Dora Greenfield left her husband because she was afraid of him. She decided six months later to return to him for the same reason. The absent Paul, haunting her with letters and telephone bells and imagined footsteps on the stairs had begun to be the greater torment. Dora suffered from guilt, and with guilt came fear.

English literature

Text 2

The oars dipped and the boat moved away slowly over the surface of the water. Delighted, Dora released her breath and sat enjoying the gliding motion and the silence of the misty lake, broken only by the dripping of water from the blades. The mist was becoming golden. Now it began to clear away…. Behind the Court the clouds were in perpetual motion, but the sky was clear at the zenith and the sunshine began to warm her. She kicked off her sandals and trailed one foot in the water over the edge of the boat. The depths below affrighted her no longer.

1   What do you learn about Dora from the opening paragraph?
2   Although it is more difficult for you to judge the ending of a novel you have not read, can you see any way in which Dora appears to have changed from the glimpse you have of her at the beginning?

CONSIDER

(a)   Dora is shown in the first passage to be both indecisive and a victim. She has no clear sense of her own identity or capacity to fashion her life in a way that suits her.
(b)   In the second passage Murdoch presents Dora's character by using the symbolism of the world around her. She is shown to have reached an understanding of her place in the world and a sense of confidence. Her confidence is shown by her ability to row and by her no longer fearing the water. The clearing mists suggest her new clarity of vision and understanding of what to do with her life.

How effective characterisation is depends on the methods used to portray it. These may include description, interaction with other characters, what others say about them and their own words and thoughts.

ACTIVITY

Read the following passage from *Emma* by Jane Austen. Emma is trying to make a match between her friend Harriet Smith and Mr Elton, unaware that he is actually in love with Emma herself. On your own or in pairs, examine the passage to see how Austen reveals Emma's character:

Emma could not feel a doubt of having given Harriet's fancy a proper direction, and raised the gratitude of her young vanity to a very good purpose; for she found her decidedly more sensible than before of Mr Elton's being a remarkably handsome man, with most agreeable manners; and as she had no hesitation in following up the assurance of his admiration by agreeable hints, she was soon pretty confident of creating as much liking on Harriet's side as there could be any occasion for. She was quite convinced of Mr Elton's being in the fairest way of falling in love, if not in love already. She had no scruple with regard to him. He talked of Harriet; and praised her so warmly that she could not suppose anything wanting which a little time would not add. His perception of the striking improvement of Harriet's manner, since her introduction at Hartfield, was not one of the least agreeable proofs of his growing attachment.

'You have given Miss Smith all that she required,' said he; 'you have made her graceful and easy. She was a beautiful creature when she came to you; but, in my opinion, the attractions you have added are infinitely superior to what she received from nature.'

'I am glad you think I have been useful to her; but Harriet only wanted drawing out, and receiving a few, a very few hints. She had all the natural grace of sweetness of temper and artlessness in herself. I have done very little.'

'If it were admissible to contradict a lady…' said the gallant Mr Elton.

'I have, perhaps, given her a little more decision of character – have taught her to think on points which had not fallen in her way before.'

'Exactly so; that is what principally strikes me. So much superadded decision of character! Skilful has been the hand!'

'Great has been the pleasure, I am sure. I never met with a disposition more truly amiable.'

'I have no doubt of it.' And it was spoken with a sort of sighing animation which had a vast deal of the lover.

CONSIDER

Here are just a few of the things that may have struck you about this passage.

(a) The scene is presented from Emma's point of view and brings us very close to her thoughts: 'She was quite convinced of Mr Elton's being in the fairest way of falling in love'; 'She had no scruple with regard to him.'

(b) That Emma is self-deluded is brought out by **irony**. There is a discrepancy between the way Emma sees her world and the way the reader sees it. It is clear to the reader that a number of things could be interpreted in more than one way, for instance the reference to the 'sighing animation which had a vast deal of the lover'. This suggests to us that Elton is in love with Emma herself rather than Harriet and throws a new light upon our interpretation of his praise of Harriet's changed character. It is also ironic that Emma refers unconsciously to Harriet's 'young vanity', unaware that she possesses the same quality herself, 'she was soon pretty confident of creating as much liking on Harriet's side…' Here she is vain about her supposed powers of matchmaking, which the reader perceives to be unfounded. Ironically Emma, complacent about her marriage-making success, disclaims responsibility 'I have done very little'.

(c) She is characterised in a number of ways: through her thoughts given in indirect speech, through direct speech in dialogue with Elton and through authorial comment, such as 'she had no hesitation in following up the assurance of his admiration by agreeable hints'. The latter comment helps the reader to realise that Emma, rather than working on a promising affection, is actually attempting to create one where no foundation for it exists.

Theme

The themes can be thought of as the central ideas of a text. It has been pointed out already that although it is convenient to discuss some of the main aspects of a novel separately, they are all interconnected. So a novel's themes or ideas are clarified by its characters and action. In *Wuthering Heights*, the themes of love and revenge are allied, because Hindley's drive for revenge on Heathcliff arises from his seeing Heathcliff replace him in his father's affections. This begins a cycle of revenge which runs through almost to the end. Heathcliff picks up the theme when he is apparently ousted from Catherine's affections by her marriage to Edgar, and the second half of the novel is largely concerned with Heathcliff's quest for revenge. We can see how the action is shaped by revenge when we consider Heathcliff's marriage to Isabella and Cathy's forced marriage to Linton. The revenge theme only comes to an end when Heathcliff, strongly influenced by the supernatural, another theme in the novel, is persuaded to seek his love in death.

It is sometimes said that in literature there are only two great themes, love and death, and

English literature

although that may be an exaggeration, they are certainly very much in evidence. Many of the themes you may identify in a novel often emanate from these two. In examinations, themes have traditionally been the focus of essay questions where candidates were asked to discuss a writer's treatment of a particular theme. Now in the new AS Level courses theme, like character, has become less of a focus for studying a novel. Rather than seeing how many themes you can identify in a novel, you should discover the central issues and see how they work in the context of the novel as a whole.

Thematic commentary

Some authors write at length about their themes in the form of moral or philosophical comment. This is a particular characteristic of Victorian writers, such as George Eliot and William Thackeray. Modern writers may equally have moral comment to make, but they tend to do it in less obvious ways. In *The Handmaid's Tale*, Margaret Atwood does not give her readers a straightforward moral commentary on the evils of repressive, totalitarian regimes such as the one she portrays. Instead she contents herself with letting her description of the actions of the regime, and their consequences for the members of that society, speak for themselves. She also subtly makes clear through extensive reference to the society which existed before Gilead (a society which is shown to be very similar to that which exists in America today), that the seeds of destruction were inherent in that society and led directly to the take-over by the Gileadean regime. In this way Atwood is able to warn her readers that the same fate could befall their/our society without having to resort to any overt moralising.

TASK

Choose a novel you are studying or have studied. Write down what you think the major themes are. Then write several paragraphs about each theme, looking carefully at the way these themes are made clear in the novel, whether through language and imagery, through moral comment, through characters or through the action of the novel. They may of course emerge in all these ways.

Setting

Every novel establishes a sense of place or setting, although its importance varies. This is one of the most vital tasks of the novelist, who needs to give the reader a sense of where they are right from the start. So the opening sentence of George Eliot's *The Mill on the Floss* is:

> A wide plain, where the broadening Floss hurries on between its green banks to the sea, and the loving tide, rushing to meet it, checks its passage with an impetuous embrace.

This immediately signals to the reader the importance of place and setting to this novel.

'Setting' and 'background' are rather inadequate terms of reference for what they describe, since they suggest something rather static or detached. 'Setting' plays an active role in many novels and its importance is often apparent from a novel's title: in *The Mill on the Floss*, both the Mill itself and the river play very important parts, they contribute to the action and themes as well as providing a location for the characters. *Wuthering Heights* similarly depends on the setting in ways that will be detailed below. In Thomas Hardy's *The Return of the Native* the title indicates both the importance of setting and its relationship with character, in this case one who is native to it.

Setting does not just indicate place, but also the conditions associated with it, in particular the atmosphere and weather conditions. The diagram below helps in working out the relationship between setting and other aspects of a novel:

Weather	Location	Atmosphere

Setting

Themes arise	Characters belong	Action takes place

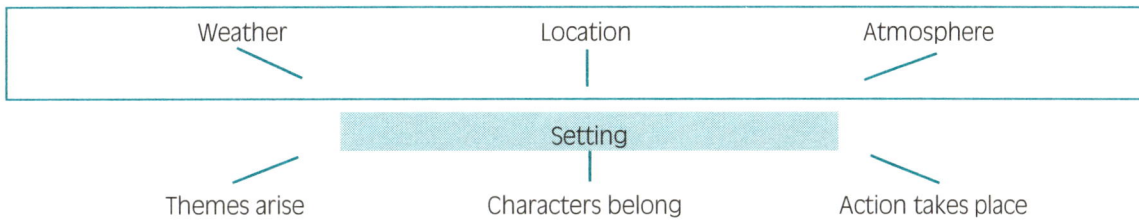

Places are sometimes associated with certain kinds of weather not just by the author and therefore the reader, but also by the characters. So in *Bleak House*, Sir Leicester Dedlock's family seat in Lincolnshire is seen from Lady Dedlock's point of view as unutterably dreary:

> The rain is ever falling, drip, drip, drip, by day and night, upon the broad flagged terrace-pavement, The Ghost's Walk. The weather is so very bad, down in Lincolnshire, that the liveliest imagination can scarcely apprehend its ever being fine again.

To Esther, on the other hand, the scene appears very different:

> There was a favourite spot of mine in the park-woods of Chesney Wold, where a seat had been erected commanding a lovely view. The wood had been cleared and opened, to improve this point of sight; and the bright sunny landscape beyond, was so beautiful that I rested there at least once every day.

The weather then mirrors the mood of the characters. This is an example of the way setting can play an active part in a novel.

ACTIVITY

Establish the setting, or settings, that are used in the novel you are studying.
1   If there is more than one, are they contrasting, for example are they rural and urban? If so, why do you think the author has chosen them?
2   Does setting play a very important part in the novel?
3   Are particular settings related to particular characters and if so, why?
4   How far does setting contribute to mood in the novel you are reading?
Make notes on all these aspects.

Place as character

Place assumes such importance in some novels that critics have frequently commented that the setting takes on the nature of another character. This is true of Hardy's *The Return of the Native*. The opening chapter is entirely given over to a description of Egdon Heath. Although Hardy speaks in general terms of the relationship between man and nature (an important theme in his work and one which indicates the close link between theme and setting), he does not introduce any of the novel's characters until the second chapter. The Heath's status as much more than a mere feature is shown by Hardy's description:

> It was at present a place perfectly accordant with man's nature – neither ghastly, hateful, nor ugly: neither commonplace, unmeaning, nor tame; but, like man, slighted and enduring; and withal singularly colossal and mysterious in its swarthy monotony. As with some persons who have long lived apart, solitude seemed to look out of its countenance. It had a lonely face, suggesting tragical possibilities.

English literature

This rather sombre picture, hinting at isolation and tragedy, perfectly prepares the reader for the tragic story shortly to be unfolded, in which the Heath itself plays a key part. By attributing human characteristics to the inanimate Heath, Hardy is using the technique of **pathetic fallacy**. Setting is supremely important for Hardy who is famous for his creation of the fictional Wessex, which is based on his native Dorset.

Place as symbol

A novel's setting can often take on a symbolic significance, as in *Wuthering Heights*, which works through a contrast between two polarised places: the Heights itself, set in a harsh and wild landscape and buffeted by the elements, and Thrushcross Grange, which although nearby, is peaceful, civilised, set in the valley and enclosed by a park and walls. These contrasts are epitomised in the two men associated with these places, Heathcliff and Edgar, the conflict between them being reinforced by their associations with place. The uninhibited passions of the Heights, even in the servant Joseph's religious rantings, is a forceful contrast to the colder natures of those at the Grange, who are at least superficially civilised and appear much more restrained than those at the Heights.

Novelists obviously choose the setting that suits them. It may be intimately connected with their life's experiences, and will also suit the story they have to tell. Dickens sets a great deal of *Bleak House* in London. In his day it was frequently fog-bound, contained appalling slums and a multitude of out-of-the-way places. All these aspects make it the ideal setting for a story that is somewhat sinister and full of secrets, being largely a thriller. The fog acquires a symbolic significance through its connection with the fog of Chancery, an unfathomable legal system:

> Fog everywhere. Fog up the river, where it flows among green aits and meadows; fog down the river, where
> it rolls defiled among the tiers of shipping, and the waterside pollutions of a great (and dirty) city.

aits   islets on the River Thames

Time

We need to know when the novel is set as well as where. Many novels are historical. Novelists may set their work one or two generations back in order to get a better sense of perspective and to enable them to speak more freely on the issues they deal with. This is true of both *Vanity Fair* and *The Mill on the Floss*. On the other hand they may be set centuries back. This kind of historical novel of course requires extensive research as well as great imagination on the part of the writer, offering as it does an authentic picture of the way life was lived at the given time as well as creating the imagined characters who people the novel.

Futuristic novels, on the other hand, depend more exclusively on the author's imaginative power. One of the difficulties a writer faces is how to make us believe in the world depicted. Atwood, in *The Handmaid's Tale*, makes her totalitarian Gileadean regime credible by using our present society as a constant point of reference. She builds up a detailed and convincing picture of the daily life of Offred, the central character, both past and present.

Setting as context

The 'context' referred to in the final Assessment Objective may refer to the setting of a novel, rather than looking for contexts outside the novel itself. For instance if you are studying *Wuthering Heights* part of a question could be how Brontë uses natural settings in the novel. Similarly, if you are studying *Huckleberry Finn*, AO5 might be targeted by asking you to write about the importance of the river.

ACTIVITY

Read the following passage from L P Hartley's novel *The Go-Between*. It describes the transforming experiences of the central character, Leo, while he was staying at Brandham Hall with a school friend during the extremely hot summer of 1900:

> The thermometer stood at eighty-four: that was satisfactory but I was confident it could do better. Not a drop of rain had fallen since I came to Brandham Hall. I was in love with the heat, I felt for it what the convert feels for his new religion. I was in league with it, and half believed that for my sake it might perform a miracle …

Leo goes on to speak about the change in himself that has resulted from his recent interest in the zodiac and the sense of power that seems to come from it:

> And the heat was a medium which made this change of outlook possible. As a liberating power with its own laws it was outside my experience. In the heat, the commonest objects changed their nature. Walls, trees, the very ground one trod on, instead of being cool were warm to the touch: and the sense of touch is the most transfiguring of all the senses. Many things to eat and drink, which one had enjoyed because they were hot, one now shunned for the same reason. Unless restrained by ice, the butter melted. Besides altering or intensifying all smells the heat had a smell of its own – a garden smell, I called it to myself, compounded of the scents of many flowers, and odours loosed from the earth, but with something peculiar to itself which defied analysis. Sounds were fewer and seemed to come from far away, as if Nature grudged the effort. In the heat the senses, the mind, the heart, the body, all told a different tale. One felt another person, one was another person.

> Although you are not looking at the passage in the context of the whole work from which it comes, you should get some sense of how the writer is using setting here. On your own or in pairs discuss and make notes on what the passage tells you about the setting and how it affects the character.

CONSIDER

This is an example of how setting is not just about place, but also about the creation of atmosphere. The heat here becomes a felt presence and has a transforming effect on Leo. L P Hartley makes us aware of how the heat changes everything, both in physical ways, such as its effect on butter and in more intangible ways, giving Leo a sense of liberation. The close connection between the heat and the boy is made plain through the references to the senses, all of which are affected, although the sun's power is most closely connected with the sense of touch. Above all, a feeling of Leo's being lost in the intensity of the moment is created.

Language

All the aspects we have considered already contribute to making an author's work distinctive and individual. The overall feel of an author's writing may be referred to as their 'idiom'. This results from a number of aspects, such as register, tone of voice, choice of language, sentence structure, use of dialogue, image and symbol. All these aspects have to do with language, which may well be regarded as the most important element of all, since it is the medium

English literature

through which everything else is conveyed. Our response to a text is greatly dependent upon its individual idiom. The following passages illustrate the vast difference which may be found in the ways individuals write. The first passage is from *The Mill on the Floss*, the second from *The Color Purple*:

Text 1

Here suddenly was an opening in the rocky wall which shut in the narrow Valley of Humiliation, where all her prospect was the remote unfathomed sky; and some of the memory-haunting earthly delights were no longer out of her reach. … It was so blameless, so good a thing that there should be friendship between her and Philip; the motives that forbade it were so unreasonable – so unchristian! – But the severe monotonous warning came again and again – that she was losing the simplicity and clearness of her life by admitting a ground of concealment, and that by forsaking the simple rule of renunciation, she was throwing herself under the seductive guidance of illimitable wants.

Text 2

Dear God,

My mama dead. She die screaming and cussing. She scream at me. She cuss at me. I'm big. I can't move fast enough. By time I git back from the well, the water be warm. By time I git the tray ready, the food be cold. By time I git all the children ready for school it be dinner time. He don't say nothing. He set there by the bed holding her hand and cryin, talking bout don't leave me, don't go.

She ast me bout the first one Whose it is? I say God's. I don't know no other man or what else to say. When I start to hurt and then my stomach start moving and then that little baby come out my pussy chewing on it fist you could have knock me over with a feather.

In the first passage Maggie is experiencing a mental conflict as to whether to become friends again with Philip when her family has forbidden it. In the second passage Celie is coping with giving birth to what she believes to be the child of her father, who has raped her. The two ways of writing could hardly be more different. George Eliot's prose is full of long, complex sentences, written in standard English using an extensive, **latinate** vocabulary. She uses metaphor and abstractions. The **register** is formal, the tone sympathetic.

Celie's English, used by Walker for her particular purposes, is non-standard and judged by reference to the standard is ungrammatical and narrow in range. Celie's Black English is perfect for Walker's purposes, to convey the situation and feelings of a black woman who is at the bottom of the heap in society. Celie's ignorance and the shocking experience of childbirth are effectively evoked by the very basic language which contains neither comment nor description. Celie speaks with immediacy and graphically portrays the situation, but her feelings are only implied. George Eliot, on the other hand, uses linguistic devices to show us the depth of Maggie's mental conflict. Her method is allied here with narrative viewpoint. George Eliot is the omniscient narrator, but to elicit sympathy here she uses an **interior monologue**, which takes us very close to Maggie's thoughts. Walker, on the other hand, is distanced from the text by her first-person narrator, but also elicits sympathy for her heroine. Celie's lack of commentary and analysis, a stark contrast to Maggie's articulate introspection, make her plight more moving and immediate to the reader.

TASK

Do a more detailed analysis of the two texts above, working from the hints already given. Look at such aspects as sentence structure and choice of words and examine how each writer uses language to make the reader sympathise with the character.

CONSIDER

(a) One of the obvious differences between the two passages is in the writers' use of sentence structure. George Eliot uses only three sentences in the given extract. This is because her sentences are complex and have a number of dependent clauses, indicated by such words as 'which', 'where', 'and' and 'But'. (A basic understanding of language and grammar is useful in the analysis of literary as well as non-literary texts. If you feel that you know very little about the language aspects of analysis, have a look at *An Introduction to Stylistics* by Urszula Clark, which sets out the basics in a straightforward way.) The complexity of the sentences helps to create the flow of thought which George Eliot is aiming for here. She also uses latinate diction, that is words which derive from latin roots, such as 'humiliation', 'renunciation' and 'illimitable'. This may make the passage more difficult for the modern reader but enables the author to explore the character in more depth; the words quoted above are all abstract words and establish Maggie as an intellectual woman, while the tone and content of the passage show her to be searching for some fulfilment.

(b) The passage from *The Color Purple* is totally different. It has a rather staccato effect, because it is composed entirely of short sentences, with monosyllabic words. The non-standard English very effectively establishes Celie's situation and background. Her inability to use the normal language for such things as pregnancy, 'I'm big', is a poignant reminder that she has not been allowed to go to school by her abusive father. Alice Walker uses repetition very effectively in 'By time I...' to establish the dull, monotonous routine to which Celie is subjected.

(c) It is interesting to compare the two writers' uses of metaphor. Celie uses the cliched expression 'you could have knock me over with a feather', which is entirely appropriate to her and brings out her bewilderment at the birth of her baby. George Eliot writes of 'the rocky wall which shut in the narrow Valley of Humiliation'. This is both metaphorical and **allegorical**. It shows the narrow constraints and deprivations of Maggie's life. The 'Valley of Humiliation' is a reference to John Bunyan's *Pilgrim's Progress*, which is an allegorical account of the experiences of a Christian coping with the day-to-day difficulties of life. It is significant that both Celie and Maggie have something in common; they are both deprived by their societies, largely because they are women, and yet in other ways they could hardly be more different.

Irony

One of the commonest tones in literature is the ironic. It often accompanies a satirical purpose, that of holding up the follies and vices of the world to scorn so that we laugh at them, but at the same time perceive an underlying serious purpose. *Huckleberry Finn* has a number of satirical targets, one of the most important being racism. Similarly Twain satirises those who hypocritically espouse the importance of brotherly love and go away from the church to murder one another. This is effectively achieved in the episode where Huck meets two feuding families, the Grangerfords and the Shepherdsons. The satire is evoked through the forthright language of Huck, who observes with a clear vision, unclouded by the taint of society. He describes the Sunday sermon:

It was pretty ornery preaching – all about brotherly love, and such-like tiresomeness; but everybody said it was a good sermon, and they all talked it over going home, and had such a

English literature

powerful lot to say about faith, and good works, and free grace, and preforedestination, and I don't know what all, that it did seem to me to be one of the roughest Sundays I had run across yet.

The irony of the feuding families talking in one way and acting in another is reinforced by Huck's plain speaking, with the use of such phrases as 'such-like tiresomeness'. Ironically Huck, who finds all this talk tedious, is the only one of them who displays any true brotherly love.

Plot and structure

Plot and structure relate to the scheme of events as designed by the novelist E M Forster in *Aspects of the Novel*, but differentiated between story and plot. Although story and plot are both narratives setting out events, the difference is that whereas a story simply puts events in sequence, in a plot there is emphasis on the causal link between those events. One thing is seen to happen as a result of another.

Although this functions as a useful definition of plot, there are innumerable ways of designing a plot, and not all of them show clearly the causality Forster was referring to. Some do, however, and tend to use linear plots, where the sequence of events is chronological, as in Jane Austen's novels. In such cases it is easier for the reader to see how one incident relates to another, because they are not displaced in time. Whereas in non-linear novels, such as *The Handmaid's Tale*, the reader is often confused and may still be confused at the closure of the novel, the more traditional form may create mysteries or suspense during the course of the novel, but will normally make everything clear in the conclusion.

The mystery novel is a type of novel which is particularly dependent upon plot. This may be said to have derived from the eighteenth century **gothic horror novel**. These novels specialised in the violent, the macabre and the sensational and were intended to be spine-chilling. Naturally the arousal of suspense through complex sequences of events was one of their main functions. One of the most famous of these authors was Mrs Radcliffe who wrote a very popular novel called *The Mysteries of Udolpho*. The novel is full of incident and relies greatly on suspense. Many of the great nineteenth-century novels make use of a thriller element in their plots and most novelists make use of suspense. The detective story is still one of the most popular genres in the twenty-first century and often Stephen King, said to be one of the most 'popular' current novelists, makes use of many of the horror elements that are associated with the Gothic horror genre.

ACTIVITY

Examine the plot of the novel you are studying to see whether you can identify the use of suspense, or any elements that you associate with the detective story or with horror stories.

Plot and character

Jane Austen, whose plots are very different from those of the Gothic horror writers, **parodies** the form in her own novel, *Northanger Abbey*. She shows us how it is not necessary for a novelist to resort to sensationalism to interest a reader in the plot. Her novels are more complex and subtle than the Gothic novels and involve the major characters in coming to a degree of self-realisation. Plot is therefore closely allied to the development of character. Another of Jane Austen's novels which shows a very different approach from that of the Gothic novelists, is *Emma*. Emma, despite having many excellent qualities does not know herself and thinks she can rearrange the lives of others to her own and their satisfaction:

> The real evils, indeed, of Emma's situation were the power of having rather too much her own way, and a disposition to think a little too well of herself;

The events of the plot are all designed to play their part in enabling Emma to come to terms gradually with her own defects and indeed Emma herself largely initiates the plot through her own unwitting blindness. So we see the causality mentioned by E M Forster; Emma, in her anxiety to make a match between her friend Harriet and the vicar, Mr Elton, pays the latter so much attention as to precipitate a proposal of marriage to herself rather than to Harriet. This gives us one of the climaxes of the plot.

Emma's shame at finding herself deceived does not prevent her from going on to make further blunders. She thinks herself in love with the son of a friend, Frank Churchill, then, realising her mistake, designs for Harriet to marry him.

Interest and suspense are aroused in a very different way from that of the Gothic novel. A mystery surrounds the arrival of a piano for a poor but talented and attractive young lady, Jane Fairfax. No-one knows who has sent the piano which plays a small but vital part in the plot. Frank Churchill, who has actually sent it, misleads Emma by pretending it has come from someone else. He is in fact in love with Jane but Emma misreads all the signs. Even when Frank hints his love, she is blind to it. The reader may misread some of the signs too, but is generally one step ahead of Emma, which creates much of the interest in the novel.

Each of the relatively trivial happenings contributes significantly to Emma's growing self-knowledge. Character and plot are intimately bound up together and the reader experiences immense satisfaction at the outcome, the traditional one for the 'novel' genre of marriage.

The non-linear plot

Although most novels have linear plots, twentieth century novels have experimental non-linear plots, Atwood's *The Handmaid's Tale* being an example of this. The novel has no clear beginning or closure and the events of Offred's story do not follow any clear chronological sequence. We have little idea as we read the opening chapter who Offred is (her name is not mentioned in the opening chapter and we never discover her real name), or quite where she is in either space or time. Information is gradually revealed, but the events of the present are constantly interrupted by flashbacks and we remain unsure of Offred's fate, despite the hints given in the Historical Notes to the story which set it in a new perspective. At various points during the story Offred gives us several alternative versions of parts of the narratives. We are never told what the definitive version is. This suggests to the reader that life is essentially not something we can finally pronounce on, because of its constantly shifting perspectives.

The non-passive reader

The effect of a non-linear plot is to put the reader into a position where he/she has to work hard reading between the lines and keeping what has been read clearly in mind, in order to put events into some understandable order. This is a feature of modern literary theory, which tends to place emphasis on the reader as an active rather than a passive participant in the triangular relationship between author, text and reader. As a student of literature you also need to think of yourself as an active part of the reading experience.

English literature

The importance of structure

We can see from the example of *The Handmaid's Tale* that structure is dependent on much more than simply the events of the plot. Most novels are divided into chapters, although this is by no means always the case in modern novels. Even where chapters exist, they are often part of a larger scheme. *The Handmaid's Tale* contains forty-six chapters, but each of these belongs to one of fifteen longer sections. The first, the last and each alternate section is entitled 'Night'. In the Night sections the heroine, who lives in a very circumscribed totalitarian society, is free to go back in time through her memories. Thus the novel is constructed around the constant contrast between past and present which makes possible the full consideration of the themes of liberty and the individual in society. It also makes clear to the reader that the novel is as much grounded in the society he or she lives in as it is in a futuristic society.

The perspective is widened by the addition of a final section entitled Historical Notes, which moves even further forward in time to June 2195. By this time, the Gileadean regime Offred suffered under, has collapsed and a more democratic society seems to have been restored, in which women are no longer denied a proper place in society. However, as we read this section we become aware that sexist attitudes still exist and that this future society has in fact learnt very little from Offred's story. So the structure of the novel is carefully manipulated to give us more than one perspective on Offred's story, despite the fact that, apart from the Historical Notes, it is a first person narrative.

The non-linear novel is by no means a modern invention. Lawrence Sterne, writing in the eighteenth century, satirises the traditional novel form with its ordered plot in *Tristram Shandy*. The novel begins with his conception, although his birth is not finally dealt with until Book III. The plot follows no logical order and has no real conclusion. Both Sterne and post-modern writers seem concerned to remind us that life is neither ordered nor predictable and that we should allow literature to reveal this through a sense of its randomness and lack of shape.

Traditional, linear novels often seem more satisfactory to the reader because they contain a beginning, a middle and an end. The reader may feel cheated when confronted by the 'post-modern' novel, John Fowles's *The French Lieutenant's Woman*. Fowles presents us with two alternative endings, thus putting the onus on the reader to effect the novel's closure. This is as far away as possible from the traditional romantic conclusions of so many nineteenth-century novels. It should make us aware that there are as many readings for a novel as there are readers. We each come to a novel with our own background, tastes and temperament and therefore there is no fixed meaning which can be assigned to it. Fowles carries this idea to what may be seen as its logical conclusion in asserting that his novel has no fixed end, any more than it has a definitive interpretation.

TECHNICAL TERMS

allegory   in allegory abstract ideas are made concrete. Bunyan in *Pilgrim's Progress* describes life as a journey with many obstacles and difficulties, so a period of doubt is represented by 'Doubting Castle' and so on.

classical realism   a way of portraying events and people as realistically as possible in their natural settings

dialogue   conversation between characters

epistolary   written in the form of letters

euphemistic written in such a way as to make the thing described seem less offensive or unpleasant, e.g. describing death as 'passing away'

gothic horror novel novel written in the latter half of the eighteenth or early part of the nineteenth century that was dependent on dramatic and violent events in romantic or exotic settings

idiolect an individual's distinctive way of speaking

imagery descriptive language in a literary work

interior monologue a way of representing a character's flow of thoughts

irony a difficult concept, but one that involves a discrepancy or incongruity between two things, such as what someone says and what they do; or the way a word is used in a particular context which has the double-edged effect of making the meaning contrary to the words

latinate derived from a Latin root

omniscient narrator an all-knowing narrator who looks on at events from the outside

parody the imitation of an author's style in order to ridicule

pathetic fallacy a kind of personification, where a writer ascribes human feelings to something which is not human, such as the landscape

persona a mechanism whereby an author takes on another identity for the purposes of his or her writing

plot the design of events in a novel, poem or drama

post-modern post-modern writers react against traditional views of form and question the possibility of attaching any definitive meaning to a text

setting the place where the events of the novel or other literary work occur

style the particular way in which an author writes; what makes their writing distinctively their own

thesis the viewpoint put forward by the author, particularly in relation to society or politics

English literature

3 | Studying poetry

In this chapter we shall be looking at how to define poetry and at the various aspects you need to be aware of when studying it, for instance the viewpoint of the poet or persona, the use of language, imagery, rhythm and metre. Some of the many different types of poems will be discussed, along with their contexts and different critical viewpoints.

It helps to put poetry into perspective when we remember that, whereas the novel genre is only around three hundred years old, poetry has been part of people's experience for thousands of years. Long before poetry was written down, it was told or sung as part of an oral tradition that stretches back into prehistory. In many civilisations poetry has played a much more important role than it may seem to do today, at least in Britain.

How can we define poetry?

What is poetry, and in what ways does it differ from the prose we were discussing in the last chapter? Since you may come across either poetic prose or prose poetry, it is impossible to define poetry and prose as completely separate forms.

TASK

From your previous study of poetry you will have some ideas about what makes poetry different from other forms of writing. Write down as many distinctive features of poetry as you can.

CONSIDER

These are all features you might expect to find in poetry, although you would certainly not find all of them in all poems. You will probably have written down some of the following:
(a) an organised arrangement of lines on the page
(b) a division into sections or **stanzas** or verses
(c) **rhythm** and **metre**
(d) **rhyme**
(e) imagery or figurative language
(f) word orders which differ from those of prose
(g) compressed wording which often leaves out connecting words that you would find in prose.

Prose, on the other hand, is usually written in complete sentences, is generally less intense than poetry and less condensed in its expression. It tends to use more common, everyday language than poetry and is often easier to read, particularly at a first glance. Poetry often makes great demands on the reader, failing to yield a meaning until you have read between the lines and made your own connections. However, when you make the effort to be an active reader, the rewards are great since poetry can bring a sense of revelation and fulfilment.

Different categories of poems

Narrative poems

There are many different types of poems, just as there are varying types of novels. Whereas almost all novels tell a story, a poem may or may not involve a narrative. A good example of a narrative poem, of great length and complexity, is Chaucer's *Canterbury Tales*. Among the set texts for AS are three parts of this work, *The Prologue*, *The Wife of Bath's Prologue* and *The Merchant's Tale*. Reference will be made to all three in this chapter. *The Canterbury Tales* is a collection of narratives, each one told by a pilgrim travelling from London to the shrine of St Thomas à Becket at Canterbury. Many of the pilgrims have little in common with each other and their tales are markedly different in style, tone, subject-matter, structure and narrative type. This is what makes the whole poem so rich and fascinating.

One of the themes that crops up many times is marriage and *The Wife of Bath's Prologue* gives an account of her five marriages. The Wife's point of view is that the woman should dominate in marriage, having 'maistrie' over her husband.

The Merchant's Tale presents interesting contrasts and comparisons with the *The Wife of Bath's Prologue*. Like the latter, it is concerned with marital relationships but it is rather more cynical in tone and looks at marriage mainly from the man's perspective. The central character is an elderly knight who decides after a lifetime as a single man who had many affairs, that he will marry. He does not, however, look for a partner of his own age, but for a young and beautiful woman. The Merchant ironically disclaims understanding of whether his decision to marry is based on 'hoolinesse or … dotage', that is whether he is pious or simply an old fool. *The Merchant's Tale* has stock romantic characters, the bride, May, and her young lover, Damyan. Damyan suffers the traditional pains of love in his courtship of May and she finally shows 'pitee and franchise', pity and generosity to him. However, she is still contracted to marry the old knight, Januarie. The names, with their obvious significance, contribute to the conventional aspect of the tale, but Januarie turns out to be a more complex character.

He is blind to the truth of his own nature and his situation; sight and blindness are motifs which play a significant part throughout the tale. Januarie is struck down by blindness and keeps a firm guard on his young wife as he is obsessively jealous. Ironically, when he thinks he has her all to himself in the garden he has devised for their encounters, her lover Damyan is waiting in a pear tree where she proceeds to have sex with him. The gods Pluto and Proserpine, also stock figures in medieval tales, look on and play their parts, each intervening on behalf of their own gender. Pluto gives Januarie back his sight, so that he can look on at his wife's infidelity, but Proserpina gives May the eloquence to prove to him that his eyes have deceived him.

The reader's response to Januarie is a complex one, alternating between pity and contempt. The main weapon Chaucer uses to achieve this and to present us with a tale of great complexity and subtlety, is the all-pervasive irony, which we shall look at in more detail later in this chapter. The tale becomes ironic because the Merchant, (or Chaucer), presents

Januarie as a very naive character, who is often unaware of the significance of what he is saying. The narrator, however, makes sure that the readers understand things more fully. Unlike the Wife's tale, this one has no happy ending, except in the deluded imagination of Januarie. It is a cynical tale.

The Canterbury Tales then are held together by the framework of the pilgrimage and by common themes, such as love and marriage, which are looked at from a variety of perspectives.

TASK

Using this brief account of *The Merchant's Tale* and any other knowledge you have of narrative poetry, write down what you think might be some of its key aspects.

CONSIDER

As it tells a story it will probably have a number of central and perhaps also minor characters.

(a) It needs a setting.

(b) The story must have a point or possibly a moral.

(c) It must be narrated by either the poet, a persona or a character within the poem.

(d) The language and tone must be suited to the narrator and the theme.

(e) These aspects will be considered more fully in relation to poetry in general later in this chapter.

Epic poems

The points made above are equally applicable to another type of narrative poem, the epic. An epic is a long narrative poem about important people and events. Some of the most famous Greek and Roman original epic poems, which influenced later writers of the genre, were Homer's *Iliad* and *Odyssey* and Virgil's *Aeneid*.

In *Paradise Lost*, Book 9, Milton takes the fall of man as his subject. He considered this to be the greatest story in human history. Despite Milton's epic being very different from the Greek epics that inspired him, he makes extensive use of Greek mythology in the poem, as well as using many devices which are based on the Greek or Roman originals. So Milton's fallen angels have a great debate in Pandemonium and range through Hell engaging in various activities. The former is the seventeenth century equivalent of Homer's meeting of the Greek leaders in the *Iliad*, while the exploration of Hell may recall the funeral games in the *Iliad*.

The narrative of *Paradise Lost* is not a straightforward, chronological one. It begins in the middle, at the point where Satan and his followers have been thrown out of Heaven after their rebellion against God. The beginning of the story is found in Books 5–8. Book 3 is set in Heaven, where God talks at length about man's freedom of choice, making clear, however, that it is paradoxically linked to predestination, God's foreknowledge that man's free choice will ultimately lead to his downfall. Book 4 introduces Adam and Eve in the Garden of Eden and the first unsuccessful tempting of Eve by Satan. Book 9 is tragic in tone, dealing with Satan's successful temptation of Eve, and Adam's decision to eat the forbidden fruit just as Eve has done because of his love for her. Bitter recriminations follow, which are resolved in Book 10, where Adam and Eve are made aware that, despite their expulsion from Paradise, good will ultimately be victorious over evil. The final two books look into the future and the poem concludes as Adam and Eve:

> *... hand in hand, with wandering steps and slow*
> *Through Eden made their solitary way*

as they exit from Eden into the mortal world of pain and suffering.

From this brief synopsis you can see the vast sweep of the story and the greatness of Milton's purpose. Poets in ancient Greece invoked one of the nine Muses (goddesses associated with particular arts or areas of interest) to give them inspiration. Milton, however, invokes the Spirit of God, the 'heavenly Muse', to give him the inspiration to deal effectively with his high subject.

As a narrative poem, *Paradise Lost* has a very different coherence from *The Canterbury Tales*. It is much more tightly structured and is all seen from the viewpoint of the poetic omniscient narrator. Chaucer's story, on the other hand, is seen from the viewpoints of a wide variety of people, although third person narration is widely used. Whereas Chaucer's overall account of the pilgrimage involves many different stories, Milton is concerned with only one story. As we have seen from the synopsis above, Milton uses retrospective narration and a variety of techniques to convey the tone and pace of the narrative: description, dialogue and dramatic incident for instance. We shall look at these in more detail in relation to Book 9 later on in this chapter.

Narrative poetry continued to be popular in the eighteenth century when much of it was satirical, such as Alexander Pope's *The Rape of the Lock*. Some of the most memorable narrative poems were produced by the Romantic poets, for example Coleridge's *The Rime of the Ancient Mariner* and *Christabel* and Keats's *The Eve of St Agnes*. The Romantic poets were a group of poets writing in the late eighteenth and early nineteenth century who placed great emphasis on the importance of the individual experience and imagination. The most famous of them were Wordsworth, Coleridge, Byron, Shelley and Keats. If you are studying Keats, *The Eve of St Agnes* will probably be among the group you will look at. Like much later narrative poetry, it has a much shorter and simpler structure than that of *Paradise Lost*. The Victorians enthusiastically continued the narrative tradition with Tennyson's *Idylls of the King*, Arnold's *Sohrab and Rustum* and Browning's *The Ring and the Book*, to mention only a very few. In the twentieth century the form has continued to be popular, although more modern narrative poems tend to be shorter again than their nineteenth century counterparts, as in Wilfred Owen's *Strange Meeting*, T S Eliot's *The Journey of the Magi* and Philip Larkin's *The Whitsun Weddings*.

Context in a narrative poem

You will realise if you're studying Chaucer or Milton, that there is a lot more involved than just studying the poem. In reading Chaucer you have to get used to a whole different language, Middle English, although it is not as different from our twenty-first century English as it might seem at first. You are also reading about a world which was entirely different from ours in social, political, cultural and religious terms. Both Chaucer and Milton write a lot about science as well, particularly in relation to the known views of the universe. To understand Chaucer you need to know something of the Ptolemaic system. This theory put forward the idea that the earth was the centre of the universe with the sun, moon and planets revolving around it. Even though this view of the universe was outdated by the time Milton was writing, he still takes it as the basis for the universe of *Paradise Lost*. In order to get an idea of the context Milton was writing in, you need to find out something about the English Civil War between the puritans and the royalists which took place in the middle of the seventeenth century.

ACTIVITY

Find out as much as you can about the background and society of the age in which the poet you are concerned with was writing. If you are studying contemporary poetry, concentrate first on what you can find out about the poet's life.

Lyric poetry

Lyric poetry derives from ancient Greece where a lyric was a song accompanied by a lyre. We still call the words of popular songs lyrics, and lyric verse developed as a form which involved the intense outpouring of emotion in a relatively brief poem. Both Romantic and Victorian poets created vast numbers of lyric poems and the lyric accounts for the majority of the poems ever written. Most of the poets named above in connection with their narrative poems, also wrote lyrics. A number of lyric poems will be examined in greater detail when we come to consider how to analyse poetry.

The Sonnet

A sonnet is a poem which has fourteen lines. These are arranged in a particular sequence and with a precise rhyming scheme. The sonnet originated in Italy and was introduced into England in the sixteenth century, becoming extremely popular. Some Elizabethan sonnets were written as individual poems or occasional verse, but many poets wrote sonnet sequences. The most famous is Shakespeare's sonnet sequence, which contains 154 poems. The sequences often contained a loose narrative. One of the criteria for being thought of as a gentleman in Elizabethan times was the ability to write a sonnet 'off the cuff', that is on the spur of the moment. Shakespeare's sonnet sequence has provided a focus for critical comment over the centuries, not just because of the brilliance of the poetry, but also because of the mystery that surrounds a dedication to 'W H' and a reference to a 'dark lady', neither of whom have ever been satisfactorily identified.

There are two main types of sonnet, the Petrarchan and the Shakespearean. The Petrarchan, named after the medieval Italian poet, has an **octet** (eight lines) and a **sestet** (six lines), the octet being composed of two **quatrains** (four lines each) with a particular rhyme scheme. The sestet is made up of two **tercets** (three lines each) with various possible rhyming schemes. In the Shakespearean sonnet the lines are grouped in three quatrains, each with alternate rhyme, followed by a final rhyming couplet. All sonnets traditionally use **iambic pentameter**.

The sonnet form has survived the centuries. Milton wrote sonnets, as did the Romantic poets and the form is still being used in the twentieth century.

TASK

Read the following sonnet, Keats's 'On First Looking into Chapman's Homer'.

Much have I travell'd in the realms of gold,
    And many goodly states and kingdoms seen;
    Round many western islands have I been
Which bards in fealty to Apollo hold.
Oft of one wide expanse had I been told,
    That deep-brow'd Homer ruled as his demesne:
    Yet did I never breathe its pure serene
Till I heard Chapman speak out loud and bold:
Then felt I like some watcher of the skies
    When a new planet swims into his ken;
Or like stout Cortez when with eagle eyes
    He stared at the Pacific – and all his men
Look'd at each other with a wild surmise,
    Silent, upon a peak in Darien.

English literature

There are various things you need to know about this poem before you can fully make sense of it. Chapman was a writer whose complete translation of the *Iliad* and the *Odyssey* was published in 1616. Keats wrote his poem when he had just read the work and found the experience, even through a translation, inspiring. Cortez was a sixteenth century Spanish explorer who discovered the Pacific and looked at it with amazement from a mountain peak in what is now Panama.

In the light of what you have already learned about the sonnet form, work out, singly or in pairs, whether this is a Petrarchan or a Shakespearean sonnet. Comment on the poet's use of the rhyme scheme and the way in which he has organised his material in relation to the structure of the poem.

CONSIDER

(a) This is of course a Petrarchan sonnet, because it is divided into two sections, one containing eight lines and one six.

(b) The way in which the poem is traditionally set out enables you to respond more easily to the rhyme scheme, since in the octet the lines rhyming 'seen', 'been', 'demesne' and 'serene' are all indented, while the other rhyming lines are not. Although the octet is divided into two quatrains, the whole is given cohesion by the strength of the rhyme scheme, which uses complete rhymes, most of which are monosyllabic.

(c) The words 'demesne', 'serene', 'surmise' and 'Darien' are highlighted by not being monosyllabic. 'Demesne' and 'serene' connect the quality of tranquillity with Homer's Greek homeland and area of influence, while the extraordinary nature of the situation as Keats imagines the exotic location and the wonder of viewing this new sea for the first time, is brought out through the rhyming of 'surmise' (suggesting the inability of the sailors to take in the truth of what is before them), with 'eyes', the agent of wonder and 'skies', the medium which connects their experience with the travellers' everyday lives.

(d) If you examine the way in which the poem is constructed, you will see that the first quatrain focuses entirely on the poet's previous reading experience, 'the realms of gold' being a metaphorical expression for the world of poetry. The second quatrain draws our attention to an area he has not previously explored, Greek literature, and offsets his previous ignorance, as expressed in the first two lines, against the Enlightenment, expressed in the next two, which comes from his experience of reading Chapman. The colon at the end of the octet makes the reader pause before being plunged into the experience through the two similes, both of which concern discovery and therefore complement his theme.

There are many types of poems you may come across, such as **dramatic monologues**, **ballads**, **odes**, **limericks**, **clerihews**, **alliterative verse**, **elegy** and **haiku** to name only a few. Most of these poems broadly fit into one of the above categories, for instance a ballad is a narrative poem.

Aspects to look at in a poem are:

◆ what the poem is saying
◆ from whose point of view it is said and to whom
◆ the setting; use of language and imagery
◆ mood and tone
◆ and rhythm and metrical form.

What the poem is saying

Although of course when you're writing an Advanced Level essay you shouldn't spend time simply describing the content of a poem. It is important to start by understanding what the poem is about in order to give effective comment on how the poet writes. You will probably need to read a poem through several times before you are at all sure of what it means. You may need to look up obscure references, although you can often get the gist of what a poem is about without necessarily understanding every detail.

The different aspects of a poem mentioned above are, of course, not always easy to separate. In determining what a poem is about, you are taking note of its setting, who is speaking, to whom and so on.

TASK
Read the following poem by John Donne, a seventeenth century poet and writer. After you have read it through several times, see if you can write down what you think it is about.

The Good Morrow

I wonder, by my troth, what thou, and I
Did, till we lov'd? were we not wean'd till then?
But suck'd on countrey pleasures, childishly?
Or snorted we in the seaven sleepers den?
T'was so; But this, all pleasures fancies bee.
If ever any beauty I did see
Which I desir'd, and got, t'was but a dream of thee

And now good morrow to our waking soules,
Which watch not one another out of fear;
For love, all love of other sights controules,
And makes one little roome, an every where.
Let sea-discoverers to new worlds have gone,
Let Maps to other, world on worlds have showne,
Let us possesse one world, each hath one, and is one.

My face in thine eye, thine in mine appears,
And true plaine hearts doe in the faces rest,
Where can we find two better hemispheares
Without sharpe North, without declining West?
What ever dyes, was not mix't equally;
If our two loves be one, or, thou and I
Love so alike, that none doe slacken, none can die.

CONSIDER
(a) The poet is asking his lover what he and she did before they fell in love. Everything they experienced previously now seems unreal and dream-like.
(b) Love has made the room which contains the lovers, their whole world. They are more satisfied with the world of their love than explorers are with new worlds they discover.
(c) Their faces are reflected in each other's eyes. They are like two hemispheres, but better

English literature

because, unlike hemispheres, they experience no alteration. Their love cannot change because each loves the other equally.
(d) It would be possible to give a much more detailed account of the poem, but what is necessary at first is a clear outline of what the poet is saying. When you begin to look at other aspects of the poem, details will begin to become clearer.

Point of view

As in a novel, the writer's point of view is very important. Sometimes poets write from their own personal point of view but often a **persona** is assumed. There are a number of reasons why poets may decide to voice their thoughts through an agent:

◆ it enables them to distance themselves from what is being said
◆ they can present us with a situation or experience which they could not reasonably have encountered in their own lives
◆ they can enter into the mind of another person and show us a conflict or crisis.

One kind of poem which does this is the **dramatic monologue**. One of the most famous writers of dramatic monologues was Robert Browning. He developed this way of writing after the almost total failure of some of the early poems he wrote in which he bared his soul too openly. His sensitivity to criticism was partly what led him to write in a different way.

Dramatic monologues at times seem contrived but Browning manages to make his characters speak spontaneously despite, or because of, the careful crafting of the poem. A good example of this is *My Last Duchess*, where the poet takes on the persona of a rich, Italian renaissance Duke. The Duke has murdered his wife, merely because she is as polite to other people as to himself:

> *She thanked men, – good; but she thanked*
> *Somehow… I know not how… as if she ranked*
> *My gift of a nine hundred years old name*
> *With anybody's gift.*

The naturalness of the speech here reveals the Duke's arrogance, snobbery and perverted values. The poet here is speaking to us through the persona of the Duke, but the Duke is also, within the context of the poem itself, speaking to an envoy. Ironically, the envoy has been sent by the Count whose daughter the Duke is negotiating to marry. The irony is heightened by the Duke showing the envoy a picture of his 'last Duchess' and quite frankly implying what has happened to her. The word 'last' is itself ambiguous, perhaps not referring simply to the wife he has just 'lost' but to the fact that she is simply the last in a line of wives.

By presenting the Duke through his own words Browning is able to persuade the reader to identify with the Duke and temporarily suspend moral judgement. The Duke's multi-faceted personality becomes more compelling than his wickedness as a murderer.

Conflicting viewpoints

There are times when the poet may himself present two conflicting views on the events he describes, as is the case with Chaucer in *The Canterbury Tales*. This is particularly noticeable in *The Prologue*. Chaucer begins the poem as a third person narrative, but at line 20 he introduces himself as a lodger at the Tabard inn:

Redy to wenden on my pilgrimage
To Caunterbury with ful devout corage,

As a pilgrim Chaucer apparently accepts the opinions of the Host who organises the pilgrimage and the telling of the stories, at face value and speaks deprecatingly of his own lack of skills as a narrator:

Also I prey yow to foryeve it me
Al have I nat set folk in hir degree,
Heere in this tale, as that they sholde stonde.
My wit is short, ye may wel understonde.

It very soon becomes clear to the reader, however, that Chaucer the narrator is very far from short of wit. He shrewdly sums up the personalities of all the assembled pilgrims, including the Host who:

spak of mirthe, amonges othere thinges,
Whan that we hadde maad oure rekenings,

Chaucer's clever way of ironically undermining one comment by the immediate addition of another is well illustrated here, when he makes a sly comment about the Host's love of money being intimately connected with his willingness to be merry. *The Prologue* contains a great deal of this kind of irony, which is made all the more effective by contrast with the portraits of the thoroughly good characters, such as the Knight and the Poor Parson, which are presented without irony.

ACTIVITY

Read the following poem 'Sleeping' by Carol Ann Duffy.

Sleeping

Under the dark warm waters of sleep
your hands part me.
I am dreaming you anyway.

Your mouth is hot fruit, wet, strange,
night-fruit I taste with my opening mouth;
my eyes closed.

You, you. Your breath flares into fervent words
which explode in my head. Then you ask, push,
for an answer.

And this is how we sleep. You're in now, hard,
demanding; so I dream more fiercely, dream
till it hurts

that this is for real, yes, I feel it.
When you hear me, you hold on tight, frantic,
as if we were drowning.

English literature

1   Singly, or in pairs, examine the point of view of the poem. Who is speaking? To whom?
2   What situation is the speaker in?

CONSIDER

This is told from a rather unusual viewpoint, that of a sleeping woman, who dreams that her lover is with her. The dream is so real that she imagines her lover is having sex with her and speaking to her. She wills herself to dream so that it seems utterly real. The poem uses the metaphor of sleep as moving in water and this image neatly opens and closes the poem. Her lover 'parts' her as you would part water, whereas at the end they are both 'drowning'.

Setting

Most poets have a strongly developed sense of place with which they achieve a variety of effects. One of the poems in which setting is powerfully exploited is Tennyson's *Mariana*. The poet takes his inspiration from 'Mariana in the moated grange', a forsaken lover in Shakespeare's *Measure for Measure*. The poem opens with a precise and detailed description:

> *With blackest moss the flower-plots*
> *   Were thickly crusted, one and all:*
> *The rusted nails fell from the knots*
> *   That held the pear to the garden-wall.*
> *The broken sheds look'd sad and strange:*
> *   Unlifted was the clinking latch;*
> *   Weeded and worn the ancient thatch*
> *Upon the lonely moated grange.*
> *   She only said, 'My life is dreary,*
> *   He cometh not,' she said;*
> *   She said, 'I am aweary, aweary,*
> *   I would that I were dead!'*

Each detail contributes to a cumulative effect of decay and desolation. The black moss, 'the rusted nails', 'the broken sheds' and the 'weeded' thatch all suggest decay, while 'sad and strange' and 'the lonely moated grange' evoke a melancholy isolation which is enhanced by Mariana's words. These words, with slight variations, are repeated at the end of each stanza, their effect always being complemented by the setting: 'The level waste, the rounding grey'; 'the glooming flats'. No human voice is heard in the poem other than that of Mariana and some ghostly 'old voices'. This human isolation is stressed by significant detail: 'Unlifted was the clinking latch' and by reference to creatures:

> *The blue fly sung in the pane; the mouse*
> *   Behind the mouldering wainscot shriek'd,*

Tennyson creates a setting which is a symbol for Mariana's inertia and melancholy, which form the heart of the poem.

Tennyson is perhaps also making a comment on the place of women in Victorian society. Their role tends to be seen as passive, unfulfilled and subject to the dominance of men. This can also be seen in *The Lady of Shallot* where Tennyson uses an Arthurian setting of an isolated tower on an island. The Lady of Shalott is effectively imprisoned there and her detached setting is contrasted with the active world of the men at Camelot. She can only experience life at one remove, through her mirror and when she turns to embrace life fully at the sight of Sir Lancelot, the result is her death.

Poets, like novelists, are often associated with places where they have lived or worked. Philip Larkin is associated with Hull, where he was the university librarian, which he writes about extensively in *The Whitsun Weddings*. 'Here', for instance, is a poem which describes the eastward journey to Hull, one of the country's most isolated large cities, 'Where only salesmen and relations come'. Hull is set in the flat landscape of the East Riding alongside the Humber and Larkin captures his scene with a swift movement from the lyrical:

piled gold clouds, the shining gull-marked mud,

to the down-to-earth reality of the city itself and its inhabitants:

And residents from raw estates, brought down
The dead straight miles by stealing flat-faced trolleys,

The last stanza, however, takes us beyond Hull, to the coast:

Here silence stands

Like heat. Here leaves unnoticed thicken,
Hidden weeds flower, neglected waters quicken,
Luminously-peopled air ascends;
And past the poppies bluish neutral distance
Ends the land suddenly beyond a beach
Of shapes and shingle. Here is unfenced existence:
Facing the sun, untalkative, out of reach.

We can see the significance of the title now. The poem moves, both through a physical and a spiritual journey, to a point of revelation. This revelation involves references to 'Here' that become more elusive. 'Unfenced existence', 'facing the sun', 'untalkative', 'out of reach' are all in some ways negative, but not absolutely so.

Poets may use place to bring out their ideas and beliefs. They do not, however, necessarily use realistic settings. Milton, for instance, in Paradise Lost, creates imaginary settings: Hell, Heaven and the Garden of Eden. In Book 9 Milton describes Satan's second attempt, in the shape of a serpent, to tempt Eve to eat of the forbidden fruit of the Tree of Knowledge. He hopes, but does not expect, to find Eve alone:

when to his wish,
Beyond his hope, Eve separate he spies,
Veil'd in a Cloud of Fragrance, where she stood,
Half spi'd. so thick the Roses bushing round
About her glowd, oft stooping to support
Each flour of slender stalk, whose head though gay
Carnations, Purple, Azure, or spect with Gold,
Hung drooping unsustaind, them she upstaies
Gently with Mirtle band, mindless the while,
her self, though fairest unsupported Flour,
From her best prop so farr, and storm so nigh.

Milton achieves a denseness of texture through his description of the roses as 'thick' and 'bushing round'; through the listed colours of the carnation and the heady effect of the 'cloud of fragrance'. The combination of the senses of sight, smell and touch creates a sensuous beauty which is underlined by the threat of the lurking serpent and the comparison of Eve herself to one of the unsupported flowers she seeks to assist.

ACTIVITY

Choose one of the poems you are studying, or a section of a longer poem, and answer the following questions:
1   What is the poem's setting?
2   Does the setting change during the course of the poem?
3   If so, why do you think that is?
4   What does the poem gain from its setting?
5   How does the poet establish the setting?

Language and Imagery

Metaphor is fundamental to poetry and one of the most important skills for the student of literature is the ability to analyse metaphor. This skill is tested by the third Assessment Objective, 'understanding of the ways in which writers' choices of form, structure and language shape meaning'. Sometimes, as in the case of Blake's *The Sick Rose*, quoted in Chapter 1 on page 130, a writer will use an extended metaphor which covers part or all of the poem. An interesting form of extended metaphor is known as a **conceit** is particularly associated with the Metaphysical poets. A conceit is noticeable because of its apparent incongruity, in that it may seem to wrench a comparison from two things that would not normally be thought of as having anything in common. A well-known example of this is to be found in Donne's *A Valediction: forbidding mourning*. The poem is spoken by the poet to his wife on his departure for the continent in 1611. Donne uses many complex images, comparing their parting to the death of a good man and to the movement of the spheres. The two most interesting images come at the end of the poem:

> *Our two soules therefore, which are one,*
>   *Though I must goe, endure not yet*
> *A breach, but an expansion,*
>   *Like gold to ayery thinnesse beate.*
>
> *If they be two, they are two so*
>   *As stiffe twin compasses are two,*
> *Thy soule the fixt foot, makes no show*
>   *To move, but doth, if th'other doe.*
>
> *And though it in the center sit,*
>   *Yet when the other far doth rome,*
> *It leanes, and hearkens after it,*
>   *And growes erect, as that comes home.*
>
> *Such wilt thou be to mee, who must*
>   *Like th'other foot, obliquely runne;*
> *Thy firmnes drawes my circle just,*
>   *And makes me end, where I begunne.*

One reason why conceits can be very effective is just because they are striking and unusual. They make us look at a situation in a way which would never have occurred to us before. However, mere ingenuity is not enough. Donne in particular and the Metaphysical poets in general, were associated with a capacity to fuse thought and feeling in their poems. The reason why the two images in the above stanzas work so well is precisely because of the way they fuse thought and feeling. Donne compares the projected parting not to a breaking apart of two 'soules' but 'an expansion' just as gold can be expanded by being finely beaten. This is a clever idea which suggests the closeness of their relationship, while also emphasising that it does not consist merely of physical proximity. The richness of their love is exemplified in the reference to 'gold' and the finely spiritual nature of the relationship is particularly well evoked by the choice of the word 'ayery'; the gold becomes so fine that it is scarcely distinguishable from air.

An even more striking conceit is developed in the final three stanzas, where Donne compares himself and his wife to a pair of compasses. This seems at first a bizarre idea, but the force and relevance of it soon becomes clear. The wife is, although at a fixed point, like the foot of the compass, both utterly central to the poet and joined spiritually in a way which cannot be broken by mere separation. So she yearns after him in his departure and her influence draws him home again. The sexual pun on 'growes erect' shows the importance of physical love to Donne, while the frequent references to the 'soule' underline that their relationship is far more than merely physical. The metaphor is brought to a conclusion in the final two lines of the poem where the 'circle' denotes the perfection and equality of their love and the wife's constancy is seen as the determining factor in the relationship.

Keats sighed for 'a life of sensations rather than thoughts'. In *Ode to a Nightingale* he desperately seeks an escape 'on the viewless wings of poesy' from the world of sorrow that surrounds him, and he describes his surroundings with sensuous detail:

> *I cannot see what flowers are at my feet,*
>   *Nor what soft incense hangs upon the boughs,*
> *But, in embalmed darkness, guess each sweet*
>   *Wherewith the seasonable month endows*
> *The grass, the thicket, and the fruit-tree wild;*
>   *White hawthorn, and the pastoral eglantine;*
>   *Fast fading violets cover'd up in leaves;*
>   *And mid-May's eldest child,*
> *The coming musk-rose, full of dewy wine,*
>   *The murmurous haunt of flies on summer eves.*

If you compare this passage with the passage quoted earlier from Book 9 of *Paradise Lost*, you will probably become aware of the influence Milton had on Keats. Both create very sensuous descriptions of the beauty of the natural world, a 'pastoral' scene. Both rely heavily on the senses, Milton's 'cloud of fragrance' being very similar to Keats's 'soft incense' which 'hangs upon the boughs'. Keats's description, however, is more strongly dependent on metaphor, often in subtle ways. The poet makes sure we do not forget his main theme of the anguish of human loss and sorrow, which we are reminded of by the word 'embalmed' with its double meaning. In poetry 'embalmed' has the sense of giving fragrance to, but in the context it also reminds us of death. Similarly the 'fast fading violets' recall the youth who 'grows pale, and spectre-thin, and dies'. The final two lines are particularly effective in their use of language. The 'musk-rose' by its name suggests fragrant beauty; and the heady effect of the scent is enhanced by the comparison of the dew it holds to wine. The last line with its

English literature

English literature

sibilance and its lingering repetition of the alliterative 'm' and assonant 'u', combines to evoke onomatopoeically the soft, pervasive buzzing of the flies.

The importance of sound in poetry

The sound of poetry is very important. If you can hear it read aloud it often helps you to grasp the meaning. Poets use a range of devices to achieve specific sound effects. One such example is onomatopoeia, where sound echoes sense, as in 'rustling', 'whispering' or 'rattling'. Different consonants have different effects, depending on whether they are hard or soft sounds, and vowels may be long or short with differing effects. The sounds made by rhyming or half-rhyming words and the use of different kinds of repetition affect our response to a poem.

ACTIVITY

Read the following stanza from Tennyson's 'The Lotos-Eaters':

There is sweet music here that softer falls
Than petals from blown roses on the grass,
Or night-dews on still waters between walls
Of shadowy granite, in a gleaming pass;
Music that gentlier on the spirit lies,
Than tir'd eyelids upon tir'd eyes;
Music that brings sweet sleep down from the blissful skies.
Here are cool mosses deep,
And thro' the moss the ivies creep,
And in the stream the long-leaved floqwers weep,
And from the craggy ledge the poppy hangs in sleep.

1. How has he used sound here?
2. What do you think Tennyson was trying to achieve here by his use of sound?

CONSIDER

He appears to be trying to achieve an effect of tranquillity. This is suggested by the content of words such as 'softer' and 'gentlier' as well as by their sounds. He uses a lot of sibilants, repeated 's' sounds, as in lines five and six of the extract. There are also soft 'w', 'f' and 'l' sounds, which are particularly effective in combination with the long vowel sound in 'falls'. Repeated long vowel sounds, as in 'sweet sleep down' draw out the line, reinforcing the idea of weariness and of time as endless. You may see the passage in different, equally valid ways.

The most important thing to remember when you are reading poetry is the necessity for alertness. It is easy to miss the significance of words and phrases if you read them casually and you will find that you often need to read a poem many times to get the most out of it.

TASK

Read the following poem, 'Family Affairs' by Elizabeth Jennings:

Family Affairs

No longer here the blaze that we'd engender
Out of pure wrath. We pick at quarrels now
As fussy women stitch at cotton, slow
Now to forget and too far to surrender.
The anger stops, apologies also.

And in this end of summer, weighted calm
(Climate of mind, I mean), we are apart
Further than ever when we wished most harm.
Indifference lays a cold hand on the heart;
We need the violence to keep us warm.

Have we then learnt at last how to untie
The bond of birth, umbilical long cored,
So that we live quite unconnected by
The blood we share? What monstrous kind of sword
Can sever veins and still we do not die?

This poem about the relationship between mother and daughter is full of imagery. Examine the images Elizabeth Jennings uses. Try to explain what is being compared to what.

CONSIDER

(a) The poet economically sets the scene for us with her opening image. We immediately understand that two people are at loggerheads but not blazingly angry with one another in the way they might have been when they were younger.

(b) The comparison between anger and a fire is one that is often used but which is made individual by the particular context. The force of the image is partly the result of the reference to 'this end of summer, weighted calm' at the beginning of the next stanza. This image of late summer suggests that the blaze of heat is over for the year, just as the opening image showed us that these women were past the stage of open fighting.

(c) That they have reached the stage of apathy is effectively evoked by the metaphor 'Indifference lays a cold hand on the heart', the word 'cold' picking up by contrast the earlier references to 'blaze' and 'summer'. This illustrates the importance, when you are examining imagery, of seeing how individual images fit into the whole context of a poem.

(d) The particular stage of hostility the two women have reached is also effectively brought out by the image of sewing, 'We pick at quarrels now/ As fussy women stitch at cotton'. The methodical and pernickety way in which the women pursue their quarrel is appropriately compared to the minute attention a careful seamstress gives to each stitch. The thoughtful, reasoned process is also ironically shown by the careful way the poet uses parenthesis '(climate of mind, I mean)' to modify her meaning as she explains the nature of the relationship to the reader.

(e) The final stanza concerns itself with the women's blood connection, signified by the umbilical cord. The separation that has been effected is compared to the severing of veins by a sword.

English literature

English literature

The shattering and painful image this summons up reveals the tragic underlying smouldering resentment which both joins and separates the two women, just as the sword paradoxically severs their veins and yet does not kill them. You may have come up with an equally valid and completely different response to the poem's language.

Rhythm and metrical form

We have looked at some of the forms in which poets write, and these are sometimes associated with particular metrical forms. For instance a limerick will always follow the same rhythmic patterns, as will a ballad. By this stage in your studies it is a good idea to become acquainted with the basic metrical forms. They can be described as the skeleton of the poem, a structure on which the poet places the flesh of his ideas and images. It may, however, be the ideas that come first and suggest an appropriate skeleton to go with them. Different poets work in different ways.

One of the most widespread metrical forms in English poetry is blank verse. Shakespeare, Milton and Wordsworth all wrote primarily in this form. It consists of unrhymed iambic pentameter lines, or lines divided up into five feet (groups of stressed and unstressed syllables), where each of the five feet is composed of an unstressed syllable followed by a stressed one. An example would be the opening of Book 9 of *Paradise Lost*:

No more of talk where God or Angel Guest
With Man, as with his Friend, familiar us'd
To sit indulgent, and with him partake
Rural repast, permitting him the while
Venial discourse unblam'd;

If you read this passage aloud you will find that the stress tends to come on the second and every alternate syllable, so in the first line there is a stress on 'more', 'talk' 'God', the first syllable of 'Angel' and 'Guest'. This is the natural rhythm of English speech, which is why it is so widespread in English poetry. The stress is not always absolutely regular. Poets use the lines flexibly to avoid monotony, so in line four the stress comes on the first syllable of 'Rural'. The flexibility of blank verse makes it an ideal medium for long poems such as Milton's epic.

The iambic pentameter line has also been much used by English poets in sequences of rhyming couplets, also known as heroic couplets. A four foot iambic line, known as an 'iambic tetrameter' has also been very popular. When the stressed syllable precedes the unstressed, the metre is 'trochaic'. Blake used trochaic metre in 'The Tyger':

Tyger! Tyger! burning bright
In the forests of the night,
What immortal hand or eye
Could frame thy fearful symmetry?

This is one of Blake's *Songs of Experience* and he makes very clever use of metrical form to achieve his purpose. A trochaic tetrameter line would normally have eight syllables, ending on an unstressed one. Blake's line, however, only has seven syllables, thus it begins and ends on a stressed syllable. Again, however, we see how the poet constantly adapts metre to his purpose. So here the last line of the quatrain has eight syllables and is in iambic metre, enabling Blake to introduce the key word 'symmetry'. The overall effect of the poem is deepened by the almost exact repetition of the first stanza in the last, with one significant difference; 'could frame' becomes 'dare frame'. So the opening question of which divine creator would have the power to create a beast of powerful natural energies like the tiger, becomes a question of which creator would dare to put such a beast into existence, with all that that implies.

Although free verse became very widespread in the twentieth century, there are plenty of twentieth century poets who make interesting and individual use of traditional metres.

Free verse

This is verse which does not make use of traditional metrical forms, but which relies on the natural rhythms of the speaking voice and the content of the poem to give it its shape or the particular relationship between stressed and unstressed syllables. There are instances of free verse going back centuries, but the most famous examples before the twentieth century were the poems of Gerard Manley Hopkins. Instead of relying on a set metre these employ what Hopkins called 'sprung rhythm'. Hopkins generally employed four stresses in a line, but the line could include any number of unstressed syllables.

ACTIVITY

Read the following poem, 'Winter Love' by Elizabeth Jennings:

Winter Love

Let us have winter loving that the heart
May be in peace and ready to partake
Of the slow pleasure spring would wish to hurry
Or that in summer harshly would awake,
And let us fall apart, O gladly weary,
The white skin shaken like a white snowflake.

In pairs or a small group, discuss the poem.

1. What kind of metrical form does it have?
2. Does it have a rhyme scheme?
3. If so, how does it work?
4. What does the poet achieve by her use of particular aspects of form?

CONSIDER

(a) The poem is a sestet in iambic pentameters, with lines two, four and six rhyming. There is also a half rhyme between lines three and five.

(b) One of the things to look for is how regular the metre is. You may immediately notice that the very first syllable departs from the iambic rhythm by putting the stress there rather than on the second syllable. You can see why: the poet wants to stress a course of action 'Let us'. The other most obvious deviation from the metrical form is in the final line, where 'white', 'skin' and 'the first syllable of 'shaken' are all stressed. These repeated stresses are called **spondees**. The effect of them is to draw attention to a climactic moment of love-making. The stress on 'white' is enhanced by the repetition of the word later in the line, with its association of purity.

(c) The whole poem is advocating the 'slow pleasure' of 'winter loving' which appears to be associated with a deep and mature love. By contrast a spring loving would be hurried and a summer loving 'harsh'.

English literature

(d) The content of the poem is echoed by the rhythm, partly through the use of mainly regular iambics and partly through the use of **enjambement** which gives a flow to the lines and therefore to the act of loving described. The flow is unbroken up to the word 'And' at the beginning of line five, where the poet pauses before talking about the time after love-making. Notice how line three has an extra syllable which suggests the drawing out of pleasure. The falling apart of the lovers after love-making is echoed in the **caesura** in the middle of the line. Again, you may have thought of very different ways of interpreting the poem from the above, although every interpretation has to fit the metrical 'facts'.

Tone and mood

Much of the effect of a poem arises from its tone and mood, yet these are often difficult to establish and to write about. Tone, as we have already seen in relation to the novel, like the tone of voice in speech, reflects the attitude of an author and/or narrator towards their subject-matter or readers. The tone may match the mood that is created. For instance in the poem we looked at on page 161, 'On First Looking into Chapman's Homer', Keats's tone is one of awed excitement as he compares himself to 'some watcher of the skies/ When a new planet swims into his ken' and the mood of the poem as a whole is one of intellectual excitement.

Setting is closely related to mood and is often used to establish it. In Keats's *The Eve of St Agnes*, the setting moves from an initial description of the bitter cold, through reference to the revelry within the castle, to the heart of the poem, which concerns itself with the lovers Madeline and Porphyro. Madeline is in a state of heightened emotion, expectant, dreaming of love, since it is said that on this evening a young girl may dream of her lover. So the mood of the poem is related to romance, but here it is spiced by danger, which is effectively evoked, first through the description of the bitter cold which surrounds them and the hostile, harsh revellers, and then through lines which bring out fear and suspense:

> *The lover's endless minutes slowly pass'd;*
> *The dame return'd, and whisper'd in his ear*
> *To follow her; with aged eyes aghast*
> *From fright of dim espial.*

The mood is unequivocally romantic at the climax of the poem:

> *Into her dream he melted, as the rose*
> *Blendeth its odour with the violet, –*
> *Solution sweet:*

However, the ideal expression of love is brief, the change of mood being signalled by the weather:

> *meantime the frost-wind blows*
> *Like Love's alarum pattering the sharp sleet*
> *Against the window-panes; St Agnes' moon hath set.*

In Donne's 'The Indifferent', the poet seems rather cynical when he says that he can love any woman so long as she is inconstant. He wonders whether women are afraid that men will prove constant and tells them not to worry about such an unlikely outcome. Venus looks into the situation on Donne's behalf:

And said, alas, Some two or three
Poore Heretiques in love there be,
Which thinks to stablish dangerous constancy.
But I have told them, since you will be true,
You shall be true to them, who'are false to you.

Although the tone is cynical, the mood is buoyant and cheerful, showing the poet energetically enjoying a variety of sexual relationships.

Tone and mood are very important in establishing the attitude of the poet to their subject-matter. However, as we have seen with Donne, the tone of a poem does not necessarily establish the mood you might expect.

ACTIVITY

Read the following poem, 'Infant Joy' by William Blake:

Infant Joy

'I have no name:
I am but two days old.'
What shall I call thee?
'I happy am,
Joy is my name.'
Sweet joy befall thee!

Pretty Joy!
Sweet Joy, but two days old!
Sweet Joy I call thee.
Thou dost smile,
I sing the while,
Sweet joy befall thee!

This poem is one of Blake's *Songs of Innocence*.

1   Singly or in pairs, establish both the mood and tone of the poem.
2   What evidence can you find to prove your assertions?
3   By what means does the poet establish mood and tone here?

CONSIDER

(a)   The mood is obviously one of joy and happiness, the tone light and cheerful. The very simplicity of the form of the poem is entirely appropriate to Blake's subject matter. The child is seen as innocent and happy in its innocence. The main stress is on 'Joy', which as both the child's state of being and its name, is constantly repeated.

(b)   The use of direct speech, in a dialogue between the child and the poet, helps to evoke the mood with directness and immediacy.

(c)   The simple rhythm and occasional fluid rhymes give the effect of a smoothly moving lullaby traditionally associated with infant joy.

English literature

English literature

The critic's viewpoint

When writing about poetry, you may well be expected to show a knowledge of different critical viewpoints. You also need to be able to look at poetry with a view to **synthesis** as well as analysis. In other words, you need to be able to give your final viewpoint on a poem or a poet, after you have looked at all the aspects discussed above. In order to achieve both these objectives, Tennyson's poem *Crossing the Bar* is printed below, along with some critical comments to which it has given rise.

ACTIVITY:

Tennyson wrote this poem in October 1889, three years before he died and expressly asked that it be put at the conclusion of all editions of his poetry. He said that the idea came to him when he was on a steamer bound for the Isle of Wight, where Tennyson had a home at Farringford.

Read the critical material also included here and then analyse the poem, referring in the course of your commentary to any of the aspects discussed in this chapter:

Crossing the Bar

Sunset and evening star,
*   And one clear call for me!*
And may there be no moaning of the bar,
*   When I put out to sea,*

But such a tide as moving seems asleep,
*   Too full for sound and foam,*
When that which drew from out the boundless deep
*   Turns again home.*

Twilight and evening bell,
*   And after that the dark!*
And may there be no sadness of farewell,
*   When I embark;*

For tho' from out our bourne of Time and Place
*   The flood may bear me far,*
I hope to see my pilot face to face
*   When I have crost the bar.*

Christopher Ricks writes about the poem as follows:

Hallam Tennyson had said: 'That is the crown of your life's work.' This is not to say that it is his greatest poem; but certainly, and without irony, it was a gift reserved for age, to set a crown upon his lifetime's effort. Its simple dignity is yet consonant with a fine patterning and subtle variety. The third line of each stanza, longer than the preceding line, swells into a release of feeling. But what saves this from self-indulgence, converting it rather to a religious indulgence or remission, is the immediate curbing effect of the stanza's shortened concluding line, reining and subduing the feeling. Two sentences, each two stanzas, each beginning with an exclamation which is vibrant rather than exclamatory and whose vibrations then die away; the poem itself 'turns again home'. The central stanzas incorporate rhymes which are disyllabic, but not as rhymes with each other; the first and last stanzas maintain only monosyllabic rhymes, and the concluding rhyme ('far' into 'bar') returns us to the first line of the poem ('star' into 'bar'). 'Face to face': did Tennyson's mind go back to Arthur Hallam and to the manuscript of In

Memoriam, the final two lines of its final section (CXXXI)? – 'And come to look on those we loved/ And that which made us, face to face.' And did his mind go even further back, moved by the deep reciprocity, to recall that it was Arthur Hallam, in a poem to Tennyson's sister Emily, who had glimpsed this distance: 'Till our souls see each other face to face'?

There may be vocabulary here that you need to look up. You also need to know that Arthur Hallam was a very dear personal friend of Tennyson in his youth, who died young and to whom Tennyson wrote his elegiac poem 'In Memoriam'. Tennyson's son, Hallam, was named after him.

Of the same poem, Roger Ebbatson writes in his *Tennyson* in the Penguin Critical Studies series:

This is one of the finest of Tennyson's later poems, and in it the poet looks steadily towards death. Stanzas three and four subtly repeat the basic rhythms and syntax of the first two verses, yet with cunning variation. In each a musing exclamation is followed by a reassurance, the long line in each case being carefully controlled and curbed by the shorter line which follows. There have been critical objections to the appearance of the Pilot in the final stanza, but the beauty and darkness of the waters has been stressed, and the poem neatly produces the paradox that the move into the boundless deep is also the turn towards the final home. Through such imagery is a final sense of plenitude produced in the poetry of a writer who may be termed the laureate of loss and absence. This short and evocative poem stands, in Hallam Tennyson's phrase, as the 'crown' of the poet's lifework, and the words 'face to face' serve to conjure up, for the final time, the dead friend of fifty years before. Although as Ricks remarks in his fine reading of the poem, there are six references to 'I' or 'me'. yet 'no poem was ever less self-absorbed'. In this final testament Tennyson leaves the reader with a sense of the full and tested humanity of a great poet.

Roger Ebbatson's reference to Christopher Ricks shows that he has read the earlier critic. You may like to consider how you would know that he had done so even if he had not explicitly mentioned him.

TECHNICAL TERMS

alliterative verse   verse which makes great use of alliteration, often alliterating the stressed syllables

ballad   a narrative poem often associated with folk tradition, in four line stanzas with a particular metre and rhyme scheme

caesura   a break in a line of poetry indicated by punctuation

clerihew   a four line verse of two rhyming couplets

conceit   a striking metaphor comparing two things not usually associated

dramatic monologue   a poem spoken by an imaginary speaker to an imaginary audience

elegy   a poem written on the death of an individual or for a particular occasion

enjambement   run-on lines in a poem

epic   a long narrative poem on a heroic scale

English literature

free verse   verse which does not use any of the established metrical forms

haeccitas   a word coined by the Victorian poet Gerard Manley Hopkins to mean individuality

haiku   a Japanese form; each poem has three lines which have five, seven and five syllables

iambic pentameter   a ten syllable line divided into five metrical divisions (or feet); each foot has one unstressed and one stressed syllable

limerick   a five line poem rhyming aabba and with a mainly anapaestic rhythm (two unstressed syllables and one stressed in a foot)

lyric   a poem of emotion rather than one that tells a story

metre   the pattern of unstressed and stressed syllables in poetry

octet   a group of eight lines in poetry

ode   a formal lyric poem with a complex stanza form

onomatopoeia   the use of words whose sound echoes their meaning, such as 'rustle' or 'twitter'

persona   the person who speaks in a poem other than the poet

prelapsarian   before the fall of man

rhythm   the movement and flow of a poem which results from its metrical form

sestet   a group of six lines in poetry

sonnet   a poem in fourteen lines which are grouped in various possible ways with particular rhyme schemes

spondee   a number of stressed syllables which follow one another

stanza   a verse of a poem

sibilance   the repeated use of letters that create a hissing sound

synthesis   a putting together of the various separate elements looked at in a work of art into a connected whole

tercet   a three line rhyming stanza

zeugma   the linking of two nouns with a verb that is not appropriate to one of them

4 | Studying a play

In this chapter we shall be considering plays from the sixteenth to the twentieth century. We shall look at how plays are structured, how themes and characters are presented, stagecraft, use of language and the contexts in which plays are written and understood.

Like poetry, drama is a very old genre, originating in ancient Greece. Much of early drama, such as the medieval miracle and mystery plays, was associated with religion. You can still see cycles of mystery plays performed in the cities of York and Chester.

A good deal of detail about the theatre of the Elizabethan and Jacobean period is given in Chapter 5 on Shakespeare. Jacobean drama was characterised by the macabre. This was especially evident in the work of John Webster, whose *The Duchess of Malfi* and *The White Devil* are still often performed today. The puritans closed the theatres during the rule of Oliver Cromwell at the end of the English Civil War in the mid seventeenth century. The theatres were not opened again until the Restoration of Charles II in 1660, which is why we call the plays that followed 'Restoration Comedies'. Many of these plays, such as Wycherley's *The Country Wife*, Congreve's *The Way of the World* and Aphra Behn's *The Rover* are still popular today.

Few of the plays written in the eighteenth and nineteenth centuries have survived in performance, the main exception being Sheridan's *The Rivals*. Nineteenth and early twentieth century plays were performed in a theatre very similar to many modern conventional theatres, with a **proscenium arch** at one end of the auditorium. Looking at the stage when the curtain is drawn back is like looking into someone's room. This generally realistic mode of drama was given the name of **the fourth wall convention**. When one wall is taken away we can look on at the characters' lives.

A German playwright who reacted against the realist theatre was Bertholt Brecht who wrote in the 1930s and 1940s. He pioneered the **alienation technique**, whereby the dramatist, far from wishing to create the illusion of reality, goes out of his way to remind us that we are watching a literary construct. He had great influence on European dramatists. When you are looking at a play it is important to determine whether or not it is realistic and whether the dramatist seems anxious to remind you that this is a play or not. Remember that even though a playwright may want the audience to think of a play as 'realistic', as a literary construct it will not really be so; it will simply create the illusion of reality.

Many plays written today are basically realist drama but one of the twentieth century movements in drama most influenced by the idea of alienation technique and non-realism has been the 'Theatre of the Absurd'. This kind of theatre originated in Europe. The best-known dramatists to write in this mode in English are Harold Pinter and Samuel Beckett.

English literature

The 'Theatre of the Absurd' is based on philosophical ideas about the absurdity of life. It gives rise to much disjointed and repetitive dialogue, plots which do not follow any logical order and some rich comedy. The most famous play of this kind written in English is Beckett's *Waiting for Godot*, which will be discussed later in this chapter.

Two famous American dramatists of the 1940s and 1950s are Arthur Miller and Tennessee Williams. Some of their plays are set for AS. Both Miller and Williams use a character as a narrator at times and they both give very detailed stage directions. Williams's stage directions include many technical aspects, because he believed that theatrical effects could best be achieved by very specific guidance to the producer and actors.

Some of the most interesting recent plays have been those of Tom Stoppard, whose *Rosencrantz and Guildenstern are Dead*, *The Real Inspector Hound* and *Arcadia* show his interest in using the stage in new and inventive ways.

If you want to get to know about what's going on in modern drama, there are lots of interesting productions around the country. Going to the theatre can be a very enjoyable experience as well as helping you to get a good grade in your AS Level.

Fitting the play you are studying into its time and context is a way of responding to the second and fifth Assessment Objectives. When you begin to think about the play's structure you are responding to the third Assessment Objective.

ACTIVITY

The brief outline above has attempted to put a number of the plays set for AS into their context.

1   Make sure you know when the play you are studying was written. Find out as much about the background of its era as you can (if it is not contemporary). If it is contemporary it may have a background and setting you need to find out more about. Has it been placed in a particular group or movement? If so, what characterises that movement? Make notes on any material you discover. If it does not appear to belong to any particular sub-genre, what are its characteristics?

2   Does it follow a traditional three or five act structure with a clear beginning, middle and end?

3   Is it realistic?

4   Does it present events in a non-logical order and give an uncertain sense of time and reality?

5   Does it seek to remind you constantly that you are watching a play?

The structure of a play

There are many possible ways of structuring a play. Elizabethan dramatists such as Shakespeare wrote plays which contained natural breaks, making it easy for later editors to make them into five act plays. Scene divisions were usually made clear by the dramatist, for instance by the use of a rhyming couplet, or the exit of actors from the stage. Most plays followed this format for nearly one hundred and fifty years until Ibsen introduced the four-act play. Most plays in the twentieth century have been in three acts or sometimes fewer, or have been written as a succession of scenes.

Three-part structure

Traditionally plays have tended to have a three-part structure, even when they have five acts, consisting of what critics refer to as the 'exposition', the 'development' and the 'resolution' or **denouement**.

The exposition

Whether the genre of the play is comedy or tragedy, the first part of the play needs to achieve the same things.

TASK

From your previous study of plays or experience of seeing them, write down what you think a playwright needs to do in the opening part of a play.

CONSIDER

(a) You probably have some or all of the following points.

(b) The playwright must set the scene, both in place and time.

(c) Characters must be introduced.

(d) Themes must be suggested.

(e) The plot needs to be initiated, with the basis for conflict indicated.

Let's look at the first scene of a Restoration comedy, *The Rover* by Aphra Behn, to see whether she establishes the aspects in our list. There are in fact a number of different versions of this Restoration comedy. The one being used here is taken from Swan Theatre Plays published by Methuen. The play is set in a Spanish colony during the time of Cromwell's rule in Britain, the main characters being exiles because they support the Cavalier cause. During the carnival, three sisters, Florinda, Hellena and Valeria, escape from supervision to meet three cavaliers, Belvile, the Rover Willmore and Frederick. The opening dialogue goes straight to the point:

Florinda: What an impertinent thing is a young girl bred in a nunnery! How full of questions! Prithee no more, Hellena; I have told thee more than thou understand'st already.

Hellena: The more's my grief. I would fain know as much as you, which makes me so inquisitive; (Florinda sighs) Nor is't enough I know you're a lover, unless you tell me to who 'tis you sigh for.

Florinda: When you're a lover I'll think you fit for a secret of that nature.

Hellena: 'Tis true, I never was a lover yet, but I begin to have a shrewd guess what 'tis to be so, and fancy it very pretty to sigh, and sing, and blush, and wish, and long and wish to see the man, and when I do, look pale and tremble, just as you did when my brother brought home the fine colonel from England to see you. What do you call him Florinda? Belvile?

A great deal is revealed quickly here. Florinda is the older, more experienced sister who tends to patronise Hellena. The inquisitive nature of the younger sister suggests the way in which the plot of the play may develop and it is clearly going to be based around the theme of love. The fact that Florinda already has a romantic entanglement with someone called Belvile is revealed and it is hinted that there is a possibility that if Hellena is not careful she may be consigned to the nunnery. After this extract Florinda goes on to reveal more about Belvile, but we are also made aware that Florinda's father wishes her to marry a rich old man called Vincentio. So the conflict between love and family duty is set up right away.

It has been said that conflict is the essence of drama and this is certainly the case in all but a few experimental plays. It is also made clear that Hellena's family intend her to become a nun. Florinda's brother, Don Pedro, offers her an alternative to marriage with Don Vincentio;

she can marry a young man of his choice, Antonio, the following day. The situation seems inescapable, but at this point the third sister, Valeria, works out a plot, whereby the three sisters go to the carnival disguised as gypsies and seek their men.

All the ingredients for conflict are clear here. There is already some kind of conflict between Florinda and Hellena, although the more important conflict is obviously the one between the father and brother on the one hand and the three sisters on the other.

This opening extract doesn't give us full information about the setting, although the Spanish names and the reference to being away from England suggest a Spanish colony. The language used is a clue that the play was written in the late seventeenth century. The rest of the scene establishes that the colony is having a carnival which the sisters plan to attend. Of course the scene is set through the visual effect of the stage setting as well as through the playwright's language.

ACTIVITY

Read the following extract from the opening of Willy Russell's *Educating Rita*. The setting for the opening of the play is Frank's study in a red brick university where he is a lecturer. He is awaiting the arrival of Rita, an Open University student:

Frank: (on telephone) Look if you're trying to induce some feeling of guilt in me over the prospect of a burnt dinner you should have prepared something other than lamb and ratatouille … . Because darling, I like my lamb done to the point of abuse and even I know that ratatouille cannot be burned … Darling, you could incinerate ratatouille and still it wouldn't burn … What do you mean am I determined to go to the pub? I don't need determination to get me into a pub …

There is a knock at the door

Look I'll have to go … There's someone at the door … Yes, yes I promise … Just a couple of pints … Four …

There is another knock at the door

(Calling in the direction of the door) Come in! (He continues on the telephone) Yes … All right … yes … Bye, bye … (He replaces the receiver) Yes, that's it, you just pop off and put your head in the oven. (Shouting) Come in! Come in!

The door swings open revealing RITA

Rita: (from the doorway) I'm comin' in, aren't I? It's that stupid bleedin' handle on the door. You wanna get it fixed! (She comes into the room)

Frank: (staring, slightly confused) Erm – yes, I suppose I always mean to …

How far does the opening succeed in giving you an idea of situation, character and possible future action?

CONSIDER

(a) The technique of opening the play with Frank in the middle of a telephone conversation, obviously with his wife, is effective in establishing a relationship even though the audience only hears one side of the conversation. It is clear that Frank has the upper hand in the relationship and that he is unhappy with his wife. He is rude to her both in the conversation and in the comment he adds after he has put the receiver down. His selfishness and tendency to drink too much are indicated, as well as his sarcasm, 'Darling ...'

(b) The fact that he is waiting for an unknown person interests the audience who wait to see who materialises. When Rita enters we realise immediately that she forms a complete contrast both to Frank and to the woman at the other end of the phone. She speaks in non-standard English, unlike Frank and immediately accuses him of not ensuring that his door handle works effectively (thus also giving another sidelight on the kind of person he is). She appears very forthright and able to speak up for herself.

(c) We are intrigued by the contrast between Frank's confused response to Rita's accusations and his patronising dominance with his wife. We may suspect that the stage is set for a triangular relationship to develop, although if you are studying the text in class you will note that Frank and Rita are the only characters in the play.

(d) The ingredients for conflict are clearly established here in the very opening of the play. The stage setting in a university study full of books suggests that education will be a key theme.

Development

The central acts or scenes of a play are referred to as the 'development'. This speaks for itself; the strands that are introduced at the beginning of the play are developed to a point of climax before the final denouement.

The Rover's development is very complicated. The sisters, wantonly disguised for the carnival, meet the three men they are destined to marry, but of course the plot is complex and drawn out. This is partly the result of disguise (which although designed to avoid difficulties, also creates them) and partly the result of Willmore, the Rover, being enamoured of a courtesan called Angellica Bianca, although he falls in love with Hellena. So the conflict becomes complicated. It is not just between the sisters and their father and brother, but also it results from the triangular relationship between Hellena, Angellica Bianca and Willmore. The fast-moving pace is maintained, the central characters are developed as fully rounded and interactive. A sub-plot concerning another prostitute, Lucetta and a country fool, Blunt, complicates matters still further.

Some difficulty arises in resolving the Angellica Bianca/Willmore plot and for a while the play seems to be moving in the direction of tragedy, but in general the central scenes run at a fast pace, with plenty of stage action, and create a situation towards the end of the play where matters have become so complicated that Florinda, because she is disguised, is in danger of being assualted by her own brother. All this of course is funny because of the comic mode in which it is presented. You can see from the above that conflict plays a vital part, both the conflict between Angellica and Willmore and the conflict between friends which arises through disguise.

ACTIVITY

Look at one of the central scenes from the play you are studying for AS or from a play you have studied before. It is helpful if you can either watch the scene on video or act it out in a group. Work out what kind of conflict is presented and how the playwright presents it, for example through violent stage action, language or gesture. How effective does it seem?

The Resolution

The three-part structure is, of course, as much applicable to a tragedy as to a comedy. To see how the resolution may be effected, we shall look at a tragedy by one of Shakespeare's contemporaries, Marlowe's *Dr Faustus*. Faustus, at the beginning of the play, decided to give

English literature

English literature

his soul up to the Devil for twenty-four years of power and pleasure. The central scenes of the play showed him enjoying those pleasures, but when the time is up, he is brought to the point of damnation. The final part of a play resolves the conflict or conflicts and in Faustus' case the conflict has been within him, between the forces of good and evil. This conflict is externalised in the play through allegorical figures, such as the Good and Bad Angels. Faustus goes to his damnation as the clock strikes midnight. His final soliloquy is one of the most powerful speeches in dramatic literature, as he tries unsuccessfully to repent. The conflict is still within him, rather than being between him and other characters as he desperately tries to think of ways to avoid damnation:

> O, I'll leap up to my God! Who pulls me down?

Time has been very important throughout the play, since Faustus' bargain was for twenty-four years. The audience is conscious of time passing, but never more so than in Faustus' final hour:

> Ah, Faustus,
>
> Now hast thou but one bare hour to live,
>
> And then thou must be damn'd perpetually.
>
> Stand still, you ever-moving spheres of heaven,
>
> That time may cease, and midnight never come.

Faustus appeals to the universe to cease its motions, but now that he needs supernatural intervention he finds it working against him. Faustus is torn between the claims of Christ and Lucifer, but being unable to repent, is finally drawn into hell. The audience is left to experience a **catharsis** here, being purged of the emotions of pity and fear which they have experienced through watching the enactment of Faustus' experience. *Dr Faustus* and *The Rover*, as a tragedy and a comedy, exemplify many of the points made about those two genres in Chapter 5 on Shakespeare.

There are various quite different ways of organising a play from the one described above. This will be the case for instance if you are studying *Waiting for Godot*. Some reference is made to its structure later in this chapter.

Some plays are much more static than others and may have an **episodic** structure. Tenessee Williams' *The Glass Menagerie* is one of these. It does not have much action and the scenes are not tightly constructed in a sequential way. The play is given unity by the use of such devices as musical motifs and symbolism.

All your work on structure relates to the third Assessment Objective.

ACTIVITY

Look at the last scene of the play you are studying.
1   How effective is it in tying up all the loose ends. Is there anything that you think has not been dealt with satisfactorily?
2   Did you see the end coming, or was it a surprise?
3   Have the characters been developed consistently?
4   Have the themes been resolved?

Language

Use of dialogue

There is a tremendous variation in the kinds of language used by dramatists, from the mixture of verse and prose used by the Elizabethans, through the long, rhetorical speeches of Shaw's characters, to the use of a much more colloquial language by many modern dramatists. Some, like Pinter and Beckett, make silence as meaningful as speech. Both wrote some extremely short plays. One of Beckett's is called *Breath* and lasts only a few seconds. It starts with a cry, then a stage full of rubble is lit up and the audience hears the sound of lungs breathing. Another cry brings the play, which represents the progress of birth, life and death, to an end.

Non-naturalistic dialogue

Non naturalistic dialogue is dialogue which does not give the illusion of normal speech. It may achieve this effect through rhetorical devices at one extreme or extreme simplicity at the other.

Apparently simple methods may have powerful effects. In Pinter's *The Caretaker*, a tramp called Davies takes up residence in a house belonging to Aston. In the first act of the play Davies explains to Aston that his papers are at Sidcup and that he needs to go there to get them:

Davies: (with great feeling). If only the weather would break! Then I'd be able to get down to Sidcup!

Aston: Sidcup?

Davies: The weather's so blasted awful, how can I get down to Sidcup in these shoes?

Aston: Why do you want to get down to Sidcup?

Davies: I got my papers there!

[Pause.]

Aston: Your what?

Davies: I got my papers there!

[Pause.]

Aston: What are they doing at Sidcup?

Davies: A man I know has got them. I left them with him. You see? They prove who I am! I can't move without them papers. They tell you who I am. You see! I'm stuck without them.

At first reading this may seem a very straightforward conversation, but in the context of the play as a whole, it is far from that. Part of the effect of the dialogue comes through repetition. Davies talks at intervals throughout the play about his papers and it becomes clear that he will never go to Sidcup (even if they are there, which is doubtful) and when Aston throws him out at the end of the play, he is still asking whether if he fetches his papers, Aston will change his mind. The business of Davies's papers is tied up in the play with the whole question of shifting identity. We are never sure who any of the characters really are and the sense of menace that is often associated with Pinter plays largely arises from the audience's uncertainty. The characters play elaborate games with one another, and in the second act, Mick, who owns the house, plays in a sinister fashion with the name Davies has given as his real one:

English literature

Mick: It's awfully nice to meet you.

[Pause.]

What did you say your name was?

Davies: Jenkins.

Mick: I beg your pardon?

Davies: Jenkins!

[Pause.]

Mick: Jen...kins.

You can begin to see here how pauses can be sinister. There is often a deliberate mismatch between what is said and the tone it's said in. So when Mick says 'It's awfully nice to meet you', the audience is far from believing him, as is Davies. There is a powerful dramatic effect as Davies becomes increasingly confused and disorientated.

This dialogue is clearly non-naturalistic, as is the dialogue in Beckett's *Waiting for Godot*, where the language varies from extreme simplicity and colloquialism to a kind of poetry:

Estragon: All the dead voices.

Vladimir: They make a noise like wings.

Estragon: Like leaves.

Vladimir: Like sand.

Estragon: Like leaves.

There is a great deal of patterned repetition and the whole structure of the two act play seems to consist of the first act being repeated in the second, with some reversals and differences of emphasis. All this is of course entirely the opposite of naturalistic, but is extremely effective in evoking a sense of uncertainty: will Godot come, or not? Who is Godot? Has anything really changed by the end of the play and will anything ever change in our own lives? In considering a play's dialogue you will be responding to the second and third Assessment Objectives.

ACTIVITY

Tom Stoppard begins his play *Arcadia* with a most effective play on words. The play opens in 'a room on the garden front of a very large country house in Derbyshire in April 1809'. Thomasina Coverly, aged 13, is having a lesson with her tutor, Septimus Hodge, aged 22. She is working on mathematics:

Thomasina: Septimus, what is carnal embrace?

Septimus: Carnal embrace is the practice of throwing one's arms around a side of beef.

Thomasina: Is that all?

Septimus: No ... a shoulder of mutton, a haunch of venison well hugged, an embrace of grouse ... caro, carnis; feminine; flesh.

Thomasina: Is it a sin?

Septimus: Not necessarily, my lady, but when carnal embrace is sinful; it is a sin of the flesh, QED. We had caro in our Gallic Wars – 'The Britons live on milk and meat' – lacte et carne vivunt'. I am sorry that the seed fell on stony ground.

Thomasina: That was the sin of Onan, wasn't it, Septimus?

Septimus: Yes. He was giving his brother's wife a Latin lesson and she was hardly the wiser after it than before. I thought you were finding a proof for Fermat's last theorem.

This is a fascinating beginning to a play that uses the same stage set to represent first the scene described above, and later, to represent the present day. You are in the same position as anyone approaching the play for the first time. What do you make of the opening dialogue and what does it reveal to you?

CONSIDER

Think about the way the dramatic context sets up some interesting questions about power and knowledge. When Thomasina asks her question, are we meant to think that she might already know the the answer, and wants to endorse her teacher – or is she genuinely naive? When Septimus replies, is he being deliberately playful because he knows that she knows – or is he indeed embarassed enough to deflect the question? The ambiguity in the language will be in part resolved, of course, by the ways in which the authors deliver the lines.

Stagecraft

There are many different ways in which playwrights attempt to indicate to a producer what the finished product, or the play on stage, should be like. In a way a play script is rather like a musical score. A composer writes down symbols that have to be translated into sound. In the same way the playwright writes down what has to be translated into something that we can both hear and see.

Stage directions

It has already been noted that some playwrights give very detailed instructions. A good example of this is in Miller's *Death of a Salesman*. These are some of the opening directions:

A melody is heard, played upon a flute. It is small and fine, telling of grass and trees and the horizon. The curtain rises.

Before us is the **Salesman's** house. We are aware of towering, angular shapes behind it, surrounding it on all sides. Only the blue light of the sky falls upon the house and forestage; the surrounding area shows an angry glow of orange. As more light appears, we see a solid vault of apartment houses around the small, fragile-seeming home. An air of the dream clings to the place, a dream rising out of reality … On a shelf over the bed a silver athletic trophy stands … .

The entire setting is wholly, or in some places, partially transparent. The roof-line of the house is one-dimensional; under and over it we see the apartment buildings. Before the house lies an apron, curving beyond the forestage into the orchestra. This forward area serves as the backyard as well as the locale of all Willy's imaginings and of his city scenes. Whenever the action is in the present the actors observe the imaginary wall-lines, entering the house only through its door at the left. But in the scenes of the past these boundaries are broken, and characters enter or leave a room by stepping 'through' a wall on to the forestage … .

English literature

From the right, **Willy Loman** the Salesman enters, carrying two large sample cases … .
Linda, his wife, has stirred in her bed at the right. She gets out and puts on a robe, listening.
Most often jovial, she has developed an iron repression of her exceptions to Willy's behaviour
– she more than loves him, she admires him. …

TASK

Write down what you think Miller wanted to show dramatically by giving these detailed instructions.

CONSIDER

(a) He gives vital details of props, the position of doors and so on and a precise idea of what the backdrop looks like.

(b) He wants the producer to see the backdrop as not just something physical, but something that has 'an angry glow'; also the surroundings make the house centre stage seem dream-like.

(c) Miller is also attempting to create a stage set which can be used to indicate whether scenes are taking place in past or present time, and a set which can be used for locations other than the obvious one.

(d) He wants the producer and actors to know some intimate details about the characters. Linda's attitude to Willy is described, rather than the playwright leaving it to her actions and dialogue to reveal that for themselves.

(e) He perhaps also wants us to work out that the athletic trophy is going to have some symbolic value in the play. He stresses the importance of flute music, which is used throughout the play, and which relates to Willy's dream. It becomes a motif connected with Willy, which gathers significance with every recurrence.

Miller is relying heavily on stage directions to perform a great many functions, while other playwrights concern themselves much more simply with setting the scene.

Originally, plays had few, if any, stage directions, and those we find in the plays of Shakespeare and his contemporaries have mostly been added by later editors. This certainly does not seem to detract from performances of these plays. In fact, it might be regarded as an advantage to leave some room for the producer and the actors to make their own interpretations. In looking at the use of stage directions you may be responding to a number of Assessment Objectives. They are part of the theatrical context for AO5, but also used by the playwright to give form to their concept for AO3, as well as being part of your response with knowledge and understanding for AO2.

Using the stage setting

In Elizabethan times the stage was very bare and unrealistic. The opposite extreme would be perhaps the stage setting for an Alan Ayckbourn play, with a fully furnished room centre stage and glimpses of other rooms to the sides and back, as well as perhaps stairs leading to another part of the house. That is what we would expect to find in a naturalistic play. A naturalistic play is one which seeks to recreate life as exactly as possible, giving the illusion of everyday speech and creating a stage setting in every detail as lifelike as possible. In England John Galsworthy and Terence Rattigan wrote plays of this kind.

In between these two extremes there are all sorts of other possibilities. Nowadays many directors use the stage with great ingenuity, so that many different locations can be suggested by one simple set technique.

Items on stage at times acquire a symbolic value, as is the case in some of Miller's plays, where for instance the sports trophy in *Death of a Salesman* comes to stand for the fulfilment

Biff will never achieve. Miller's plays, although they use a lot of realistic detail, are not purely naturalistic plays. They often use symbolism, they sometimes use a narrator, as in *A View From the Bridge* (another technique which reminds the audience they are watching a play, as the narrator mediates between the audience and the actors) and they use music and sound effects in non-realistic ways.

As mentioned earlier, Miller uses a complex set in *Death of a Salesman* which enables the audience to differentiate between the past and the present. When the characters observe the 'imaginary wall-lines' they are in the present, 'But in the scenes of the past these boundaries are broken, and characters enter or leave a room by stepping 'through' a wall on to the forestage'. This makes it possible for Miller constantly to move between past and present, illustrating the way in which everything that happens in the present is the product of what happened in the past, and making those past events very vivid to the audience. To fulfil Miller's intentions fully an **apron stage** is needed.

The 'Theatre of the Absurd', does not use stage settings, any more than it uses language, in a realistic way. *Waiting for Godot* is an excellent example. The title itself is puzzling and ambivalent. When we look at the text, we see that the setting is described as 'A Country Road. A tree. Evening.' This may seem quite precise, but it soon becomes clear that this is no normal setting. The main stage feature is a low mound on which Estragon sits pulling his boots on and off. Neither of the two main characters, Vladimir and Estragon, is fully characterised and they are not defined by class or position. So they seem perhaps to be representative of humankind. The setting then also takes on a representative nature, as do Estragon's boots and Vladimir's hat. These respectively preoccupy them throughout the play. The second act, as mentioned above, seems to repeat the first, but there are some vital differences. For instance the tree, which was bare in Act One, has sprouted four or five leaves in the second act. Naturally we might assume that this means something good is happening; some growth or development. However, the end of the play does not seem to suggest this. Estragon opens the play with the words 'Nothing to be done' as he sits on the mound. Although in the conclusion he says 'Yes, let's go' to Vladimir's question 'Shall we go?' this suggestion of movement is negated by the stage direction 'They do not move'. The movement of the play, if there is movement at all, is cyclical and this is given emphasis by the unchanging stage set.

In writing about stage setting you will still be responding to AO3 but also to the context in which the play is produced, AO5.

ACTIVITY

1   Look at the stage setting of the play you are studying. Are the instructions about it complex or simple?
2   What kind of setting is it, realistic or not? If it is not realistic, what do you think the playwright is trying to do with it?
3   Is it symbolic?
4   Are there a number of changes of setting or does all the action take place in the same place. If it changes locations, can you think of ways of staging it without having to have several elaborate sets?

English literature

Relationship between actors and audience

Most of us probably assume that everything that is said on stage is directed towards the audience, but some critics interpret a soliloquy as a speech in which a character is talking to themselves, whereas others interpret it as that character talking to the audience. The use of soliloquy, much less common in modern plays than in the Elizabethan theatre, is itself a non-naturalistic technique. It can be used in a variety of ways, for instance to reassure the audience that what the character says is sincere, since there is no-one else on stage to exert any influence on what is said. In Pinter's *The Caretaker*, there are a number of speeches which, while not technically soliloquies, are long outpourings of emotion not apparently addressed to another character on stage. They therefore have more in common with soliloquy than with dialogue. Soliloquies often represent emotional climaxes in a play.

The use of a narrator

It is certainly the case that there are some plays where there is much more direct linking between stage and auditorium. This is obvious in plays that have a narrator, such as Miller's *A View From the Bridge*. Alfieri, an Italian immigrant lawyer, acts as a mediator between the characters and the audience. Although he is one of them, he is able to look at the characters to some extent dispassionately, and his narration helps to involve the audience in the events of the play. This is true also of Tom Wingfield in *The Glass Menagerie*. He is one of the main characters, but also plays the part of narrator. He introduces scenes in a fairly detached way, summing up his family's characteristics as a novelist might, only to be plunged into the action himself as he completes his narration. He speaks directly to the audience as narrator and identifies himself with them in time, going back in time for the events of the play. So he not only informs the audience of all the background detail, biographical, sociological and historical facts that they need to know, again like a novelist; he also forms a link between past and present.

The distinction between real life and theatre

One of the most complicated plays as far as actor and audience relationship is concerned is Stoppard's *Rosencrantz and Guildenstern are Dead*. The two characters from Hamlet seem at the beginning of the play to be living out lives beyond the boundaries of the play they belong to. The situation is further complicated when, as well as being characters let loose from a play, they become a potential audience for a play performed by a group of travelling actors, themselves forming an obvious parallel with the group of actors who play 'The Mouse-trap' in *Hamlet*. The two characters refuse to see a play, but then become part of their original play when other characters from Hamlet appear and the audience is treated to extracts from Shakespeare's play. All this places the audience of Stoppard's play in a very confusing situation, so that it becomes difficult to determine the boundaries between real life and theatre.

Similarly in *Waiting for Godot*, there are times when Vladimir and Estragon show awareness of the audience in a way that allows Beckett to make some jokes at the audience's expense. For instance at one point the two characters are trying to escape and:

(Vladimir takes Estragon by the arm and drags him towards the front. Gesture towards auditorium.) There! Not a soul in sight! Off you go. Quick! (He pushes Estragon towards auditorium. Estragon recoils in horror) You won't? (He contemplates the auditorium). Well I can understand that.

The audience is spoken of here ironically as so insignificant that there's 'Not a soul in sight' and also as so horrifying to the actors that going in their direction would only be a very last resort. These ways of referring to the audience within the play are of course ways of reminding us that we are watching a play. We are made to think about the significance of that and about the sometimes blurred distinctions between the stage and the world.

So although there are naturalistic plays, as there are novels, which aim to help you forget that you are an audience and that what you are watching is not real, it is always a good idea to try to be as alert as you can and see how the playwright is trying to manipulate you. In considering the relationship between actors and audience you are again thinking about context responding to AO5 but also about the way form and structure express meaning, answering AO3.

ACTIVITY

Read the following passage, which is the opening of Robert Bolt's *A Man for All Seasons*:

[When the curtain rises, the set is in darkness but for a single spot which descends vertically upon the COMMON MAN, who stands in front of a big property basket.]

Common man: It is perverse! To start a play made up of Kings and Cardinals in speaking costumes and intellectuals with embroidered mouths, with me.

If a King, or a Cardinal had done the prologue he'd have had the right materials. And an intellectual would have shown enough majestic meanings, coloured propositions, and closely woven liturgical stuff to dress the House of Lords! But this!

Is this a costume? Does this say anything?

It barely covers one man's nakedness! A bit of black material to reduce Old Adam to the Common Man.

Oh, if they'd let me come on naked, I could have shown you something of my own. Which would have told you without words! ... Something I've forgotten ... Old Adam's muffled up.

(Backing towards basket.) Well, for a proposition of my own, I need a costume. (Takes out and puts on the coat and hat of STEWARD.)

Matthew! The Household Steward of Sir Thomas More! (Lights come up swiftly on set. He takes from the basket five silver goblets. ... A burst of conversational merriment off ... There's company to dinner ...

All right! A Common Man! A Sixteenth-Century Butler! (He drinks from the jug.) All right – the Six- (Breaks off, agreeably surprised by the quality of the liquor, regards the jug respectfully and drinks again.) The Sixteenth Century is the Century of the Common Man. (Puts down the jug.) Like all the other centuries. (Crossing right.) And that's my proposition.

1   What does this opening passage reveal to us about Robert Bolt's attitude towards the relationship between audience and actors?
2   Is the audience detached or drawn in?
3   Is the playwright trying to create a realistic setting or otherwise?

English literature

> **CONSIDER**
>
> (a) It is immediately obvious that Bolt is not trying to create a sense of realism. This is made clear when he draws attention to the whole business of theatricality and staging a play by having the Common Man on stage with a large property basket.
>
> (b) The way in which the Common Man immediately starts commenting on the playwright and the choices he has made is also extremely self-conscious and makes it impossible for the audience not to be drawn in to considering that process too.
>
> (c) The actors seem to exist apart from the way they are envisaged by the playwright, since the Common Man chooses his costume from the basket, making his own decision as to the part he plays, except in so far as it is made plain that he represents the Common Man throughout the ages. This is of course another way of departing from tradition where playwrights did as the Common Man evidently thinks Bolt should do here, put all the words into the mouths of the important characters.
>
> (d) Paradoxically, however, the fact that Bolt puts so many words into the mouth of the Common Man in the end makes the play much more real to us. Everything the Common Man says here relates to the dramatic process. He speaks of doing the prologue and starting a play for instance. The transferred words 'speaking' and 'embroidered' also draw attention to the dramatic process by being apparently out of place. We would have expected him to speak of 'embroidered costumes and intellectuals with speaking mouths'. All these aspects tend to absorb and intrigue the audience, thus keeping them on their toes, waiting to find out what happens next.

The playwright's purposes

Entertainment

You may ask yourself why any piece of writing was written. In the case of a play, it is likely that one answer will be to entertain an audience.

Making a moral point

However, at times dramatists also see their purposes as didactic and may experiment to try to get their points across in ways that do not necessarily 'entertain' their audiences. Miller usually has a didactic purpose, as when he wrote *The Crucible*, which made oblique comment on the anti-Communist Senator McCarthy and his Unamerican Activities Committee. Miller does not do this directly, but shows the hysterical and prejudiced behaviour of the people living in the New England town of Salem in the seventeenth century who sought out people as witches. This draws a parallel with McCarthy's committee, which sought people out as communists or communist sympathisers. This must have been most uncomfortable viewing for many of the audience and although the play was a great success worldwide its conservative first-night audience did not receive it well.

The same is true of many plays that have disturbed audiences and reminded them of their own short-comings. One of the playwrights who often made audiences feel uncomfortable was Shaw, who was always prepared to confront difficult issues in his writing. Ironically, after all his criticisms of society, religion and politics, Shaw eventually went on to become a British institution. To get the most out of studying these plays it is of course necessary to know the circumstances in which they were written, their 'context'.

Purpose and genre

The playwright's purposes are of course also related to the genres they use. If they write a tragedy they want to arouse pity and fear; if they write a comedy they want to arouse laughter, but, as has been said elsewhere, that does not mean that comedy may not have a serious purpose. In *St Joan*, the form Shaw uses interestingly reveal his purposes. The play is apparently a tragedy and the six scenes support this, leading to Joan's death at the stake. However, Shaw adds an epilogue in which he changes the scene first to 1456, the year in which Joan was declared not to be a heretic or a witch, and then to 1920, the year in which she was declared a saint. The ghosts of all those who were involved in her story are brought in to comment on the later events. This part of the play alters the attitude of the audience towards Shaw's purposes. He cannot see her story as a tragedy or he would not have written the rather comical, somewhat surreal epilogue. The form and structure of the play then leads the audience to assess and reassess the writer's purposes. They may conclude in this instance that the playwright was more concerned with the ways in which society reacts to exceptional people than he was with the death of Joan of Arc. Thinking about the playwright's purposes in relation to how they structure their plays is a way of targeting the third assessment objective. Your understanding of their purposes also relates to AO2.

ACTIVITY

Look again at the play you are studying.
1   What do you think are the playwright's purposes. Do they seek to entertain, to moralise, to do both, or neither?
2   What leads you to your conclusions?
3   Are you influenced by the form of the play or the language used?

Revelation of character in drama

In the course of looking at use of dialogue, stage directions, allegory and the various possible structures of a play, we have in fact already said quite a lot about revelation of character. It is clear that some characters are hardly developed at all, while others are profound studies of the human mind. Much of what was said about 'flat' and 'round' characters in Chapter 2 on the novel on page 143 is relevant here. An allegorical character, like the Bad Angel in *Dr Faustus* is a flat character, while Faustus himself is a round one.

Characters are revealed in a number of ways. The most obvious ways are through their own speech and actions, but they are often spoken about when they are not present in ways that are enlightening to the audience. In Act One of *Death of a Salesman*, Linda, Willy's wife, talks frankly with her sons about Willy and how he is really a failure and has tried to commit suicide. However, when she is talking to Willy, she bolsters him up in his impossible dream because she loves him. Biff, although he knows things about his father that Linda doesn't, and has concluded that he is a 'fake', spends a lot of the play deceiving himself about his life but ends up with a realisation of the truth and expresses it clearly at the end of the play. Because the play contains scenes from both past and present, the audience is given two sets of material to compare and contrast in coming to an assessment of the characters. Minor characters, such as Bernard and his father, who are consistent and honest throughout, point up the self-deceptions of the Loman family by contrast. **Expressionist** devices, such as the use of Willy's flute music to remind us of his impossible dream, and symbolism, also help in the revelation of character.

English literature

Character in the 'Theatre of the Absurd'

Characters like Vladimir and Estragon in *Waiting for Godot* are far removed from real life. We cannot imagine anyone in a real life situation speaking as they do. Near the beginning of Act One, Vladimir inspects his hat and Estragon finally removes his boot and examines it:

> **Vladimir**: Well?
>
> **Estragon**: Nothing.
>
> **Vladimir**: Show.
>
> **Estragon**: There's nothing to show.
>
> **Vladimir**: Try and put it on again.
>
> **Estragon**: (having examined his foot). I'll air it for a bit.
>
> **Vladimir**: There's a man all over for you, blaming on his boots the faults of his feet. (He takes off his hat again, looks inside it, feels about inside it, knocks on the crown, blows into it, puts it on again.) This is getting alarming. (Silence. Vladimir deep in thought, Estragon pulling at his toes.) One of the thieves was saved. (Pause.) It's a reasonable percentage. (Pause.)

This is a most mysterious conversation from any normal point of view. One of its characteristics is inconsequentiality; the comment about the thief being saved is apparently suggested by nothing in the immediate dialogue, but serves the purpose of intimating to the audience that there is perhaps a Christian dimension to the work. Critics point out that Beckett probably had a passage from St Augustine in mind here. He said: 'Do not despair; one of the thieves was saved. Do not presume; one of the thieves was damned'. Beckett pointed out also that Estragon's feet had an equal chance of salvation or damnation, which may explain why he fiddles continually with one boot. However, it would be difficult for a member of the audience to work that out for themselves.

Not much detail is revealed about the main characters. Vladimir here appears contradictory and inconsistent in criticisng Estragon for his preoccupation with his boots, while he is equally preoccupied with his hat. No kind of progression is made here; if anything the dialogue suggests no progression is possible. It seems that Beckett is much more concerned with philosophical ideas about the nature of mankind's situation and his responses to it than he is with psychological delineation of character. The patterned, repetitive dialogue and the association of one character with the head/mind through the hat and 'stinking breath' and the other with the body through the boots and 'stinking feet', also intimate that Beckett is not particularly concerned with realistic characterisation. So again we are back to the playwright's purposes; the kind of characters created depends on the purposes for which the writer is creating them. Your analysis of the ways in which character is revealed in drama relates to AO3.

ACTIVITY

Look at the opening scene of the play you are studying.

1   How are the characters introduced?
2   Do they speak briefly, or at length?
3   Does their language appear natural or not?
4   Do they speak in prose or verse, rhetorically or simply? How do they interact with one another?
5   Does the dialogue suggest one is dominant? If so, how is this achieved?

Different viewpoints on a play

Remember that the fourth Assessment Objective requires you to have your own independent judgements on a text as well as being aware of the views of others. In order to come to your own judgement what you need most is a good knowledge of the text and, in the case of drama, some awareness of different possible ways of producing the play you are studying. The best way to gain this experience is to see the play performed on stage, ideally to see it performed in different ways. Since this is not always possible, the next best way of getting a sense of the play on stage is to watch it on video, again if possible seeing at least two different videos.

It is also very useful to compare the way a play is produced on stage with the way it is produced as a film. For instance we have looked at the way Miller uses the stage set in *Death of a Salesman* to show past and present simultaneously. This is an ingenious way of using the stage but would not work for a film. A film, however, can use different techniques to show past and present, most obviously flashback. It is then helpful to discuss what is gained or lost by the different methods. Flashbacks can create a more realistic sense of the past, showing characters in different clothes, looking younger and so on. However, Miller was trying to do something more complicated than simply using flashback. He wanted to illustrate that time past and time present overlap and that both exist simultaneously within us. What we are in the present is determined by what we have done in the past. Miller said that he wanted to show that if Willy Loman could be made to remember enough he would kill himself, and he does. This cannot be achieved nearly so effectively with the use of flashback as with the stage setting which can represent past and present simultaneously.

One of the things you will notice if you are studying one of those plays with very detailed directions is that often producers ignore most of them and do things in their own way. Every time a producer picks up a play and makes a decision, a different interpretation is born. Actors bring their own interpretation to the part. Plays with both tragic and comic aspects are particularly likely to be interpreted in a variety of ways. There is much that is comic for instance in *Waiting for Godot,* in the pantomime actions and the complicated games the characters play and in their language. Different producers may stress the humour to a greater or lesser degree depending on their own interpretation of the play.

There are also many ways of interpreting plays in the study as well as in the theatre and it is helpful to read both critical works and theatre reviews to find out what some of these different viewpoints are. If you are going to see a performance on stage, or a new film comes out of a play you are studying, get hold of the reviews and compare what the critics think with your own point of view.

ACTIVITY

Write a review of either a video or stage production. Think about some of the aspects discussed in this chapter: the use of stage set; how the stage directions were interpreted; how effectively dialogue was delivered and character revealed. Were the opening and ending effective? You may also be aware of aspects we have not touched on here, such as lighting, which is particularly important in some plays. If possible compare your review with another, either that of another student or of a professional critic.

English literature

Context

The context of the play itself

The fifth Assessment Objective will also be important to you in studying a play. Context can take a number of different forms.

Contemporary background and theatre

It helps to have an understanding of the period in which the play was written and the kind of theatre it was written for. For instance in studying *The Crucible* you would need to know about the contemporary attitude to communism as well as about the seventeenth century and witch hunts. In order to make sense of *Dr Faustus* it helps to have a working knowledge of sixteenth century attitudes to hell and damnation. A study of *The Rover* is helped by a knowledge of the background of puritanism which has exiled the characters to a Spanish colony, and a knowledge of the Restoration theatre.

Fitting the play into the playwright's complete works

You should find out where the play you are studying comes in the list of works and what other plays the playwright has written and whether a particular one was written early or late in the playwright's career.

The literary context

Where does the play fit into the literary scene as a whole? Can it be placed in a sub-genre such as the Theatre of the Absurd? If so, what are the particular features which identify it in this way? It's worth remembering that a good play, even though it may belong to a sub-genre of this kind will be unique, so that you need to be as much aware of its unique features as of those which it shares with other plays by different playwrights.

The language context

It's important to look at the kind of language used to determine whether it's naturalistic, colloquial, **ritualistic** or **dialectal** for instance. The language will reflect the era when the play was written. Why do you think the writer chose to use the particular kind of language they did?

The context in which the play is received and understood

If you go to see a seventeenth century play today you will see it in a twenty-first century context. Your study of it needs to take that into account. Try to think of the differences between a response to *The Rover* in 1677 and a response to it in 2000. This understanding of context also overlaps with the fourth Assessment Objective (AO4) because the different contexts in which plays are read and seen give rise to different interpretations. Our very different attitudes to women and their position in society would mean that we would respond to the play in a very different way from most of its contemporary audience.

ACTIVITY

Pick one of the six aspects of context discussed above and write about how it relates to the play you are studying. Of course if you are studying a contemporary play you can't compare a modern reception with an earlier one, but you might consider the possibility of different responses from two different kinds of audiences.

TECHNICAL TERMS

alienation   a way of reminding the audience that they are watching a play, not observing something that is real

apron stage   a stage such as the Elizabethan stage, which projects a long way out into the auditorium

catharsis   the process of releasing pent-up emotion. The feeling an audience should have of being purged of pity and fear at the end of a tradegy

denouement   the last part of a play which resolves all the problems and ties up the loose ends

dialectal   relating to 'dialect', the kind of language spoken by a particular geographical group; also used in relation to differences resulting from class and occupation

didactic   having a message to get over to the reader or audience

episodic   loosely constructed in episodes or sections

fourth wall convention   looking on at a traditional stage with the curtain drawn aside to show what looks like a room with one wall removed; usually the audience seems to be looking at something very like real life

proscenium arch   the arch which separates the stage from the auditorium

rhetoric   the use of language to persuade

ritualistic language   formal, patterned language such as you would expect to find in a 'rite', that is a formal procedure associated with a particular ceremony

5 | Studying a Shakespeare play

In this chapter we shall be looking at a range of plays, including comedies, tragedies and histories and what makes them distinctive. Structure, language, critical viewpoint and context will be considered in relation to Shakespearean theatre.

The study of one play by Shakespeare is a requirement of every specification for AS English Literature, whether through coursework or through an examination. You will almost certainly have already studied one or more plays by Shakespeare and may have some idea of where those plays fit into the Shakespeare cycle.

Since one of the main Assessment Objectives tested in relation to the study of Shakespeare is AO5, the contextual one, one of the first things you can usefully do is to find out the date that the play you are studying was written. The relationship between the work you are studying and other works by the same writer, along with the period of the writer's work represented by a particular text, are relevant aspects of context.

You are probably already aware that any given Shakespearean play will fit into one of a number of categories, such as comedy, history or tragedy. It may, however, have a slightly more complicated designation, such as late romance, problem play or Roman play. A play may, of course, fit into two categories, like *Antony and Cleopatra*, which is both a tragedy and a Roman play.

ACTIVITY

Find a reference book which gives a complete chronology of Shakespeare's plays and make a note of where the play you are studying fits into the list. Then go on to find out which category the play belongs to.

How to go about studying a Shakespeare play

You will spend a lot of time looking at the details of the text but it is a good idea first of all to read through the play quickly to get a general idea of what it is about. Don't worry about the many details that you don't understand. The important thing at this stage is to get an overview. Reading the whole play before you start your study also has the advantage of enabling you as you go through the play in detail to see the part you are looking at in relation

English literature

English literature

to the whole, so that you are more aware of such things as dramatic irony.

Aristotle, a fifth century BC Greek writer and one of the earliest literary critics, said that there were six aspects of a play: plot, theme, character, language, music and spectacle. You can already see that most of these aspects are similar to the aspects we have looked at in relation to other genres. The major difference is indicated by the last two aspects. Music played a very important part in ancient Greek drama and, although it was far less important by the Elizabethan age, it plays a very important part in some of Shakespeare's plays. One of the best examples is in *Twelfth Night*, which opens with the words, addressed to a musician on stage:

> *If music be the food of love, play on,*
> *Give me excess of it ...*

The most important difference, however, between the genres we have already considered and the dramatic genre, is 'spectacle'. What Aristotle means by this is the visual impact that the play has on the audience. It is important to be aware that the play is intended to be performed on stage and to think of yourself as a member of the audience rather than a reader, although of course you should be both. Take any opportunity you can to go to see Shakespeare in the theatre. Many of the suggested areas for coursework tasks relate to performance, production and reviews of both film and plays. If it's not possible for you to see the play on stage, see it on film or video. The wider your experience, the more assured your written commentary will be. Questions on Shakespeare can vary greatly and you may need to be able to answer questions which involve an understanding of how a producer might look at a scene or scenes and to comment on the meanings and effects of language and structure, as well as on different critical opinions and context.

The Shakespearean theatre

One particularly important aspect of context is the Elizabethan/Jacobean theatre. To arrive at an understanding of the plays it can be helpful to visualise the contemporary Shakespearean theatre and compare it with more modern variants.

The Globe, built in 1598, is the theatre with which Shakespeare was particularly associated and where most of his plays were performed. There is a newly reconstructed Globe Theatre in London. If you get the chance it would be worth a visit. The original theatre was built in 1600 and burnt down in 1621. It was open to the sky; there was no artificial lighting except in a few private theatres until the Jacobean period. Shakespeare's last plays, *Cymbeline*, *The Winter's Tale* and *The Tempest*, were performed in the Blackfriars theatre, which had elaborate music, painted backcloths and footlights.

A notable feature of the Elizabethan theatre was its apron stage, which projected a long way into the auditorium and round three sides of which the audience crowded. Although in the twentieth century we have often come back to a similar stage, or to **theatre in the round**, stages at other times have tended to be more detached from the audience and able to be closed off by curtains. This gave a greater sense of realism and of looking into a room where people revealed themselves as they really were. In fact, of course, as pointed out more fully in the chapter on drama, they were not really doing so at all. The whole question of different types of staging, which is of course equally relevant to the performance of Shakespearean plays, is considered more fully in Chapter 4 on drama on pages 187-189.

Lack of realism

There was little sense of realism in the Elizabethan theatre. Men and boys played all the parts, both male and female. Costumes were not elaborate and there was no scenery (although the canopy which protected the apron stage was painted with heavenly bodies to suggest the sky). The Forest of Arden in *As You Like It* would have been indicated by a board or a few property shrubs. There was a recess at the back of the stage, which could be curtained off, and which was used for a variety of purposes, such as the bedroom where Desdemona is smothered in *Othello*, or Prospero's cell in *The Tempest*. On either side of the recessed area were doors which led to the 'tiring room' and up to the next level. The balcony would again have played a variety of parts: the most obvious would be the balcony in *Romeo and Juliet*, but it would also have served as the walls of Corioli in *Coriolanus* and one of the places where Ariel periodically appeared in *The Tempest*. If you climbed the stairs from the balcony, you would have come out at the top of the theatre where a trumpeter sounded a flourish to indicate that the performance was about to start.

ACTIVITY

Look for examples from the play you are studying of the uses of the different parts of the stage as detailed above.

Demands of Elizabethan theatre on the audience

Elizabethan drama made great demands on its audience, requiring the extensive use of the imagination. For instance, if you were watching *King Lear*, there would have been no elaborate simulation of the storm. Instead it would have been suggested by the power of language and metaphor:

> *Blow, winds, and crack your cheeks! rage! blow!*
> *You cataracts and hurricanoes, spout*
> *Till you have drench'd our steeples, drown'd the cocks!*
> *You sulph'rous and thought-executing fires,*
> *Vaunt-couriers of oak-cleaving thunderbolts,*
> *Singe my white head! And thou, all-shaking thunder,*
> *Strike flat the thick rotundity o' th'world!*
> *Crack Nature's moulds, all germens spill at once*
> *That makes ingrateful man!*

The power of Lear's feelings is represented here by the storm and the power of both by his words and metaphor. The opening line for instance uses the rhythm very flexibly to suggest the violent squalls of the wind, which are brought out by the monosyllables, the spondees, 'cheeks! rage! blow!' and the repetition of 'Blow' at the end of the line.

English literature

ACTIVITY

Singly, or in pairs, analyse Shakespeare's use of language in the speech quoted above to show how effectively you feel it serves the purpose of making the audience aware of the play's setting. Then go on to choose an extract from the play you are studying to show how Shakespeare similarly uses language to evoke a setting.

CONSIDER

(a) You may have noticed how the power and force of the rain are suggested by 'cataracts and hurricanoes' and by the alliterative 'drench'd' and 'drown'd'. The effect of 'cataracts and hurricanoes', both polysyllabic, latinate words, is enhanced by their being surrounded by monosyllables. The use of enjambement helps to give the feel of the unrelenting storm.

(b) When Shakespeare describes the lightning, he uses two hyphenated words, one of which, 'thought-executing', is his own coinage. The latter is particularly effective in suggesting the speed of lightning, which is compared to the rapidity of thought. Two more hyphenated words, 'oak-cleaving' and 'all-shaking' evoke the power of the thunder.

(c) The whole passage is made effective also by the imperatives 'Blow', 'Singe', 'Strike' and 'Crack' all positioned at the opening of the line; by its exclamatory style and by being addressed directly to the elements.

(d) The destructive power of the elements, which Lear particularly invokes, is brought out by his final metaphor of 'Nature's moulds' where she prepares the seeds of mankind and which Lear wishes to see smashed to atoms to prevent the birth of any more ungrateful children like his own. You may see some quite different effects when you consider the language here.

Plot and structure

Order and disorder

Most plays follow a three-stage pattern of exposition, development and resolution and Shakespeare's plays are no exception. This was discussed in Chapter 4 on pages 181-184. The exposition is the opening part of the play, which sets the scene and introduces the characters and the basis of the action. One way of interpreting Shakespeare's plays is to look at them in terms of order and disorder. This broad idea is just one way among many of looking at a Shakespeare play. A play will tend to start with a state of order and move towards chaos and disruption. These, in their turn, will be resolved at the end of the play. This is true of both comedies and tragedies, although obviously their resolutions will be very different. The onset of disorder tends to result from people following their natural feelings, as Viola does in *Twelfth Night* when, having disguised herself as a man in order to serve at Count Orsino's court, she then proceeds to fall in love with him. Love is of course the main feeling with which the comedies concern themselves. In tragedy what has often been referred to as the tragic flaw of the main character tends to be the catalyst for chaos: Macbeth's ambition, Othello's jealousy, Hamlet's irresolution or Lear's egotism. Of course in each case the situation is more complex than this might suggest, with a number of factors contributing to the situation.

The central three acts then develop the disorder to a point of climax, the problems being resolved in the denouement of the final act. The forces of disorder are evident at most points in a Shakespeare play. If we look at one of Shakespeare's mature comedies, *Twelfth Night*, examining in turn the beginning, middle and end of the play, we can see how the themes of order and disorder are shown, bearing in mind that this of course is only one way of looking at the play.

At the beginning the Duke is lovesick for Olivia. Although he doesn't really know her, he has given up all his normal pursuits in order to indulge his love with music and introspection. The opening may at first seem ordered, since the Duke is in a settled state he has clearly been in for some time. However, it soon becomes clear that this settled state is a form of disorder, since it is unnatural and involves the rejection of normal life. Ironically the Duke refuses to 'hunt', although of course that is what he is actually doing, hunting Olivia, a point that is emphasised by Shakespeare's pun on the word 'hart', meaning both a stag and the bodily organ. The sense of disorder is enhanced in the Duke's opening speech by his assertion of the volatility and instability of love:

> *O spirit of love, how quick and fresh thou art,*
> *That notwithstanding thy capacity*
> *Receiveth as the sea, nought enters there,*
> *Of what validity and pitch soe'er,*
> *But falls into abatement and low price,*
> *Even in a minute!*

However, such order as exists in the Duke's and Olivia's life-defying routines, is rudely disrupted by the arrival of Viola, who creates an impossible triangle where Olivia loves her, thinking her to be a man, she loves the Duke and the Duke imagines that he loves Olivia.

At the heart of the play, the sense of disorder is particularly shown through Olivia's hopeless and unwitting love for another woman:

> *Cesario, by the roses of the spring,*
> *By maidhood, honour, truth, and everything,*
> *I love thee so, that maugre all thy pride,*
> *Nor wit nor reason can my passion hide.*

Disorder largely arises from the use of deception. Viola appears to be one thing but is in fact another. Her disguise is, however, essentially an innocent one and one that leads in the end to the re-establishment of the forces of order. Similarly Olivia's love is essentially honest and right, but she has to wait for it to be returned by Sebastian (Viola's identical twin), the object of her love in its undisguised shape, before it can be fully realised. So the forces of order are shown in the above speech, through the essential goodness of Olivia's love, and the forces of disorder through her unwittingly bestowing it on the wrong object. This expresses the essence of the disorder in the play, which all has to do with appearance and reality and the failure of the characters to recognise each other's true natures.

All is resolved at the end of the play, largely because by this time some of the characters have gone through a learning process. Olivia has learnt that the best way to show a true love for a dead brother is to channel your energies into the complex business of living and loving, and the Duke has learned that his views of love were essentially false, being based on a lack of true understanding of the nature of love and of the object of his affections. The resolution of his new understanding in marriage rounds the play off. This, as stressed above, is only one way of looking at a complex play. Other people, yourself included, may interpret it in quite different and equally valid ways.

ACTIVITY

Re-read the play you are studying, to identify what it is in the opening act that causes a disintegration of order. Find some examples from the three central acts of the processes of order and disorder in conflict and note how a resolution is brought about at the end.

English literature

English literature

Time, place and action

What we have looked at so far is only the broad outline, but it should give you some idea of how a play works. There are, however, great differences between the plays in the ways in which they are constructed. The ancient Greek dramatists believed that a play should only have one action, that is plot; that it should only cover a time period of twenty four hours and that it should all be set in the same location. We do not have to look far in Shakespeare to see that he departed widely from such restrictions. *Antony and Cleopatra* for instance, works effectively through its contrasting Egyptian and Roman scenes; *The Winter's Tale* has a time gap of sixteen years between Acts 3 and 4 and many of the plays have sub-plots.

The *Othello* time scheme

The questions about time and place are particularly relevant to *Othello*. It has often been observed by critics that the play seems to have two simultaneous time schemes: on the one hand the events of the play are swift and overwhelming; on the other hand the text makes reference to a much slower and lengthier time scheme. The events of the play take place over a very few days and the temptation scene (Act 3, Scene 3) covers an hour or two at most. And yet, within that space of time Shakespeare has moved us from a world of innocence and happiness to a world of distrust, torment and revenge. This is only possible because of the extreme subtlety of the way Iago goes to work on Othello and because of its powerful dramatic effect on us. The overall effect of the play depends greatly on our response to the speed of events and our persuasion, through the astuteness of Shakespeare's psychology, that this could really have happened. On the other hand, the play makes reference throughout to things which suggest a different time scale altogether. For instance Iago gives Othello the impression that Desdemona and Cassio have been having a long-term relationship:

> *'Tis pitiful; but yet Iago knows*
> *That she with Cassio hath the act of shame*
> *A thousand times committed;*

This is impossible since Desdemona and Othello have only just married and have not even had time to consummate their marriage fully yet. However, in theatrical terms we tend not to notice these logical flaws, just as Othello himself does not notice them. So the two-time schemes work in conjunction to give an overwhelming sense of the tragic inevitability of the fast unrolling events of the play.

Place in *Othello*

Location is also extremely important in *Othello*. The opening scenes take place in the civilised setting of Venice, but the main events occur in Cyprus, away from civilisation and against a background of war. Although the change that takes place in Othello is obviously engineered by Iago, there is a feeling that the surroundings also play an important part. In Venice we see Othello as the civilised soldier, completely in command of himself:

> *Keep up your bright swords, for the dew will rust them.*
> *Good signior, you shall more command with years*
> *Than with your weapons.*

In Cyprus, however, he shows a tendency to succumb to his passions before there is any hint of a problem with his relationship with Desdemona. Being alerted to the brawl which is designed to demote Cassio, Othello says:

Now, by heaven,
My blood begins my safer guides to rule,
And passion, having my best judgement collied,
Assays to lead the way.

We may attribute this to the fact that he has just been roused from his first chance to consummate his marriage with Desdemona, but there seems to be a suggestion that away from the secure and civilising influence of Venice he is essentially more vulnerable.

Plot and sub-plot

So time and place are both of great importance in Othello. Action is supremely important too. There is only one plot and the deadly effect of Iago's intrigues would have been lessened by the introduction of a sub-plot. However sub-plots can be extremely effective, as Shakespeare shows in his handling of *King Lear*. Here all the aspects of the main plot are echoed in the Gloucester plot: a father has both good and evil children; the evil children hoodwink their parents into thinking they are good; the good children are cast off and eventually prove their goodness through their treatment of their parents. Why, then, does Shakespeare in the case of *Othello* choose to have one plot only, while he uses parallel plots in *King Lear*?

There are many possible answers to this question, as there are many possible critical interpretations of any given play. Your own answer to the above question can be incorporated into the following activity.

TASK

Shakespeare constructs his plays in so many different ways that it is impossible to generalise about them. What you need to be aware of is what to look out for when you are analysing the structure of the play you are studying. It is helpful if you think in terms of time, place and action. Answer the following questions in relation to the play you are studying:

1   How does Shakespeare use time in the play?
2   Over how long a period are the events of the play set?
3   Does the location change and if so what effect does this have?
4   How many plots are there and what difference would it make if a sub-plot were removed?

Comedies, tragedies and histories

It is noticeable that of all the plays specified by the various Examination Boards only one, *The Winter's Tale*, falls outside the three major categories. Some of the complex issues relating to the major genres are discussed below.

Comedies

Shakespeare's comedies were written over a long period, from the late 1580s to the early 1600s. They therefore vary a great deal in their style, method and themes. The only example of an early comedy specified by an Examination Board is *The Taming of the Shrew*, which is sometimes regarded as a farcical comedy. Farce, as a type of comedy, may be regarded as one of its sub-genres. More mature romantic comedies are *The Merchant of Venice* (*c.*1596) and *Much Ado About Nothing* (*c.*1598–99). *Twelfth Night* (*c.*1600–1601) is the last of the romantic comedies. So the specified texts cover three periods of Shakespeare's comic writing. Although there are considerable differences between these plays, they also have much in common.

As the name 'romantic comedy' suggests, these plays are mainly concerned with love and the bringing of relationships to fruition. All the comedies end with marriages, very often multiple marriages. It is observed by Lysander in *A Midsummer Night's Dream* that 'the course of true love never did run smooth' and this sums up much of what we find in the comedies. They are essentially about the obstacles that lie in the path of establishing successful relationships. Of course it may be argued that the main object of the plays is to entertain an audience. However, it would be a mistake to assume that that is all they are about. When you look more closely you can see that there are always serious messages even within the comic mode. This is especially true where irony is employed, as it is in all of Shakespeare's plays. The plays contain universal truths about human nature and relationships which enrich our lives as we watch or read them.

Comic conventions

There are certain comic conventions which we have to get used to before we can get the most out of Shakespearean comedy. Comedies deal largely with the all-pervasive Shakespearean theme of appearance and reality. Shakespeare was obsessed with the difference between people's appearances and the reality that lay beneath them. This takes a particular form in the comedies, where we frequently come upon people in disguise. This is not a realistic convention. The fact that any normal person would recognise who it really was in two minutes has to be forgotten. In the play's context we accept that people fail to recognise others that they know well after they have put on different clothes. Another convention relating to mistaken identity was the use of twins, which we find both in the early comedy, *A Comedy of Errors*, and in the mature comedy *Twelfth Night*.

A conventional scene which occurs to great comic effect in both *Much Ado About Nothing* and *Twelfth Night*, is the eavesdropping scene. Again it is assumed that the characters who are being listened to will remain oblivious of the listeners even in the most unlikely circumstances. Comedies are inevitably much dependent on coincidences, staged fights, tricks (such as the bed-trick in *Measure for Measure*), misleading messages and a host of other aspects. All of these, and the disguisings and eavesdroppings mentioned above, contribute to the obstacles which the lovers have to win through in order to attain their goal. None of the comedies presents a truly realistic scenario.

ACTIVITY

Read the following three speeches from Act 3, Scene 1 of *Much Ado about Nothing*. The first speech begins the scene, the second is part of the conversation designed to persuade Beatrice, who is against marriage, that Benedick is in love with her, and the third is her response to what she has overheard:

Text 1

Hero: *Good Margaret, run thee to the parlour;*
There shalt thou find my cousin Beatrice
Proposing with the Prince and Claudio.
Whisper her ear, and tell her I and Ursula
Walk in the orchard, and our whole discourse
Is all of her; say that thou overheardst us,
And bid her steal into the pleached bower,
Where honeysuckles, ripened by the sun,
Forbid the sun to enter …

Text 2

Hero: *O god of love! I know he doth deserve*
As much as may be yielded to a man;
But nature never framed a woman's heart
Of prouder stuff than that of Beatrice.
Disdain and scorn ride sparkling in her eyes,
Misprizing what they look on, and her wit
Values itself so highly that to her
All matter else seems weak. She cannopt love,
Nor take no shape nor project of affection,
She is so self-endeared…

Text 3

Beatrice (coming forward):
What fire is in mine ears? Can this be true?
Stand I condemned for pride and scorn so much?
Contempt farewell and maiden pride adieu!
No glory lives behind the back of such.
And Benedick, love on, I will requite thee,
Taming my wild heart to thy loving hand …

Working in pairs analyse the above passages for conventional comic elements.

CONSIDER

The eavesdropping itself is of course a comic convention, as is the ease with which the listener is convinced. Despite Beatrice's great intelligence it does not occur to her that a trick might be being played on her. This is also part of the comic convention. Beatrice sheds her former persona without a second thought, although she does have some second thoughts later. An element of exaggeration is thus evident throughout. The group who are playing the trick exaggerate Beatrice's faults for dramatic effect. The language is also worth looking at from the point of view of convention. The scene is set in a conventional romantic way in a 'pleached bower' overhung with 'honeysuckle'.

Twelfth Night, a mature comedy

Twelfth Night explores the nature of love, including homosexual love and is often interpreted in a way which moves towards tragedy in the treatment of Malvolio. In *Twelfth Night*, unlike some of the earlier and more farcical comedies such as *The Taming of the Shrew*, all the characters are fully realised and there are many searching dialogues in which the characters discuss the nature of their feelings. The ironic perversity of love is well evoked in the following dialogues:

Olivia: *Your lord does know my mind, I cannot love him.*
Yet I suppose him vurtuous, know him noble,
Of great estate, of fresh and stainless youth;
In voices well divulg'd, free, learn'd and valiant,
And in dimension, and the shape of nature
A gracious person. But yet I cannot love him:
He might have took his answer long ago.

English literature

Viola: If I did love you in my master's flame,
     With such a suff'ring, such a deadly life,
     In your denial I would find no sense,
     I would not understand it.

Olivia: Why, what would you?

Viola: Make me a willow cabin at your gate,
     And call upon my soul within the house;
     Write loyal cantons of contemned love,
     And sing them loud even in the dead of night;
     Halloo your name to the reverberate hills,
     And make the babbling gossip of the air
     Cry out 'Olivia!' O. you should not rest
     Between the elements of air and earth,
     But you should pity me.

Olivia: You might do much.

This is a good passage to illustrate the complexity of the play. Part of that complexity relates to disguise and you need to be aware that, not only is Viola acting the part of a woman disguised as a man, but that on the Elizabethan stage her part would be played by a boy. The central irony of the passage arises from Olivia's assertion that a would-be lover should be willing to recognise that a woman may simply be unable to love him. The irony is that, within a very short time (the process is already beginning as she says 'You might do much'), she herself is falling in love with Viola, an impossible object for her affections. It is also ironic that Viola speaks as eloquently as she does on behalf of Orsino because she herself is in love with him, but only succeeds in arousing Olivia's love for herself. The beautiful and moving poetry of the 'willow cabin' speech is typical of *Twelfth Night*.

TASK

Look at the following passage from *Twelfth Night* where Duke Orsino enlists the help of Viola disguised as Cesario to win the love of Olivia.

Duke: (To Viola) Cesario,
     Thou know'st no less than all: I have unclasp'd
     To thee the book even of my secret soul.
     Therefore, good youth, address thy gait unto her,
     Be not denied access, stand at her doors,
     And tell them, there thy fixed foot shall grow
     Till thou have audience.

Viola: Sure, my noble lord,
     If she be so abandon'd to her sorrow
     As it is spoke, she never will admit me.

Duke: Be clamorous, and leap all civil bounds,
     Rather than make unprofited return.

> *Viola*: Say I do speak with her, my lord, what then?
>
> *Duke*: O then unfold the passion of my love,
>   Surprise her with discourse of my dear faith;
>   It shall become thee well to act my woes:
>
> Here the Duke is seeking to attain the object of his love. Analyse the passage, with particular attention to language, to see how he goes about it.

Orsino wants to override Olivia's denial of access and subject her to a lengthy audience with Viola who will 'leap all civil bounds', that is be rude, in telling Olivia at length how much Orsino loves her. It's interesting to note that Orsino woos by proxy rather than in person. He is romantic in his love, describing it in terms of 'passion' and 'woes' which are so strong that they cannot be denied. However, he appears to have very little interest in the object of his love as a person, being far more concerned with his own feelings than with her as an individual, and having little respect for her privacy. Orsino speaks of unclasping 'the book even of my secret soul'. This is a romantic metaphor, comparing as it does his innermost feelings to the words hidden in a book and suggesting that his love to him is a religion, through the use of the word 'soul'. This is echoed later by the phrase 'my dear faith'. There is a sense that he desires to bring the object of his affections into submission through his barrage of words and through his actions. Again, of course this is one way of interpreting the above lines. Others might analyse them in very different ways.

Histories

The most well-known history plays are those which fall into two groups of four (tetralogies), the first four being *Henry IV, Part I*, *Henry IV, Part II*, *Henry V* and *Richard II*. The second group comprises *Henry VI, Parts I, II* and *III* and *Richard III*. This, however, represents their chronological order, not the order in which they were written. The latter four plays were in fact the first four plays Shakespeare wrote, the former appearing, again not in chronological order, between 1595 and 1599.

Sources and background

Shakespeare's main sources were Edward Hall's *Chronicles* and Holinshed's *Chronicles*. These works were pro-Tudor propaganda, seeking to justify the status quo largely through fear of civil war. Shakespeare took up this theme of civil war and the dangers it posed, linking it with the importance of order and hierarchy, another Elizabethan preoccupation. The Elizabethans believed that everyone and even every thing had its own place in the order of things and that any attempt to move out of that position would precipitate disorder. This applied most importantly at the top of the hierarchy with the King, who was divinely appointed by God. The usurpation of this divinely appointed position was a gross sin. Equally the rejection of one's divinely appointed role would precipitate chaos, as we see when King Lear abdicates.

Shakespeare appears to subscribe to the importance of order, but he examines the situation in a complex and subtle way. Clearly the system only works effectively if you have a good as well as a divinely appointed king. This issue is explored in *Richard II* where Shakespeare portrays Richard as the true king, but the usurping Bolingbroke as a potentially much more effective king. The tension between these two positions leads to the tragic dimension of Richard and the uncomfortable feeling that Henry will have a lot of atoning to do.

English literature

So Richard states:

Not all the water in the rough rude sea
Can wash the balm off from an anointed king;

In tacit acceptance of this, Henry, having usurped the throne, says:

I'll make a voyage to the Holy Land,
To wash this blood off from my guilty hand.
March sadly after; grace my mournings here
In weeping after this untimely bier.

These are the concluding lines of the play and Shakespeare does not show either king as the ideal monarch. Indeed the rest of the second tetralogy shows Henry and his successor being dogged by feelings of guilt. As Henry IV says 'Uneasy lies the head that wears a crown'. His son, however, strives to make England great by conquering France and he is seen as a good monarch, upholding order:

Therefore doth heaven divide
The state of man in divers functions,
Setting endeavour in continual motion:
To which is fixed, as an aim or butt,
Obedience: for so work the honey-bees,
Creatures that by a rule in nature teach
The act of order to a peopled kingdom.

Henry V is seen as a good king because he carries out his responsibilities. Richard II on the other hand, although very much aware of his rights, had little understanding of his responsibilities.

Shakespeare shifts the emphasis of the play as he writes, so that the early acts show Richard's inadequacies and incline the audience to have little sympathy for this inept king. However, as we reach the point where Bolingbroke takes over, the balance changes: Shakespeare begins to develop Richard as a tragic figure and at the same time to show Bolingbroke as a less attractive figure. If you are studying a history play primarily with a view to the importance of context, you should consider the relationship between the Elizabethan views of hierarchy and the Divine Right of Kings in relation to the way in which Shakespeare portrays the two kings in the play. The particular perspective from which you view a play will of course affect the critical view you have of it. If you see the play in the theatre, you will naturally be affected by the way the producer and the actors interpret the roles. The parts of Richard and Bolingbroke, for instance, can be interpreted in a great variety of ways, so that the audience's sympathy may not necessarily lie where they thought it would before entering the theatre.

TASK

Look at the following passage from Act 4, Scene 1, the deposition scene in *Richard II*:

Richard: Alack, why am I sent for to a king
Before I have shook off the regal thoughts
Wherewith I reign'd? I hardly yet have learn'd
To insinuate, flatter, bow and bend my knee.
Give sorrow leave awhile to tutor me
To this submission. Yet I well remember
The favours of these men. Were they not mine?
Did they not sometime cry 'All hail!' to me?
So Judas did to Christ. But he, in twelve,
Found truth in all but one; I, in twelve thousand, none.
God save the king! Will no man say amen?
Am I both priest and clerk? well then, amen.
God save the king! although I be not he;
And yet, amen, if heaven do think him me.
To do what service am I sent for hither?

York: The resignation of thy state and crown
To Henry Bolingbroke.

Richard: Give me the crown. Here, cousin, seize the crown.
Here cousin,
On this side my hand, and on that side thine.
Now is this golden crown like a deep well
That owes two buckets, filling one another,
The emptier ever dancing in the air,
The other down, unseen, and full of water.
That bucket down and full of tears am I,
Drinking my griefs, whilst you mount up on high.

Bol.: I thought you had been willing to resign?

Analyse this passage in the light of your understanding of Elizabethan views on order and kingship. How has Shakespeare used those concepts to inform his writing and how do they affect your response to the passage?

CONSIDER

(a) The passage is apparently designed to appeal to the sympathies of the audience, although their potential sympathy may be offset by a negative reaction to Richard's self-pity. Richard's opening lines suggest that the transition from kingship to deposition has been too sudden and that he needs time to become accustomed to it. This reminds us that Richard is by legal inheritance a king and engages our sympathy with his sorrow. This idea is linked with the idea of betrayal and the idea that God divinely appoints the king gains importance from the analogy between the betrayed Richard and Christ. Richard's rather histrionic repetition of 'God save the king' reminds us that Richard both is and is not the king and makes it difficult to have a simple response to the situation.

(b) You will notice that Bolingbroke says very little here. He seems to think he is entitled to a simple response, saying rather naively ''I thought you had been willing to resign'. The number of lines given to Richard here and the brevity of Bolingbroke's contribution again enforce sympathy from the audience and begin to turn us against the usurping Bolingbroke. The reversal of order is well shown in the image of the buckets, which shows Richard and Bolingbroke exchanging places and at the same time highlights Richard's sorrow. This would serve the dual purpose of showing the changing hierarchy and deepening the tragic aspect of Richard. As stressed in relation to other scenes, however, this one also may be interpreted in a variety of different ways.

Tragedies

We can again look back to the Greek and Roman originals to see where Shakespeare got his inspiration for the writing of tragedies.

Aristotle, in his *Poetics,* wrote about the constituents of tragedy. He described a typical tragic hero as:

a man not pre-eminently virtuous and just, whose misfortune, however, is brought upon him not by vice or depravity but by some error of judgement ...

What Aristotle describes here is what has come to be known as the hero's 'fatal flaw', Macbeth's ambition, Hamlet's indecisiveness and so on. This error combined with external circumstances to bring about the downfall of the hero. For example Oedipus, hero of Sophocles' play *Oedipus Rex*, had flaws of character which led him to a fate which was in any case predestined: that he would kill his father and marry his mother. So in Shakespeare's plays external and internal factors combine to bring about the fall of the central character. Macbeth's ambition alone might not have proved fatal to him had it not been in combination with Lady Macbeth's incitement and the effect of the witches.

Inevitability

As has already been implied, inevitability is another feature which most tragedies have in common. There should be a sense that once the plot has been set in motion nothing can stop the chain of events from unfolding. So in *Antony and Cleopatra*, although Antony makes a supreme effort to concentrate on war rather than love and wins the battle at Alexandria, we know instinctively that this is merely a brief respite and his incapacity to reconcile the opposing roles of soldier and lover, which we have already seen at the battle of Actium, will lead to his death. In the end his sense of honour determines his suicide.

A sense of waste

Antony's suicide brings out another major aspect of tragedy, that is a sense of waste. He is a noble soldier, conqueror of the world and gives it all up for love. Within the context of the play this sacrifice is judged in very different ways. To the Romans Antony's behaviour is 'dotage', while to Cleopatra he is 'The crown o' th'earth' whose 'legs bestrid the ocean'. The audience is likely to judge Antony finally more with an Egyptian than a Roman eye, as a great man who gave the world for love.

Growth to self-knowledge

In tragedy, the central character will experience a great fall, but should compensate for that to some extent by learning more about themselves and the world they inhabit. We may at times wonder whether there is much point in the self-knowledge attained, when the one who has reached it has done so only to die. This, of course, increases the sense of waste and the tragic irony. Lear, for instance, begins the play as a selfish, arrogant old man, but learns fundamental, philosophical truths about the world in his madness on the heath. He understands the lot of the poor, 'Poor naked wretches' and realises that we are all essentially the same when our 'robes and furr'd gowns' are stripped away to reveal us as 'unaccommodated man'.

In every Shakespearean tragedy there are moments of astounding insight, achieved by people driven to the very edge in life. Macbeth, before the final battle, Othello, before he kills his wife, Hamlet, just before his death are just three examples of characters who stop to reflect on the significance of what is about to happen.

Catharsis

However, even though we may feel a sense of waste on the death of the hero, Aristotle also felt that the audience should experience catharsis, that is a purging of pity and fear, at the conclusion of a tragedy. This should follow on from our experience of both pity and fear as we watch the events unfolding, as can be illustrated from *King Lear*. The sense of pity may be evoked from quite an early stage in the play, despite Lear being in many ways, as one critic described him, 'an arrogant old idiot, destitute of any decent human quality and incapable of any reasonable act'. Lear's suffering in the storm, both mental and physical, and his climactic and heart-breaking meeting with the blind Gloucester on the heath, may arouse deep pathos. So too can Desdemona's death scene, even though here too, there is even the possibility that we could see Othello as arrogant and foolish.

If the 'tragedy' genre is successful, then, we should perhaps feel that in experiencing the sufferings of those on stage and seeing them transcend those sorrows, we are finally purged of pity and fear.

We may as an audience respond quite differently to a play. Our reaction is dependent on many factors, such as the point of view of the producer and the particular ways in which the actors portray their roles. There are many ways of interpreting Shakespearean tragedies. However, the above categories are some of the traditional ones with which it is helpful for you to be familiar.

ACTIVITY

If you are studying a tragedy, look at it from the point of view of the above list of aspects of a tragedy to see how far they are apparent.

English literature

Aspects relating to all plays

Irony

Shakespeare makes effective use of irony throughout his plays. This is often what is referred to as **dramatic irony**. Dramatic irony is something that arises when there is a discrepancy between the audience's knowledge and that of a character or characters on stage. In relation to comedy, for instance, it is extremely ironic when Viola talks to Duke Orsino about the different ways in which men and women love, since the Duke thinks he is talking to a man, whereas the audience is aware that he is in fact not only talking to a woman, but to a woman who is in love with him. Dramatic irony, of course, tends to arouse laughter in comedy.

It is just as much a feature of tragedy, but of course has a quite different effect. One of the most intense and agonising scenes of extended dramatic irony is the long temptation scene in *Othello*, (Act 3, Scene 3). Here Iago persuades Othello that his wife is unfaithful, while the audience is well aware that she is true and pure.

Apart from dramatic irony there are more general examples of irony in all of the plays. In *Richard II* for instance, it is ironic that Richard, who claims to have a great love for his country and who weeps 'for joy. To stand upon my kingdom once again', has in fact ignored John of Gaunt's patriotic speech about the kingdom, 'This royal throne of kings, this sceptred isle', and so neglects England that the gardener talking about a garden which serves as an analogy for Richard's kingdom, describes Richard as 'He that hath suffered this disordered spring'.

TASK

Find a number of examples from several different Shakespeare plays of the use of dramatic irony. Try to say what effect each example has.

The intermingling of tragic and comic

All Shakespeare's tragedies have comic elements included in them, through for instance the Gravedigger in *Hamlet*; the porter in *Macbeth* or the Fool in *King Lear*. As we watch the plays, however, we realise that comedy in these circumstances, although it may entertain, also enhances the tragic tone. Through the first three acts of *King Lear*, for instance, the Fool comments continually on the stupidity of what Lear has done in abdicating as king and dividing his kingdom between his two evil daughters. The Fool's comment, although comic, is also cutting and continually touches a raw nerve, reminding both the King and the audience of Lear's stupidity and the disastrous effect it has had:

> **Fool**: *Nuncle, give me an egg, and I'll give thee two crowns.*
> **Lear**: *What two crowns shall they be?*
> **Fool**: *Why, after I have cut the egg i'th'middle and eat up the meat, the two crowns of the egg. When thou clovest thy crown I' th'middle, and gav'st away both parts, thou bor'st thine ass on thy back o'er the dirt: thou hadst little wit in thy bald crown when thou gav'st thy golden one away. If I speak like myself in this, let him be whipp'd that first finds it so.*

Shakespeare's language

One of the most interesting aspects of the study of Shakespeare is the development of his writing. There is not time here to discuss this fully, but you should be aware that the date of composition of the text you are studying will indicate something about the style of writing you may expect to find. For instance the earlier plays make much more use of prose, and the verse, which is less flexible than the lauguage of the later plays, often rhymes. If you have studied *Romeo and Juliet* at Key Stage 3 you probably noticed that there was a lot of rhyme and whole sonnets were used within the dialogue. The verse there is highly ornamented and at times seems elaborated for its own sake as much as for its necessity to the scheme of the play.

On the other hand *Macbeth*, which you may have studied at Key Stage 4, and which was written eleven or twelve years later than *Romeo and Juliet*, although rich in imagery, moves at a very fast pace and contains nothing that seems static or inessential to the overall design. This is also shown in *King Lear*, when, in the final scene, Lear comes on carrying the dead Cordelia in his arms and shortly after makes his final speech:

> *And my poor fool is hang'd! No, no, no life!*
> *Why should a dog, a horse, a rat, have life,*
> *And thou no breath at all? Thou'lt come no more,*
> *Never, never, never, never, never!*
> *Pray you, undo this button: thank you, Sir.*
> *Do you see this? Look on her, look, her lips,*
> *Look there, look there!*

Here Shakespeare carries his use of language to its limits. The speech is bare of metaphor, simple and stark. In the course of his experiences Lear has seen mankind stripped to his essence as a 'poor, bare, forked animal' and he goes to his death with this new insight. Language is stripped of ornament, as man is. The insights Lear has acquired can only be communicated in this basic way to achieve their effect.

Of course, it is impossible to generalise and the rich, poetic language of the ending of *Othello* was written only a year before the very different language we have looked at above. We need to look at what Shakespeare is aiming to do, as well as the period in which he is writing. Othello makes use of two very different kinds of language for particular effect. From the beginning Othello's speech is richly poetic. We note the irony of his saying:

> *Rude am I in my speech,*
> *And little bless'd with the soft phrase of peace*

and we note also that he has wooed Desdemona with his stories of his past life. One of the most disturbing aspects of the play then, is to see how Othello, when influenced by Iago into thinking his wife is unfaithful, gradually takes on Iago's crude language and speaks incoherently in prose:

> *It is not words that shake me thus. Pish! Noses, ears, and lips. Is it possible? —*
> *Confess! – Handkerchief! – O devil!*

English literature

English literature

Importantly, however, although Othello of course dies, he is restored to his true self before the end and in understanding what has happened to him, recovers the former beauty of his language:

I pray you, in your letters, ...
Speak of me as I am ...
*   of one whose hand,*
Like the base Indian, threw a pearl away
Richer than all his tribe; of one whose subdu'd eyes
Albeit unused to the melting mood,
Drop tears as fast as the Arabian trees
Their med'cinable gum.

Shakespeare characterises people through their language so it is appropriate that when a great change occurs in a character that change should be noticeable in their language.

ACTIVITY

See if you can find a character in the play you are studying who undergoes change and development during the course of the play. Having found a suitable example, examine four or five speeches taken from different parts of the play and try to see if you can find evidence of language change or development.

Iterative imagery

One of the most distinctive features of Shakespeare's language is his use of **iterative imagery**; that is imagery which is repeated throughout the play. So for instance images of blood and sleep recur throughout *Macbeth*, while *King Lear* contains many images relating to wild animals and much reference to physical suffering and torture. To look at this aspect in more detail, we may turn to *Twelfth Night*. It opens, as mentioned earlier, with an image of music as 'the food of love' and images of music can be found throughout the play. The romantic images of the Duke give way to the rowdy part-songs of Sir Toby and Sir Andrew:

But shall we make the welkin dance indeed? Shall we rouse the night-owl in a catch that will draw three souls out of one weaver?

The power of music is shown in very different ways here by both serious and comic characters. Similarly the sea gives some powerful iterative imagery to the play. Viola is cast up by the sea, while her brother 'like Arion on the dolphin's back' held 'acquaintance with the waves/So long as I could see'. The image is taken up by the Duke in describing his love:

But mine is all as hungry as the sea,
And can digest as much. Make no compare
Between that love a woman can bear me
And that I owe Olivia.

Here the Duke sees love as an appetite to be satisfied, arrogantly assuming that a man's appetite is superior to a woman's. He is proved wrong by Viola, of whom Sebastian mistakenly says:

I had a sister
Whom the blind waves and surges have devour'd:

Here the idea of the sea as related to appetite is taken up again by 'devour'd' which in turn makes a link between the sea and love, also an appetite. The fact that the waves are 'blind' also links with 'blind Cupid' the god of love. Blindness in fact seems to be as much a characteristic of the people involved as of the sea. Viola is also deceived about her brother. She thinks he went to a 'watery tomb'. The sea seems to be a symbol in the play for instability, danger and chaos. These are all symptomatic of comedy, where the problems are caused by anarchic instincts.

Some of the best examples of iterative imagery can be found in *Hamlet*. Particularly pervasive is imagery of disease. Hamlet, speaking to his mother about what he considers her corrupt action in marrying his uncle, says:

Mother, for love of grace,
Lay not that flattering unction to your soul,
That not your trespass but my madness speaks.
It will but skin and film the ulcerous place,
Whilst rank corruption, mining all within,
Infects unsees.

The comparison here is between 'unction', or healing balm, being applied to the soul and Hamlet's mother flattering herself that she is not acting wrongly. If she does delude herself in this way her delusion will be like a skin or film which covers up an ulcer but cannot prevent it from continuing to infect the body. The metaphor of 'mining' is also effectively used in this powerful metaphor which expresses Hamlet's agony at his mother's action. You may think of other interesting ways of interpreting the same images.

ACTIVITY

Look again at the play you are studying. Identify the main image strands in it, then pick one of them for more detailed study. Find four or five examples of reference to the particular image and analyse them to show how effective they are? What difference does it make that they are used repeatedly rather than just once?

Verse and prose

You will notice that Shakespeare frequently uses prose and you need to think about the reasons for this. It is generally true that the lower life characters tend more often to speak in prose, while upper class characters speak in verse. This is, however, a considerable oversimplification. We have noted above that a significant portion of *The Taming of the Shrew* is in prose. This is partly accounted for by the fact that it is an early play; you will find the same is true for instance of *Love's Labour's Lost*. In both instances also Shakespeare is moving at a fast pace and not dwelling on the finer points of feeling as he does in the mature comedies.

Prose may be used for contrast, as in the opening of *King Lear*, where the play opens with the sub-plot in prose and then moves on to the main plot, with the immediate impact of Lear's

English literature

English literature

abdication and its consequences, which are in verse. Prose is often used by Shakespeare to denote madness. Lear falls into prose at one point during his madness and Edgar, when he feigns madness, speaks in prose too. Hamlet does so also. The fact that Hamlet speaks in prose in Act 2, after discovering from the ghost that his father was murdered, may seem to suggest that he is mad. However, when he is alone again, he speaks in verse, 'O, what a rogue and peasant slave am I!' This may indicate that his madness is only feigned. However, critics have been debating this point for many years and have not yet come to any definitive conclusion.

You will realise from the above discussion that it is not a simple matter to decide why Shakespeare chooses verse or prose and that you need to think carefully also about the effects it has.

TECHNICAL TERMS

dramatic irony   when the audience has a greater knowledge of events than some or all of the characters on stage

farce   a form of comedy with a lot of physical action

fatal flaw   the predominant characteristic of the hero which helps to bring about his downfall

in the round   a way of performing a play where the audience sits on all sides of the performers

iterative imagery   strands of imagery which recur throughout a play

spectacle   the visual aspect of a play

sub-plot   a minor plot which runs in tandem with the main plot

the three unities   a Greek concept requiring plays to take place in one location within twenty-four hours and with only one plot

 stage such as

Glossary of technical terms

acronyms	a word composed of the initials of other words, and pronounced as a whole word i.e. ASH, Action on Smoking and Health
alienation	a way of reminding the audience that they are watching a play, not observing something that is real
allegory	in allegory abstract ideas are made concrete. Bunyan in *Pilgrim's Progress* describes life as a journey with many obstacles and difficulties, so a period of doubt is represented by 'Doubting Castle' and so on.
alliteration	the use of repeated consonants at the beginnings of words
alliterative verse	verse which makes great use of alliteration, often alliterating the stressed syllables
apron stage	a stage such as the Elizabethan stage, which projects a long way out into the auditorium
ballad	a narrative poem often associated with folk tradition, in four line stanzas with a particular metre and rhyme scheme
caesura	a break in a line of poetry indicated by punctuation
catharsis	the feeling an audience should have of being purged of pity and fear at the end of a tragedy
characterisation	the way characters are presented by an author
chronology	the sequence of time, a traditional chronology arranges events in the sequence in which they occur
classical realism	a way of portraying events and people as realistically as possible in their natural settings
clerihew	a four line verse of two rhyming couplets
closure	the way a text comes to an obvious conclusion
cohesion	refers to the way texts hold together, the ways parts connect. This connection can be through words, grammar and ideas

AS level English

collocation	the way certain words frequently appear together, often in a certain order
colloquial language	the informal vocabulary used in everyday conversation
conceit	a striking metaphor comparing two things not usually associated
complex clause	a main clause with subordinate parts
compound clause	mixture of parts to make a whole clause
co-ordinate clause	equal parts of a whole or compound clauses making a sentence
connectives	words which connect different parts of sentences or utterances. They are also known as conjunctions.
connotation	the connotations of a word are the associations it creates
construct	a literary structure created by the writer, either the whole of it, as in a novel or a play, or part of it, as in a character
culture specific references	references to objects and ideas which have a certain meaning within a culture or cultural group
denouement	the last part of a play which resolves all the problems and ties up the loose ends
dialect	a language variety in which features of vocabulary and grammar show the user belonging to a particular social or regional group
dialectal	relating to 'dialect', a kind of language spoken by a particular geographical group; also used in relation to differences resulting from class and occupation
dialogue	conversation between characters
didactic	having a message to get over to the reader or audience
discourse	used in various ways by linguists. It can refer to a continuous piece of written or spoken text, but as used here it refers to more than this. Here it refers to the way texts cohere (see cohesion above) and the ways in which readers recognise this.
dramatic irony	when the audience has a greater knowledge of events than some or all of the characters on stage
dramatic monologue	a poem spoken by an imaginary speaker to an imaginary audience
elegy	a poem written on the death of an individual or for a particular occasion
ellipsis	the omission of part of a word, or of a word or words from a sentence, while still making sense
enjambement	run-on lines in a poem
epic	a long narrative poem on a heroic scale
episodic	loosely constructed in episodes or sections

epistolary	written in the form of letters
euphemism	the use of a mild word or phrase instead of one which carries more force in its meaning
euphemistic	written in such a way as to make the thing described seem less offensive or unpleasant, e.g. describing death as 'passing away'
eyewitness account	an account of something seen by the person who recounts it
farce	a form of comedy with a lot of physical action
fatal flaw	the predominant characteristic of the hero which helps to bring about his downfall
field	the topic of a text, its subject matter
fillers	sounds that fill up pauses in speech
first person narrative	the use of a character within the novel as narrator, using the first person 'I'
formality	involves a scale of social use relating to situations which are 'tight' or 'loose'. Linguists talk of 'levels' of formality.
fourth wall convention	looking on at a traditional stage with the curtain drawn aside to show what looks like a room with one wall removed; usually the audience seems to be looking at something very like real life
free verse	verse which does not use any of the established metrical forms
function	the purpose of a text, why it has been produced
genre	a word for types of texts. It can refer broadly to such things as poetry, prose, drama, but also more specifically to types of text within those broad areas, such as crime fiction, narrative poetry etc.
genre conventions	these are features typically found in a certain type of text e.g. crime writing
gobbledygook	a word used to describe occupational language that is impossible for outsiders to understand
gothic horror novel	novel written in the latter half of the eighteenth or early part of the nineteenth century that was dependent on dramatic and violent events in romantic or exotic settings
grammar	the system by which texts and meanings are constructed
graphology	involves looking at the way the appearance of a text influences how it is read and understood
haeccitas	a word coined by the Victorian poet Gerard Manley Hopkins to mean individuality
haiku	a Japanese form; each poem has three lines which have five, seven and five syllables
iambic pentameter	a ten syllables line divided into five metrical divisions (or feet); each foot has one unstressed and one stressed syllable

ideology	a set of ideas and values held by a group or an individual
idiolect	an individual's distinctive way of speaking
imagery	descriptive language in a literary work
imperative	a form of command
initialisms	a collection of the initials of the name of a group or organisation to form a short title. Unlike an acronym they do not form a word.
in the round	a way of performing a play where the audience sits on all sides of the performers
interior monologue	a way of representing a character's flow of thoughts
intertextuality	the relationship of one text to another, through linguistic echoes or similarities in theme or meaning
irony	a difficult concept, but one that involves a discrepancy or incongruity between two things, such as what someone says and what they do, or the way a word is used in a particular context
iterative imagery	the use of recurring images throughout a text
jargon	the technical language of a certain occupation. The word is often used critically, as with *gobbledygook* above.
latinate	derived from a Latin root
lexis	the vocabulary of a language
limerick	a five line poem rhyming aabba and with a mainly anapaestic rhythm (two unstressed syllables and one stressed in a foot)
linear narrative	one where events are largely told in chronological order
litotes	deliberate understatement
lyric	a poem of emotion rather than one that tells a story
markedness	this is when a word indicates that it is not the norm, e.g. 'waitress' is marked by the 'ess' denoting a female waiter
masque	a form of entertainment popular in the sixteenth and seventeenth centuries which combined song/drama, music and dance in poetic form. The actors presented a kind of pageant, often representing figures from mythology or figures that stood for a particular quality
metamorphosis	process of transforming from one form into another through magic or by natural development
metaphor	a comparison where one thing is described in terms of another, without using the words 'as' or 'like'
metre	the pattern of unstressed and stressed syllables in poetry
mode	the sort of text being produced, and its possible genre
morphology	the study of the structure of words

motif	a dominant idea expressed through a recurring image
narrative/first person	a story told using the 'I' form
narrative/third person	a story about others using she/he etc.
narratee	the 'ideal' constructed reader who reads the text
narrator	the constructed voice that 'speaks' a text
non-linear narrative	a story which is not told in chronological order. It may shift between past and present, making use of flashbacks and other devices to tell the tale
obituary	a review of the life of a dead person
octet	a group of eight lines in poetry
ode	a formal lyric poem with a complex stanza form
omniscient narrator	an all-knowing narrator who looks on at events from the outside
onomatopoeia	the use of words whose sound echoes their meaning, such as 'rustle' or 'twitter'
parody	the imitation of an author's style in order to ridicule
pastiche	imitating some aspects of a genre convention, but changing others for comic or satirical effect
pathetic fallacy	a kind of personification, where a writer ascribes human feelings to something which is not human, such as the landscape
persona	a mechanism whereby an author takes on another identity for the purposes of his or her writing
phatic conventions	utterances such as 'how are you?' which establish and maintain social contact
phonology	the study of the way sound operates in a language
play within the play	a short play which exists within the structure of the play as a whole, like the 'mouse-trap' play in *Hamlet*
plot	the design of events in a novel, poem or drama
point of view	the angle from which the events of a novel or subject-matter of a poem are seen. This may be the point of view of the writer or that of a created character.
post-modern	post-modern writers react against traditional views of form and question the possibility of attaching any definitive meaning to a text
pragmatics	the way meanings in a text, written or spoken, can work beyond the apparent surface meaning
prelapsarian	before the fall of man
pronouns	words which substitute for nouns and noun phrases i.e. 'I' 'mine'
proscenium arch	the arch which separates the stage from the auditorium

AS level English

prosody	prosodic features refer to aspects of sound such as rhythm, speed, pitch
rhetoric	the use of language to persuade
rhythm	the movement and flow of a poem which results from its metrical form
ritualistic language	formal, patterned language such as you would expect to find in a 'rite', that is a formal procedure associated with particular ceremony
salient	stands out as important
semantic field	a group of words that are related in meaning through being connected in certain context
sestet	a group of six lines in poetry
setting	the place where the events of the novel or other literary work occur
sibilants	the repeated use of letters that create a hissing sound
sociolinguistics	the study of the ways in which language is used in social contexts reflecting its influence on, and by, different social groups
sonnet	a poem in fourteen lines which are grouped in various possible ways with particular rhyme schemes
spectacle	the visual aspect of a play
spondee	a number of stressed syllables which follow one another
stanza	a verse of a poem
style	the particular way in which an author writes; what makes their writing distinctively their own
sub-plot	a minor plot which runs in tandem with the main plot
superlative	the highest degree of comparison
symbol	an image which acquires a significance beyond what would normally be attributed to it, like the Cross for Christianity or a rose for beauty
syntax	the way sentences are constructed
synthesis	a putting together of the various separate elements looked at in a work of art into a connected whole
tenor	the tone used in a text
tercet	a three line rhyming stanza
the three unities	a Greek concept requiring plays to take place in one location within twenty-four hours and with only one plot
theme	one of the ideas on which a work is based
thesis	the viewpoint put forward by the author, particularly in relation to society or politics
third person verb	one which is used with 'he', 'she' or 'it' or 'they'

tone	the voice in which the writer speaks, which may be humorous, serious, bullying and so on.
verb tenses	these indicate the time in which something happens
zeugma	the linking of two nouns with a verb that is not normally appropriate to one of them.

Sources and Acknowledgements

Kate Atkinson: from *Behind the Scenes at the Museum* (Doubleday, 1995); Pat Barker: from *Regeneration* (Viking, 1991), © Pat Barker, 1991, reprinted by permission of Penguin UK; Samuel Beckett: from *Waiting for Godot* (Faber, 1956); Robert Bolt: from *A Man for All Seasons* (Methuen Drama, 1996); Donald Crowhurst: from *The Strange Last Voyage of Donald Crowhurst* by Nicholas Tomalin and Ron Hall (Adlard Coles Nautical, 1995), reprinted by permission of Hodder & Stoughton Ltd; Roald Dahl: from *The BFG* (Jonathan Cape, 1982), reprinted by permission of David Higham Associates; the *Daily Telegraph*: An obituary of Captain David Goodwin from the *Daily Telegraph* (18 March, 1999); Carol Ann Duffy: 'Sleeping' from *Mean Time* (Anvil Press Poetry, 1993), reprinted by permission of the publisher; Roger Ebbatson: from *Penguin Critical Studies: Tennyson* (Penguin Books, 1998), © Roger Ebbatson, 1998, reprinted by permission of the publisher; E. M. Forster: from *A Passage to India* (Penguin Twentieth Century Classics, 1989), reprinted by permission of The Provost and Scholars of King's College, Cambridge and The Society of Authors as the Literary Representatives of the E. M. Forster Estate; David Giles: 'I want to tell you a story...', reprinted by permission of the author; George & Weedon Grossmith: from *Diary of a Nobody* (n.e.Wordsworth Classics, 1994); L. P. Hartley: from *The Go-Between* (Hamish Hamilton, 1953; Penguin Twentieth-Century Classics, 1997), copyright 1953 by L. P. Hartley; copyright © Douglas Brooks-Davies, 1997, reprinted by permission of Penguin Books; Department of Health: 'Choose The Right Remedy This Winter' (NHS) from *Radio Times* (Christmas Issue, 1999), reprinted by permission of the Publications Information Unit; Ernest Hemingway: from *A Farewell to Arms* (Jonathan Cape, 1929), reprinted by permission of The Random House Archive & Library; Susan Hill: from *I'm the King of the Castle* (Penguin Books, 1974); *The Independent*: 'Lady of Shalott' and 'Perfect Winter Soup', reprinted by permission of the publisher; Kazuo Ishiguro: from *The Remains of the Day* (Faber & Faber, 1989), reprinted by permission of the publisher; Elizabeth Jennings: 'Winter Love' and 'Family Affairs' from *Collected Poems* (Carcanet Press, 1986), reprinted by permission of David Higham Associates; Philip Larkin: from 'Here' from *Collected Poems*, edited by Anthony Thwaite (Faber & Faber, 1990), © the Estate of Philip Larkin, 1988, reprinted by permission of the publisher; Penelope Lively: from *Oleander, Jacaranda: A Childhood Perceived* (Penguin Books, 1995); Arthur Miller: from *The Death of a Salesman* (Penguin Twentieth Century Classics, 1989); Iris Murdoch: from *The Bell* (Chatto & Windus, 1984), reprinted by permission of The Random House Archive & Library; Newcastle City Council: from *Your Guide to Road Safety in Newcastle upon Tyne*, from information supplied by the Traffic Accident Data Unit (TADU), Gateshead and collected by Northumbria Police (Publications UK Ltd, January 2000), reprinted by permission of Newcastle City Council; Northumbrian Water: a letter from Customer Contact Centre (28 October 1997), reprinted by permission of Northumbrian Water; Jamie Oliver: A recipe for 'Moroccan Preserved Lemons' from *Radio Times* (Christmas Issue, 1999), reprinted by permission of the author; P. J. O'Rourke: from *Holidays in Hell* (Pan Books, 1989); Wilfred Owen: 'Anthem for Doomed Youth', 'Exposure', 'Mental Cases', 'Strange Meeting' from *The Collected Poems of Wilfred Owen* (Chatto & Windus, 1963); Oxford University Press: from *The Young Oxford Book of Britain and Ireland* (OUP, 1996), reprinted by permission of the publisher; Harold Pinter: from *The Caretaker* (Faber & Faber, 1991), reprinted by permission of the pub-

Sources and Acknowledgements

lisher; Philip Pullman: from *Northern Lights* (Point, 1995), reprinted by permission of Scholastic Ltd; Christopher Ricks: from *Tennyson* (Macmillan, 1989), reprinted by permission of the publisher; The Rough Guides: from *The Rough Guide to Italy*. 4th Edition, edited by Ros Belford *et al.* (Rough Guides, 1999), reprinted by permission of the publisher; Willy Russell: from 'Educating Rita' from *Educating Rita WITH Blood Brothers AND Stags and Hens* (Methuen, 1986), reprinted by permission of the publisher; Tom Stoppard: from *Arcadia* (Faber & Faber, 1993), reprinted by permission of the publisher; Thomson Travel: from *Holiday Guide 2000*; Sue Townsend: from *The Adrian Mole Diaries* (Methuen, 1985), reprinted by permission of The Random House Archive & Library; Alice Walker: from *The Color Purple*, published in Great Britain by The Women's Press Ltd, 1983, 34 Great Sutton Street, London EC1V 0LQ, reprinted by permission of David Higham Associates.

We acknowledge with thanks the following agencies for permission to reproduce the advertisements in this book

'Did you know you can lose your licence the following day?'- Beer
'Please don't drink and d i e'
'How are you getting home after the party?' - Rum
'Please don't drink and d i e'
(Courtesy: DETR. © Crown Copyright 1999. Reproduced with the permission of the Controller of her Majesty's Stationery Office)

'Millennium Madness – 1/3 Off Debt. Don't Settle For Cheap Discounts. End Third World Debt Now'
(Courtesy: Christian Aid and Partners BDDH)

'Yes, They Look Daft. But They Get The Job Done'
'Nivea For Men'
(Courtesy: Beiersdorf UK)

'Suzuki 175PS GSX1300R Hayabusa'
(Courtesy: Suzuki Information Department and The National Trust)

'A pain in the neck for planespotters'
(Courtesy: British Airways)

'George Willerby – gravestone'
(Courtesy: Different Advertising, Design & Marketing Limited)

Every effort has been made to trace or contact all copyright holders. The publishers would be pleased to rectify any omissions brought to their notice at the earliest opportunity.